T0304013

Volume 13

ENTREPRENEURSHIP AND THE NEW FIRM

ENTREPRENEURSHIP AND THE NEW FIRM

DAVID J. STOREY

Routledge
Taylor & Francis Group

LONDON AND NEW YORK

First published in 1982 by Croom Helm Ltd

This edition first published in 2016
by Routledge
2 Park Square, Milton Park, Abingdon, Oxon OX14 4RN

and by Routledge
711 Third Avenue, New York, NY 10017

Routledge is an imprint of the Taylor & Francis Group, an informa business

British Library Cataloguing in Publication Data
A catalogue record for this book is available from the British Library

ISBN: 978-1-138-67308-3 (Set)
ISBN: 978-1-315-54266-9 (Set) (ebk)
ISBN: 978-1-138-68340-2 (Volume 13) (hbk)
ISBN: 978-1-315-54450-2 (Volume 13) (ebk)

Publisher's Note
The publisher has gone to great lengths to ensure the quality of this reprint but points out that some imperfections in the original copies may be apparent.

Disclaimer
The publisher has made every effort to trace copyright holders and would welcome correspondence from those they have been unable to trace.

ENTREPRENEURSHIP AND THE NEW FIRM

D.J. STOREY

CROOM HELM
London & Canberra

© 1982 D.J. Storey
Croom Helm Ltd, Provident House, Burrell Row,
Beckenham, Kent BR3 1AT
Croom Helm Australia Pty Ltd, 28 Kembla Street,
Fyshwick, ACT 2609, Australia
Reprinted 1984

British Library Cataloguing in Publication Data

Storey, D.J.
    Entrepreneurship and the new firm.
    1. Small business – Great Britain
    2. New business enterprises – Great Britain
    3. Regional planning – Great Britain
    I. Title
    338.6'42'0941   HD2346.G7

    ISBN 0-7099-2347-3

Printed and bound in Great Britain by
Billing and Sons Limited, Worcester

CONTENTS

Acknowledgements

ACKNOWLEDGEMENTS

This book was conceived during a study of local employment changes in the county of Cleveland which I undertook with Fred Robinson for the now defunct Centre for Environmental Studies (CES). In this work I have been selflessly assisted by many individuals. My greatest debt is to those in the Research and Intelligence Unit at Cleveland County Council who organised for me the interviewing of firms new to the county. Without the person-power which the Unit provided, together with the support of its Director, Reg Fox, this work could not have been undertaken. During 1979 and 1980 I worked closely with Eric Smith who supervised the computation of the replies. He provided an initial draft of Chapter 9, and has commented extensively upon Chapters 5 to 9, inclusive. The interviewing was efficiently co-ordinated by Geoff Sharp and conducted by ladies, so numerous that they will have to remain anonymous. They struggled manfully (or should it be woman-fully?) with a complex questionnaire. Finally at Cleveland, Tim Mobbs, Vic Gallant, John Harris and Judith Green assisted in the study, either in its formative stages or by commenting upon drafts. To all I offer my thanks.

Bert Nicholson, Steve Fothergill and Graham Gudgin were former colleagues at CES who convinced me that small firms were a worth-while subject for study. I am grateful to them for providing me with many stimulating conversations. My thanks are also extended to the University of Durham who granted me an Honorary Research Fellow-ship in the Department of Economics in order to advance this work. I particularly valued the encouragement and detailed comments on parts of the text which I received from Denis O'Brien, and I learnt a great deal from Mike Cross and Peter Johnson. It only remains to absolve the above individuals or organisations from any opinions, errors or stylistic clumsiness which remain in the book.

Finally and most importantly I have to thank both my wife and son for accepting my frequent absences from family occasions, and the Gatsby Charitable Foundation for financing the bulk of this research. No kept man could ever have had a more understanding benefactor.

PART ONE

THE SMALL FIRM

1 INTRODUCTION

Few readers of the biographies of the great entrepreneurs can have been unimpressed by the energy, talent and tenacity which such individuals directed towards the establishment and growth of their businesses. Several came from relatively humble backgrounds, whilst all had to battle against short-sighted bankers, hardhearted creditors and even wicked relatives. It is impossible not to feel admiration for their single-mindedness. The tradition of the Arkwrights and the Wedgwoods is maintained by the modern Sinclairs and Barretts.

For every Laurie Barrett there are, however, thousands of 'plodding men of business', some choosing to start their firms primarily to increase their income knowing that they have 'a good idea'. Others may begin out of a sense of frustration with what they perceive to be the stupidity of their employer, whilst some are captivated by the notion of independence which they associate with forming their own firm and becoming their own boss. A final, but numerically significant, group recognises that in times of high unemployment, entrepreneurship is preferable to life on the dole.

This variety of motivations and aspirations is reflected in the variety of types of firms established. For every boffin businessman, intending to manufacture and market a wholly new and technically sophisticated product, there are scores of insurance agents, garage mechanics, hairdressers and carpenters who will begin in business providing very familiar goods and services. The experience of management which individuals bring to their enterprise varies considerably, as do their ages and their social background. Perhaps only those from the poorest sections of society, at least in most developed countries, are infrequently represented amongst the entrepreneurial classes.

A book which attempts to describe the process of new firm formation must, in many senses reflect, within its pages, this diversity of motivation, experience and achievement. It cannot be exclusively theoretical since this risks a loss of the richness which only description can provide. On the other hand it cannot be wholly descriptive. It must attempt to derive general patterns and themes which are of interest, in particular to those in the public sector who have a responsibility for creating an environment favourable to wealth creation. Decisions have to be made at local, regional and national levels on an

1

appropriate mix of incentives and controls (if any) upon industry, to enable desired combinations of goods and services to be produced and employment generated.

Increasingly, the small and new firm sector has become regarded as an important vehicle for the production of goods and services. The final product is local, and thus more likely to be amenable to local public initiatives than that produced by a large multinational corporation. It is therefore not surprising that local governments should be making strenuous efforts to assist the creation of new enterprises. On the other hand national governments, having been disappointed with the employment consequences of assisting large enterprises, have also begun to reconsider the role of new and small firms in advanced economies.

This book reviews the resurrection of the small firm, partly by a multi-disciplined examination of the existing literature on small and new firms and partly by reporting the results of a study of firms new to the county of Cleveland, in north-east England. It attempts to combine the theory and the practice — the 'blackboard' and the 'real' economy, with the accent rather less upon analytical rigour and rather more on obtaining a broad view on trends and policies.

The book is divided into four parts, with Chapter 2 dealing with the role of small firms in the economies of the developed and less developed countries. It also deals with the role of small firms as sources of potential or actual competition, and their role in research and innovation are articulated, together with a review of empirical work testing the extent to which in practice, small firms fulfil this function.

Whilst virtually all new firms are small, according to almost any definition, the majority of small firms are not new. Indeed a sizeable proportion of the stock of small firms have been in existence for 20 or more years and are likely to have significantly different problems from the new, dynamic but probably highly unstable new enterprise. Parts Two and Three are concerned with this subset of small firms — the new enterprise.

In Part Two the theoretical foundations for the study of entrepreneurs and their new firms are laid, using concepts from a cross section of the social sciences. In economics, or at least to some economists, an entrepreneur may be both the owner and the manager of a firm; he may provide the capital, organise production and bear at least part of the risk of being unable to sell the output at a price which he feels rewards him with adequate profit. In large firms the owners of the firm (the shareholders) have little influence upon managerial decision taking, although in new and small firms ownership and control are often jointly combined in the person of a single, or a group of, individuals. In this book, however, it should already be clear that the term 'entrepreneurship' will be used to cover the establishment of a new firm by an individual or group. The contrasting approaches to entrepreneurship, or new firm formation, are illustrated in Part Two. Traditionally, economists have viewed the formation of new firms in a given industry as a response to the opportunities for profit-making in that industry. Entry rates are thus dependent upon expected post-entry profitability and the real or perceived entry barriers. In essence, according to Kilby (1971) economics has ignored the supply side of entrepreneurship assuming that if barriers fall, or profits rise sufficiently, entry will be induced. Conversely explanations, not having their roots in economics, have concentrated almost exclusively upon these supply-side characteristics, so that social psychologists have investigated the factors which motivate an individual to establish his own firm. Sociologists have observed that certain social groupings are more likely to enter entrepreneurship than others. The complexity of factors at work means that whilst explanations of the propensity of groups with certain attributes to be strongly represented amongst entrepreneurs is valid in some situations, it has no explanatory power in others. Nevertheless the purpose of Part Two of the book is to provide the reader with a view of matters to which it is possible, in principle, to have recourse to the facts provided in Part Three.

In Part Three some of the theories outlined in Part Two are tested on a sample of firms new to Cleveland in North East England. Chapter 5 describes the derivation of a representative sample of firms new to Cleveland, about half of which were wholly new firms. These firms were 'born' into what appeared at that time to be a fairly hostile environment, with unemployment in the area well above the average for the UK as a whole. The region as a whole could, at best, be described as antipathetic to the individualistic idealism of entrepreneurship. The remainder of the chapters in Part Three review the problems which these entrepreneurs faced in starting and developing their business and the impact which such businesses had upon the local economy. In discussing the characteristics of those starting their own firms an attempt is made to distinguish between successful and unsuccessful new firms.

Part Four reviews the lessons of the above chapters for both the regional and national economy of the United Kingdom. It suggests that governments at national and local level have unreasonably high expectations of the new firm sector as a source of wealth and employment in future. From these pages it should become clear that whilst today's new firms will make a useful contribution to employment and wealth in the next two decades, the performance of the British economy will be determined by the ability of medium and large firms to be efficient and competitive. An emphasis upon small scale enterprises is no simple solution to reversing a century of industrial decline.

2 THE SMALL FIRM

The survival of small firms is thus dependent upon a series of factors not very creditable to our economic system; monopsonistic exploitation of labour, imperfection of markets due to 'irrational' reasons, unemployment and the gambling preference of small entrepreneurs, with all the waste of energy attendant on the high 'turnover' of small businesses. – J. Steindl (1945), p. 61

During the Afghan and Iranian crises President Carter cancelled all speaking engagements except that to 2,000 entrepreneurs attending a White House Conference on Small Businesses. This is an indication of the esteem in which the small firm and its owner is now held by the White House. – Anne Reilly in *Duns Review*, 1980, p. 69

2.1 Introduction

In virtually every country in the world the small firm is, and has always been, the typical unit of production. Small firms, however defined, constitute at least 90 per cent of the population of enterprises but in many developed countries the two decades following 1945 saw a decline in the proportion of total output produced by such firms.

There is now evidence to suggest that this decline has ceased and even been reversed. The last ten years has seen the small firm undergo a remarkable metamorphosis. In the fifties and sixties the emphasis of government policies in many countries was to create large enterprises which would be able to compete internationally. It was argued that modern industrial development was in industries where economies of scale were of paramount importance. Only large firms could hope to produce output in sufficient quantities to take advantage of these economies. It was believed that scale economies were at the plant (technical) level, so that larger establishments would have lower unit costs of production than small establishments. Managerial diseconomies were thought to be negligible, whereas large firms were more likely to have access to the capital necessary to undertake research and development and to finance advertising. Large firms were likely to be able to borrow money at lower interest rates because they represented a lower risk to the bank than did a small firm. The bank itself was likely to prefer to deal with several large customers since it would find monitoring company developments easier than a portfolio consisting of many small companies.

These factors suggested that the small firm was likely to become progressively less important. Indeed it seemed that the extent to which the small firm sector had declined represented an index of development. The small firm was equated with technological backwardness, and with barely competent management. The manager in the large enterprise, with his DCF, MBO and his job enrichment was contrasted with the 'belt and braces' approach of the small firm owner/manager. The quotation from Steindl, at the beginning of this chapter, summarises an attitude to small firms which pervaded popular opinion for at least 20 years after 1945. Matters have now changed for the small firm, with its owner becoming progressively more courted by governments, as is shown in the recent quotation from *Duns Review*. In some countries, notably Japan, small firms have always played a central role in economic development, whilst the independence and aspiration of the entrepreneur has always been part of the national culture in the United States. Nevertheless even these countries, as well as in Western Europe, have seen a resurgence of the small firm in the last decade.

This chapter begins with some definitions of the small firm and reviews the extent to which the number of small firms varies both between countries and between industries. It then outlines the functions which small firms serve in the economy. Finally, since this is a book about new, rather than small, firms, data on birth and death rates of firms from several countries is provided as background to the theoretical chapters of new firm formation in Part Two.

2.2 The Small Firm: Definitions, Importance and Trends

The term 'small firm' is in such common use that the unwary reader might be forgiven for thinking that there was some uniformly accepted definition of what constitutes a small firm. Nothing could be further from the truth! The distinction between 'big' and 'small' is arbitrary and, in those industries where definitions are according to value of work done, vary from year to year because of inflation. Neck (1977) quotes an American study in 1975 of small firm definitions which identified more than 50 different statistical definitions in 75 countries. Not surprisingly Neck suggests the criteria for 'small' vary according to the context, with an upper limit of small for financiers being based on fixed assets or net worth. Other definitions might be based on total employment (including or excluding 'outworkers), total sales, energy consumption, number of customers, etc. Clearly firms which are small in some of these contexts are far from small in others.

It is therefore necessary to identify those characteristics of the small firm which epitomise its operations. First, the small firm generally has a small share of the market, although it could also have a large share of a very small market. Secondly, it is normally managed by the owners, rather than by employees on behalf of shareholders. Thirdly, the owners are legally independent in taking their decisions – although in practice probably extremely dependent upon the goodwill of their bankers. Other characteristics are that the small firm normally produces either a single product or a set of closely related products, generally at a single establishment. Its operations are generally local with the obvious exceptions of importing and exporting.

For statistical purposes it is necessary to have definitions of the small firm, but the variety of contexts and uses noted above, means that definitions in most countries vary according to the industry in which the small firm is found. In Britain, the Business Statistics Office in 1976 identified 1,300,000 small businesses, with these constituting 96 per cent of all firms. Only 100,000 small firms were in manufacturing. The BSO definitions illustrate the sectoral variations; in manufacturing a small firm is defined according to whether or not it has less than 200 employees, while in construction the upper limit is 25. In all other sectors the small firm is defined according to turnover; in wholesaling the limit for a small firm is £600,000; in the motor trades it is £300,000, and for all other sectors it is £150,000 (at 1976 prices).

In Australia the small firm is defined as having less than 100 employees in manufacturing and less than 20 employees in all other sectors. The United States uses the 100 employee definition for manufacturing but uses output definitions for other sectors. For Germany the statistical data are on an establishment (plant) basis, rather than upon a single ownership (firm) basis, making comparison even more difficult.

These variations in definition make it extremely difficult to undertake valid comparisons of the importance of small firms in various countries. In practice the only meaningful comparisons are between the role of small firms in the manufacturing sector which, at least in Britain, contains under 10 per cent of all small firms. Table 2.1 shows that even allowing for the variety of dates at which the surveys were made, the UK has a lower proportion of its total manufacturing employment in small firms than in most other developed countries. The contrast with Japan, which has over half of its manufacturing employment in firms employing less than 100 people, compared with a UK figure of 17.1 per cent, might suggest that the economic performance of countries is positively influenced by the proportion of employment in small manufacturing establishments. This tempting hypothesis is weakened statistically by the position of Italy; more importantly it is unclear whether economic growth in a country induces the creation of many small firms, or whether the presence of many small firms is an inducement to economic growth.

Table 2.1: Contribution of Smaller Enterprises to Employment in Manufacturing

Country	Year of Data	% of Manufacturing Employment in Small Firms	
		1 - 99 %	1 - 199 %
United Kingdom	1976	17.1	22.6
Denmark[a, b]	1973	36.3	52.1
Ireland[b]	1968	33.0	49.8
Italy[a]	1971	n.a.	47.3
Netherlands	1973	36.0	47.8
Belgium	1970	33.2	43.4
Germany	1970	28.8	37.0
France	1976	25.2	34.2
Luxembourg	1973	19.1	28.2
Japan	1970	51.6	n.a.
USA	1972	24.8	n.a.

Notes: a. Includes energy and water industries.

b. Figures for these countries exclude employment in very small enterprises and understate the contribution of small enterprises.

Source: Commission of the European Communities (1980); Department of Industry (1976).

The importance of small firms in the period since the 1950s has generally declined in most countries, at least until the mid-1970s. In Table 2.2 it can be seen that in four out of the eight countries where comparable data were available the share of total manufacturing employment by establishments with less than 200 employees declined continuously, whilst in other countries small firms had a mixed performance. The data in Table 2.2 refer to establishments, whereas those in Table 2.1 refer to enterprises, so that direct comparison between the tables is not possible. Nevertheless, the decline in relative importance of small firms in the 20 years after 1945 seems to have occurred in most developed countries, although it went further in Britain than elsewhere.

Table 2.2: Changes in the Share of Total Manufacturing Employment in Establishments with Less than 200 Employees

Countries with: Continuous Decline						
	Year	%	Year	%	Year	%
Germany	1953	40	1963	34	1976	31
Sweden	1950	56	1965	53	1975	41
Norway	1953	70	1963	65	1975	58
France[a]	1954	58	1963	51	1975	41
Countries with: Increases and Decreases						
UK	1954	33	1968	29	1976	31
Switzerland	1955	66	1965	61	1975	64
Canada	1955	46	1964	47	1975	44
USA	1954	37	1963	39	1972	38

Note: [a] Small establishments in France, although classified as having experienced continuous decline, increased their share of employment between 1963 and 1965.

Source: Bannock (1981a), Bolton (1971).

From the late 1960s, at least in Britain, these trends have not only been arrested but reversed. Interestingly this started at a time when government became publicly convinced that large manufacturing enterprises offered the best prospects for creating wealth, and began policies to assist the creation of giant corporations. The British government's only apparent concern was whether the small firm was likely to disappear altogether and hence reduce the competition faced by existing large firms.

It was, therefore, something of a surprise when in July 1969 the President of the Board of Trade announced that he had asked Mr J.E. Bolton to inquire into 'the role of small firms in the national economy, the facilities available to them, and the problems confronting them; and to make recommendations'. The Bolton Committee presented a report in 1971 which, although about 'anachronistic survivals in a world of promising technology' (Yamey (1972)), commanded great interest because of the insights it offered and because, with hindsight, it represented the finest exposition available of the role and contribution of small firms in a developed economy.

The most important recommendation by the Committee was that it felt there to be no case, at that time, for positively discriminating in favour of small firms, although it suggested that this matter should be reviewed if small firms continued to decline. Despite the small firm sector in Britain having been in decline for 30 years Bolton, with remarkable foresight, suggested that such decline was unlikely to continue. There were forces around, the Committee thought, which would lead to a stabilisation of the small firm sector – notably increased income leading to a demand for more 'one-off' goods which the small firm sector was most suited to supplying.

The accuracy of Bolton's predictions are illustrated in Table 2.3 which shows that the 1968 data, upon which the Committee had based its prediction, in fact represented the low point of the small firm population. Since then it has climbed from this level, fairly continuously.

Table 2.3: Employment in UK Manufacturing Enterprises: Small Firms as Per Cent of Total

1935	1958	1963	1968	1970	1972	1974	1976
38.0	24.0	21.3	20.8	21.3	21.5	21.5	22.6

Source: Bolton (1971); Department of Industry (1976).

The reasons why small firms have produced an increasing share of total output and employment since 1968 could be that they have grown faster than large firms, but it is equally possible that they have declined less rapidly. In other words, these statistics might equally well illustrate, not that small firms in the UK have performed particularly well, but merely that large firms have performed very badly since 1968.

Some support for the latter hypothesis is provided in Prais (1976) in his study of the role of giant firms. Figure 2.1 taken from Prais and the Department of Industry (1976) shows that for the United Kingdom and the United States the temporal patterns of growth of large enterprises are remarkably similar, except that the rate of growth in importance of the hundred largest establishments in Britain has been more rapid than in the USA. It shows that the period from 1910 to the mid-1930s saw a fairly continuous increase in the importance of giant enterprises but that after this, in both countries, their importance fell. Prais explains this partly by noting that between the 1930s and 1948 there were fewer joint returns of the census forms but the fact that similar patterns were apparent in the USA suggests there were 'real' as well as 'statistical' factors at work. After the Second World War, once productive capacity

Figure 2.1: Share of the Hundred Largest Enterprises in Manufacturing Net Output in the UK, 1924-77 and USA 1931-70. Share of Small Enterprises and Establishments in Manufacturing Net Output in the UK 1924-77

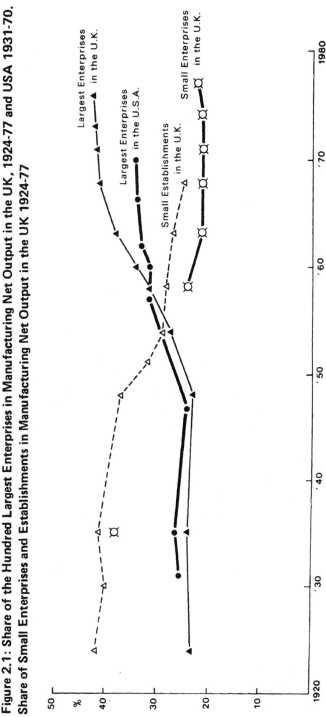

had been replaced, the large enterprise grew in importance until the late 1960s, and for the 1970s their share remained fairly constant.

Figure 2.1 suggests that during periods of national economic growth, notably the post-war years, the giant enterprise obtains an increasing share of manufacturing net output, whether this is due to internally generated growth, or to acquisition (see the debate between Hannah and Kay (1981), Prais (1981) and Hart (1981)) or even to the 'Gibrat effect'. During periods of low growth – the 1930s and the 1970s – these trends seem to be reversed with the performance of giant firms being poorer than other sizes of firm. These trends are apparent in both the United States and the UK, suggesting that when economies are undergoing major structural change it is the small firm sector with its greater flexibility which performs better than the large firm, which sheds labour but probably remains in existence awaiting a period of more steady growth in demand.

It is unclear whether the trend towards increased industrial concentration in the developed countries of the world will restart in the future. The emergence of newly industrialised nations producing 'standard' industrial goods, is of great importance. Goods such as motor vehicles and cutlery have been produced by giant enterprises in the developed countries which are now finding it increasingly difficult to compete with firms in developing countries able to combine low wages with high labour productivity. It now appears that developed countries have to move out of standard product industries in which large firms had a controlling interest, and into the production of goods where the technological content is higher, but where large production runs are less economic. In essence the entry of the newly industrialised countries means that goods in which scale economies are important, are likely to represent a decreasing proportion of the industrial output of developed countries. Scale economies, a *raison d'être* for the giant corporation, therefore become a less influential factor encouraging further industrial concentration in developed countries.

A second factor suggesting that there will be no resumption of increased concentration in Britain is the increase in the price of oil since 1974. Higher energy prices have led to increased transport costs which, in turn, have led to some markets becoming more isolated and less economically served by a single production unit. This has served both to reduce the optimum size of plant in the industry and to increase the opportunity for small locally based suppliers.

Thirdly, the existence of monopoly legislation in the developed countries may reduce the likelihood of bouts of acquisition as occurred in the late 1960s and early 1970s, normally with the (at least tacit) support of government.

The law of proportionate growth, outlined by Gibrat, may still lead to increased industrial concentration, since if all firms in an industry grow at the same rate this will lead to an increase in industrial concentration, and an increase in the share of output, etc. produced by the few largest firms. It may be therefore that although small firms have the balance of advantage over the large firms this may be only temporary whilst the world economy is in a state of recession and readjustment. Once growth is re-established the giant corporation may find it worthwhile to acquire many of the small firms currently being spawned.

2.3 The Role of the Small Firm

Despite the heterogeneity of the small firm population, such firms are thought to perform a set of common functions:

(a) Small firms provide a source of competition (potential or actual) to larger firms in their industry, limiting the latter's ability to raise prices and/or be technically inefficient in the use of factors of production.

(b) Small firms have become increasingly acclaimed as major creators of new jobs in developed countries since standardised products, which have traditionally been produced in large enterprises, are now increasingly produced by the developing countries.

(c) Small firms provide the seed corn from which the giant corporations of future years will grow.

(d) In the developing countries small firms can co-exist with large foreign-owned enterprises and, by using an appropriate local technology, make a valuable contribution to growth.

(e) Small firms can provide a harmonious working environment where owner and employee work, shoulder to shoulder, for their mutual benefit. This is likely to be reflected in fewer industrial disputes and lower absenteeism.

(f) The inner city areas of the industrialised nations contain heavy concentrations of the social problems of unemployment, low incomes and poor housing. It is argued that small firms can make an important contribution to the regeneration of such areas.

(g) Small firms are likely to be innovative, being found in industries where technical development is essential for survival. The low capital requirements in modern micro-electronics make this industry particularly suited, at present, to new small firms.

The extent to which in practice small firms fulfil the roles claimed for them is reviewed in this section. It illustrates the difficulty of deriving testable hypotheses from the above statements, each of which is reviewed in turn. In addition there are several claims made for small firms which seem either to be based on no evidence (other than casual observation) or which are virtually untestable. For example, it is often claimed that major fluctuations in the demand for certain products mean small firms move into and out of these industries with great frequency. They react to the signals of the market place by taking risks that are unacceptable to larger firms, and by doing so make the market system more responsive to the demands of the consumer. The extent to which localised markets, protected by increasing transportation costs or consumer tastes, have influenced the small firm sector is also frequently debated but rarely quantified.

(a) Small Firms as Competitors

It is not easy to test the extent to which small firms compete with larger firms so reducing the latter's ability to determine market prices. Davies and Kelly (1971) found that over 50 per cent of small firms encountered their main competition from other small firms, whilst only 28 per cent thought they were competing directly with large firms (the remainder felt their competition came primarily from overseas companies).

Lydall (1958) categorised small firms as either 'jobbers' or 'marketeers'. Jobbers were essentially complementary to, rather than competitive with, large firms since they were producing output for a specific (normally large) customer such as a retail chain or a large firm. These firms are important in industries such as metal manufacturing, engineering, wood products, paper and printing and, as Table 2.4, taken from Lydall shows, the proportion of jobbers increases as firm size declines. The marketeers, on the other hand, compete directly with the large firm. Since Lydall's study there has been a sharp increase in industrial concentration making it likely that the number of marketeering firms will have declined.

The work by Hitchens (1977) on the UK iron foundry industry tends to support these findings. He found, in that industry, 59.8 per cent of firms viewed themselves as competing with less than ten firms with this competition coming, in their view, from firms of a similar size. Nevertheless, it is interesting to note that of those firms who felt themselves to be competing primarily with firms of a different size, 78.7 per cent thought their competition was with larger firms and only 21.3 per cent with smaller firms.

Table 2.4: Type of Work Done Analysed by Size of Firm

Number of Employees	Mainly Specification Orders (Jobbers)	Percentages Mainly Own Products (Marketeers)	About Equal (Mixed)	Total Per Cent	No. of Firms
10-19	58	38	4	100	149
20-39	46	47	7	100	153
30-9	52	44	5	100	126
40-9	53	43	3	100	86
50-74	49	44	7	100	125
75-99	41	56	4	100	54
100-99	37	55	8	100	110
200-499	25	68	7	100	57
Total	47	47	6	100	872

Source: Lydall (1958).

In a study of Australian small firms, Johns, Dunlop and Sheehan (1978) found that the most important source of competition for the small manufacturing firm was other small firms in the immediate locality. There were, of course, substantial industrial variations in this pattern, with 51 per cent of the timber firms identifying small local firms as the main source, yet only 21 per cent of chemical and oil firms. In aggregate, 38 per cent of all small firms surveyed regarded their prime source of competition as being from small local firms, compared to 33 per cent who viewed it as coming from large non-local firms.

The dependence of small business upon large customers is, of course, not necessarily an indication of a weakness in the small firm sector. In Table 2.1 it was shown that Japan has the highest proportion of total manufacturing employment in small firms of any of the developed countries, yet the majority of these small firms are directly dependent upon the large enterprises for their business. In the immediate post-war years the Japanese motor industry developed primarily upon a subcontracting basis. Yamanaka and Kobayashi (1957), in their study of this industry, found that with fluctuations in demand it was easier to regulate the need for components if this function was subcontracted to small firms rather than provided within the company. They also found that the subcontractors could employ labour at lower wage rates.

Clark (1979) shows this relationship has continued to exist in Japan, since 60 per cent of small and medium sized enterprises are still engaged in subcontracting. He also notes that although major differences in value added per head exist between small and large firms, the two continue to co-exist even though large food, printing and electrical companies produce an output per head 2½ times greater than that of small firms employing less than 30 people. Large firms in Japan also maintain their advantage over small firms since the latter, in 1973, had 54 per cent of all current assets financed by promissary notes and bills. Clark believes this enables large firms more easily to take advantage of suppliers during a credit squeeze by slower settlement of accounts, than in countries where the small firms have access to other sources of funding.

The fact that most small firms are not competitors with large firms, and are in fact crucially dependent upon the development of large firms, does not mean that such a sector will show sluggish rates of growth. The example of Japan, where most small firms are jobbers, yet where the small firm sector has made an important contribution to that country's growth, illustrates it is not necessary to have small firms in direct competition with the large firms. It is more important for small firms to offer at least the threat of competition.

(b) Small Firms and Employment[1]

Birch (1979) showed, from a study of 82 per cent of all manufacturing and private sector service establishments in the United States, that two-thirds of *net* new jobs were created in firms employing less than 20 people. He argued that the small independent business was the prime source of employment growth in the USA, whilst larger firms were redistributing rather than creating employment.

Birch stated that there was an absence of knowledge about which types of companies created jobs, and about which were most likely to respond to government incentives. Consequently, he argued, government had to rely upon aggregate, macro-economic policies such as tax incentives and alterations in public expenditure, rather than being able to direct incentives towards those companies and individuals likely to be most responsive. Birch examined employment changes in 5.6 million business *establishments* (the number of *firms* or companies was substantially lower) in the manufacturing and private service sectors of the United States between 1969 and 1976. His analysis was conducted by using a components of change or job accounting technique. The technique accounts for net changes in numbers of jobs by isolating the gross components. Jobs are created through expansions of companies plus openings, and lost through company closures and contractions, with the full terminology used being set out in Figure 2.2. (The terms in brackets are synonyms for the unbracketed terms.)

Figure 2.2: The Job Generation Process

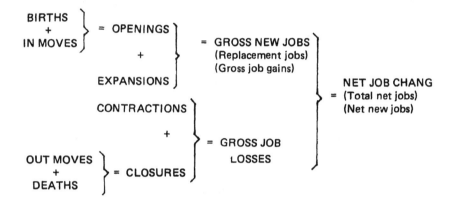

Birch's main conclusions for the USA were:

(i) Gross job loss through contraction and closure was about eight per cent per annum.

(ii) In 'replacing' these jobs, i.e. gross job gains — about 50 per cent were created through expansions of existing companies and about 50 per cent through new openings.

(iii) About 50 per cent of gross jobs created by openings were produced by independent free-standing entrepreneurs (births) and 50 per cent by multi-plant corporations (in moves).

(iv) Firms employing less than 20 people generated 66 per cent of net new jobs in the United States.

Birch was impressed by the contribution to employment made by the new, young, small independent firm which was committed to seeking out new and profitable ventures. Such firms were the major creators of employment. The contribution of small firms is shown on the upper line of Table 2.5. It shows that 66 per cent of net new jobs were created by firms employing less than 20 people. The policy implications of these results were, however, not immediately clear, even to Birch, who says:

> The job generating firm tends to be small. It tends to be dynamic (or unstable depending on your viewpoint) . . . the kind of firm that banks feel very uncomfortable about. It tends to be young. In short, the firms that can and do generate the most jobs are the ones that are most difficult to reach through conventional policy initiatives.

Table 2.5: Percentages of Net New Jobs Generated by Size in the USA 1969-76

Firm/Establishment Size	0-20	21-50	51-100	101-500	500+	Total
USA (All)	66.0	11.2	4.3	5.2	13.3	100
USA (Manufacturing)	360.0	61.7	−27.3	−168.4	−326.7	−100

Source: Birch (1979).

In addition, Birch might well have added that, not only are small firms the most difficult to reach, but even when contacted are reluctant to accept assistance and advice, often because of a fierce desire, on the part of their founder, to be independent. To many proprietors of small firms the seeking of advice is equated with an admission of failure.

The measures used by Birch, in determining the contribution of very small firms to job creation, are less simple than they initially appear. The upper line of Table 2.5 shows that two-thirds of *net* new jobs were created in firms employing less than 20 people. From Figure 2.2, however, it should be clear that this is not the same as saying either that two-thirds of *all* new jobs or of *gross* new jobs were created in such firms. Many distinguished financial commentators have made this mistake – some indeed have reported that Birch found two-thirds of all new jobs were created by small firms.

It is vitally important to distinguish between gross and net job creation, and to understand when either or both are valid measures of the contribution of large and small firms to employment change. Simply stated the rule is that where employment in all size bands increases, the proportionate contribution of small and large firms is validly measured by net changes, but where employment declines, either in total or only in individual size bands, net change may be an invalid measure. The latter is the case for manufacturing employment as reported by Birch for the USA. His data are reproduced on the lower line of Table 2.5. It shows that a negative number of *net* manufacturing jobs were created by large firms and a positive number by small manufacturing firms, so it is not possible to determine the *relative net* contribution of large and small firms. This can only be done by examining gross job losses and gross job gains, data which Birch does not provide.

Comparisons of the manufacturing sectors of Britain and the USA have been made by Fothergill and Gudgin (1979). Using data for the East Midlands, which may be reasonably representative of the UK as a whole, they show a startling similarity in terms of job-generation by size, between US manufacturing industry 1969-76 and East Midlands manufacturing 1968-75. This is shown in Table 2.6.

Table 2.6: Manufacturing Employment Change by Size, in Britain and the United States, as a Percentage of Total Manufacturing Employment in Base Year

	Size of Firm					
	0-20	21-50	51-100	101-500	500+	Total
USA 1969-76	+3.2	+0.5	−0.2	−1.5	−2.9	−0.9
East Midlands[a]	+2.7	+2.3	+1.5	−2.2	−5.9	−1.5

Note: a. Openings for East Midlands are placed in 1975 size band, but in-situ plants and closures according to 1968 size. The procedure is assumed to be identical to that adopted by Birch.
Source: East Midlands: Fothergill and Gudgin (1979).
USA: Birch (1979).

During these years, in both the USA and the East Midlands of England, firms employing more than 100 showed an aggregate decline in employment, whereas the very small firm sector showed an aggregate increase in employment.

These 'tests' of employment change are, however, unsatisfactory because new firms are placed in a size category according to their final year's employment, whereas existing firms are categorised according to a base year and expressed as a percentage of total employment in that size band. This excludes the effect of openings, but gives a more realistic picture of employment change due to expansions, contractions and closures.

Finally, Birch's analysis is conducted primarily on a firm, rather than an establishment, basis. This means that a firm, which originally had a single establishment in a prosperous area, but which decides to transfer its manufacturing operations to a less prosperous area, and by doing so reduces its total employment, is classified as a declining firm. Nevertheless, the transferred employment is still a gain to the less prosperous area and may also benefit the prosperous area in terms of reduced pressure on the local labour market. Hence, although large companies are only redistributing operations this may not be undesirable, since it is not only the total employment in an economy which is important, but also its regional distribution.

Birch stated that over eight years approximately 50 per cent of gross new jobs in the US were attributable to openings of new firms and of these, half were generated by independent 'free standing' entrepreneurs, i.e. about 25 per cent of gross new jobs are created by such entrepreneurs. Table 2.7 shows that for four selected areas in Britain which have substantially different economic bases, but where roughly comparable data exists, wholly new establishments contribute approximately half of gross new jobs, in openings, only in the West Midlands. In other regions the proportion attributable to new establishments is around 20 per cent.

Table 2.7: Jobs Created in Openings of New Manufacturing Establishments

Area	Date	Total Jobs Created in Openings	Total Jobs Created by Openings of Wholly New Manufacturing Establishments (Births)	%
Central Clydeside	1958-68	33,452	6,039	18.05
Clydeside	1963-72	34,456	5,128	14.88
West Midlands	1963-72	13,632	7,295	53.51
East Midlands	1968-75	55,586	23,214	41.76
Cleveland	1965-76	16,322	3,056	19.95

Source: Clydeside and West Midlands: Firn and Swales (1978); East Midlands: data privately supplied by Steve Fothergill, University of Cambridge; Cleveland: Cleveland County Council Data Bank.

For Britain as a whole, it is unlikely that more than 50 per cent of gross new manufacturing jobs per decade are created by wholly new establishments. In the prosperous regions approximately 30 per cent of gross new jobs are created by openings — with half of these being created by wholly new firms (births). In the assisted areas, however, about 70 per cent of gross new jobs are created by openings (30 per cent through expansions) but as shown in Table 2.7 only about 20 per cent of these, i.e. 14 per cent, are attributable to wholly new establishments (births) — the rest are created primarily by existing firms moving branches or subsidiaries into the area. In both the assisted and the prosperous areas, therefore, the proportion of gross new jobs created by new establishments is unlikely to exceed 15 per cent of gross new manufacturing jobs. Fothergill and Gudgin, for example, show for the East Midlands that 15.1 per cent of *gross* new manufacturing jobs per decade are created by wholly new firms, whereas in Cleveland about 12 per cent of *gross* new jobs are created by new firms.

The contribution which small firms can make to job creation in future remains a matter of some dispute. It is clear that as a group, small firms are increasing their labour forces at a time when large firms are decreasing their payrolls. The detailed data on which job accounting can be undertaken are currently available in Europe only for the manufacturing sector which has been a net shedder of labour to the services sector — hence comparisons with the Birch data are difficult. Nevertheless, it seems clear that the contribution which the small firm sector can make to employment generation is nowhere near as high as is suggested by those who misquote the Birch results. In particular the employment which is created by surviving wholly new firms is unlikely to contribute more than 1.5 per cent annually to the gross stock of jobs over a decade.

(c) Small Firms as Seed Corn

Today's giant corporations were once back street enterprises. In most instances they grew as their industry grew, but there are several cases of new firms in a well established industry growing through their ability either to produce existing products more cheaply or through producing an improved product.

In the above sections we have already seen that small manufacturing firms as a group in Britain have been increasing employment since the mid-1960s whilst large firms have declined. The probability of an individual firm achieving a growth rate, in terms of employment, equal to the arithmetic mean of the group is, however, substantially less than 0.5. This is because the growth patterns of small firms are positively skewed with a few firms growing rapidly but the majority growing at a rate equal to or less than the mean. This is illustrated by Table 2.8, which traces the changes in cohorts of firms in the county of Cleveland of a given size. Reading across the rows we can see that of all firms employing less than ten people in 1965, 26 per cent had gone out of business, and 61 per cent continued to employ less than ten people by

1976. Hence only 13 per cent of all firms in this size category showed an increase in employment sufficient to push them into a larger size category. Similar results were derived by Whitelegg (1976).

Table 2.8: Deaths and Movements Between Size Bands of Establishments in Cleveland, 1965-76

Employment Size in 1965	Deaths	Employment Size Band in 1976							
		1-9	10-24	25-49	50-99	100-249	250-499	500-999	1,000+
1-9	.26	.61	.09	.02	.01	0	.01	0	0
10-24	.19	.15	.46	.15	.03	0	.01	.01	0
25-49	.32	.05	.12	.34	.09	.08	0	0	0
50-99	.31	.02	0	.20	.38	.09	0	0	0
100-249	.26	.02	0	.08	.20	.34	.06	.04	0
250-499	.27	0	0	0	.0	.23	.31	.11	.04
500-999	.27	0	0	0	.06	.06	.17	.44	0
1000+	.05	0	0	0	0	0	.09	.09	.77

Table 2.9 shows the arithmetic mean growth rates of all size cohorts. The arithmetic mean growth of the cohort of firms employing less than ten people in 1965 was 54.5 per cent. Yet the probability of a firm moving into a higher size category was 0.13. This has to be contrasted with the cohort of firms employing between 250 and 499 in 1965. Of this group of firms 15 per cent had, by 1976, moved into a higher size bracket, yet the arithmetic mean employment of this cohort fell by 14.9 per cent.[2]

These discrepancies occur because a calculation of the arithmetic mean employment change of a group of firms contains an implicit bias which serves apparently to inflate the group performance of small firms. This occurs because when the very small firm closes it can only lose a maximum of nine jobs, whereas there is no upper limit to which the small firm may grow.

Hence it must be stressed that the performance of the very small firm sector, as measured by its arithmetic mean performance, should not be interpreted as being typical of the small firm sector. Put bluntly, the chances are that today's small firm will show virtually no growth, and that the next most likely outcome is that it will not exist in ten years time. Very few prosper, but those who do, can more than compensate both for those which die and those who fail to grow. Using data for wholly new manufacturing firms created in the East and West Midlands of England, together with data for Cleveland current estimates suggest that the probability of a wholly new firm employing more than

100 people in a decade is between ½ and ¾ of one per cent.

Table 2.9: Changes in Employment of Different Sized Manufacturing Establishments in Cleveland, 1965-76

Establishment Size	1-9	10-49	50-99	100-249	500-999	1,000-1,999	2,000+
Expansions	+596	+2,007	+590	+1,551	+311	+510	+729
Contractions	− 62	− 474	−391	−1,352	−2,106	−3,318	−15,615
Closures	−180	−1,076	−816	−1,376	−2,071	−2,194	0
Total	+354	+ 457	−617	−1,177	−3,866	−5,002	−14,886
% Change	+54.4	+11.6	−20.4	−14.9	−34.6	−31.1	−23.3

(d) Small Firms in Developing Countries

It has been persuasively argued by Schumacher (1972) that the failure of aid to accelerate growth in many less developed countries (LDCs) is partly attributable to its being tied to an inappropriate technology. Too frequently large plants have been established on the basis of foreign aid in the LDCs to produce output in an inefficient manner. Instead it would have been better to have stimulated the informal sector which in LDCs embodies all the characteristics of the small firm sector in the developed countries − ease of entry, reliance on indigenous resources, family ownership, small scale operation, labour intensive and adapted technology, skills acquired outside the formal school system and unregulated and competitive markets (ILO, 1972).

This debate over the relevance of the informal sector as a vehicle for growth parallels in many respects the debates over small firms in the developed countries. Those who favour supporting the informal sector believe that its growth in the past has been hampered by the low incomes of those who purchase its services and by the unreasonable reluctance of government officials to deal with the sector, resulting in a low demand by government for its services. They also believe that governments have positively discriminated in favour of firms in the 'formal' sector by offering access to credit, foreign exchange concessions and work permits for foreign technicians. According to the ILO report on Kenya such firms are also the prime beneficiaries of tariff restrictions and licensing arrangements. This has enabled many large foreign-owned plants to become technically inefficient behind the barrier of protection, in contrast with the small firm in the informal sector which, because of the nature of competition which it faces, is 'forced' to be technically efficient.

These views of the 'formal' and 'informal' sector in developing countries have been strongly challenged by Leys (1973). He argues that discrimination in favour of small indigenous enterprises in the informal sector would be 'to direct business to low wage African-owned enterprises, and to enable a new stratum of the `African petty-bourgeoisie to transcend the limitations of the competitive market and achieve a measure of protection among the ranks of the auxilliary bourgeoisie'. These comments are strongly reminiscent of those deliberations of the Bolton Committee in its examination of whether the small firm in Britain should receive positive discrimination. After considerable soul-searching Bolton decided that whilst the small firm was essential to the fabric of the competitive market system, the redistribution of income which positive discrimination in its favour would involve could not be justified. In other words, equity considerations outweighed those of efficiency.

The implications for income distribution have not, however, prevented governments in many LDCs becoming disillusioned with the performance of large firms. This is closely associated with nationalistic sentiments, and with rejecting what is seen to be the evils of foreign ownership. The small scale enterprise is now, because of its numerical dominance, receiving assistance from governments — although often in a haphazard manner. Harper and Soon (1979) assert, after presenting 21 case studies of small firms in developing countries, that government can do little to influence the rates of new firm formation in a locality. Many entrepreneurs see government agencies as the architects of expensive and irrelevant regulations whose enforcement provides widespread opportunities for corruption. The problems facing the small firm in these areas continue to be those of shortage of finance, government regulations and relatively unsophisticated management.

Nevertheless, the much greater importance of the small firm sector in developing areas such as Africa compels the use of a small firms policy. For example in Sierra Leone the average employment in a small industrial establishment was 1.9. In Western Nigeria in 1973 the average number per industrial unit was three. In Senegal only 15 to 20 per cent of enterprises employ more than six people. Many of these entrepreneurs are poorly educated. Aluko (1973) for example found that 88.8 per cent had less than primary schooling, although there is no evidence that this significantly reduced the likelihood of the entrepreneur's ultimate success in business. Marris and Somerset (1971), in fact, found a negative correlation between schooling and entrepreneurial success amongst founders of firms in the footwear industry. Similar results were reported by Kilby (1971).

Many LDCs continue to face the problem of a shortage of successful entrepreneurs, so that whilst a reliance upon small firms has the benefit of local ownership and control it leads to growth rates which fail to bring about significant improvements in living standards. Several explanations of the shortage of successful entrepreneurs, familiar to those studying small firms in the developed countries, have been proposed. The attractions of paid salaries and secure employment in large firms in the formal sector is frequently cited, but almost certainly cultural attitudes stressed by De Missie (1975) are of paramount importance.

(e) The Working Environment

The conventional view, supported by the Bolton Committee, is that whilst the small firm is not necessarily the most technically advanced, it provides a pleasant environment in which workplace conflicts are minimised.

It is argued that the worker in a small firm has direct access to the boss of the firm who has it within his power to make decisions upon grievances. This contrasts with a large organisation where senior management has little contact with those on the shop floor, since they are 'protected' by intermediaries such as middle management or the foreman. Unfortunately middle management is often insufficiently autonomous to make decisions and hence tends to leave the decision to senior staff who may have less 'feel' for the problem. For his part the worker on the shop floor may feel frustrated that, although the decision may be communicated to him by intermediaries, they are not responsible for the decision. The opportunity for debating the matter is limited to either 'making an issue', with its implications for worker/ management relations, or resentfully accepting the decision.

In a small firm there is greater opportunity for face-to-face negotiation. The boss may be approached and he will give a decision which then can be disputed by the workers, leading to a more generally satisfactory compromise. It is important that the workforce see those who are responsible for making decisions and this, it is argued, is more likely to be found in a small than a large firm.

The large organisation is also often characterised by division of labour which means the work is repetitive and boring, and stripped of non-material rewards such as pride in workmanship or recognition of achievement. On the other hand, in the small firm there is less specialisation and hence tasks tend to be complex, with the experience gained representing valuable (yet enjoyable) training.

The existence of middle management is the inevitable consequence of size and, according to Schumacher (1972), this is incompatible with entrepreneurship.

> In any organisation, large or small there must be a certain clarity and orderliness; if things fall into disorder nothing can be accomplished. Yet, orderliness, as such, is static and lifeless; so there must also be plenty of elbow-room and scope for breaking through the established order, to do the thing never done before, never anticipated by the guardians of orderliness, the new, unpredicted and unpredictable outcome of a man's creative idea.

> Therefore any organisation has to strive continuously for the orderliness of *order* and the disorderliness of creative freedom. And the specific danger inherent in large scale organisations is that its natural bias and tendency favour order, at the expense of creative freedom.

All these factors suggest that the small workplace is likely to be a more satisfactory environment than the giant enterprise, but the evidence to support this hypothesis is somewhat equivocal. Several forms of testing could be tried. The obvious strategy is to examine the extent to which strikes vary according to the size of the workforce.

Table 2.10 appears to provide fairly conclusive evidence that large plants are more prone to strikes than small, even though it is true that collection of data from small plants is less comprehensive.

Table 2.10: Annual Average Strike-proneness of UK Plants, 1971-3

Plant Size Employment	Probability of Strike in a Year
11-24	0.002
25-99	0.011
100-99	0.029
200-499	0.061
500-999	0.143
1,000-1,999	0.252
2,000-4,999	0.440
5,000+	0.758

Source: Prais (1976).

Upon reflection, it should be appreciated that this need not necessarily mean that the probability of a conflict breaking out between two individuals is any higher in a large firm than a small firm, although the consequences to other workers are more serious in large firms. Instead it may simply be the result of large numbers of people being grouped together that a dispute between any two of them could cause a strike. Prais (1976) in fact showed that the data in Table 2.10 was quite compatible with a hypothesis that the probability of conflict between two individuals was independent of size, but that it is the combination of these probabilities that leads to their observed higher strike frequency. In essence, Prais argues that although it may be more boring and repetitive to work in a large plant, and although channels of communication are certainly longer and possibly weaker, either this is offset by advantages of scale such as higher pay, better sports and canteen facilities, or that repetitive work and boredom do not cause strikes.

Strikes are only one manifestation of the existence or absence of conflict in the workplace. Since small firms are less unionised than large firms, and since strikes are positively related to the degree of unionisation, then other indices of disharmony may be more relevant. For example, high rates of labour turnover, absenteeism and even accidents at work, may reflect more accurately the nature of job satisfaction in plants of varying size.

The work of Ingham (1970) continues to be the most comprehensive review of these matters in Britain and although available at the time contrasts with the Bolton notion of small firms as offering much higher non-monetary rewards than large firms. Careful reading of his research results, and his reviews of previous work, suggests Ingham was, at best, agnostic about the workplace benefits provided by small firms. He finds no clear evidence, either in his study, or in his reviews, of a relationship between size of establishment and various measures of labour turnover. He finds that only in 'exceptional cases' do absentee rates rise with organisation size, whilst the relationships between organisation size and productivity do not show any evidence of greater productivity in small than in large establishments despite small scale methods and (probably) a low capital intensity of production. Bolton, however, had stated 'the turnover of staffs in small firms is very low and strikes and other kinds of industrial dispute are relatively infrequent'. Bolton attributed this to management being more flexible and direct, with working rules being varied to suit the individual.

Ingham explains his results by suggesting that the motivation of workers in large establishments differs from that in small. In his terms the large plant workers were 'economistic and instrumental in their work orientation'. This means that whilst small firm workers were unlikely to be absent from work primarily through a feeling of 'letting the side down', absentee rates were also likely to be low in large organisations where workers realise that the financial penalty is greater. The congruence of aims in large organisations occurs through the cash nexus, whereas in small firms it occurs through a 'responsibility-nexus'. This congruence may in turn be due to the nature of workers recruited, with small firms tending to recruit workers who were more likely to be influenced by considerations of responsibility, and large firms recruiting workers more motivated by financial reward.

The above description illustrates the difficulty of identifying the direction of causation especially when it is shown that small sized establishments are correlated both with low wage rates and low unionisation. These in turn are correlated with low propensity to strike, which may be an indication of the quality of industrial relations in a plant.

Curran and Stanworth (1981a) have attempted to overcome these difficulties by interviewing workers in small and large sized establishments in the printing and electronics industry. They do not find any evidence of employees in small firms being anti-union, and the vast majority would join a union if firms allowed. The main result of their research is that firm size has markedly less influence upon industrial relations than the industry concerned, variations in local and community structures and national political and economic considerations.

In a subsequent paper, Curran and Stanworth (1981b) show that factors such as the age of respondents and their family life-cycle position are important factors influencing perceived levels of job satisfaction. Once these and specific industry characteristics are taken into account Curran and Stanworth can find no support for a relationship between firm size and reported job satisfaction amongst the workforce.

The evidence suggests it remains unproven that the small firm workplace is significantly less prone to conflict, absenteeism or high labour turnover, or to other indices of high job satisfaction. Instead it demonstrates that a significant proportion of the labour force is prepared to work in generally poorer conditions without facilities such as sports grounds, canteen, etc. at lower wages in order to obtain job satisfaction. The remainder are prepared to accept low job satisfaction in return for higher wages and better facilities.

(f) Small Firms and the Inner City

The inner cities of most developed countries exhibit similar characteristics. They have poor housing and social facilities, high unemployment and are often populated by unskilled whites and ethnic minorities with low incomes. They have normally been subject to substantial population decline with the more affluent residents having moved out to the suburbs leaving a decaying community which co-exists with high property values because of the industrial and commercial demand for land only short distances away.

It has been strongly argued by Falk (1978) that the small firm is an appropriate vehicle for the regeneration of these areas, even though it is the disappearance of small firms in such areas, together with the declining employment in locally based enterprises such as docks, that is the major 'component' of employment decline. He argues that the small firm has several major advantages over larger firms. The first is that it requires relatively small sites to produce its output and secondly that it uses a relatively labour intensive production process. The inner city with its expensive sites may be appropriate for firms which require only small amounts of land. The use of labour intensive production methods means that it is likely to have the maximum impact upon local unemployment. These ideas received official support in the White Paper on Inner Cities (Department of the Environment, 1977).

Falk also argues that the small firm in the inner city is likely to have easy access to a relatively rich market since transportation costs will be negligible. In addition it is more likely to be able to obtain access to supplies than, for example, the firm situated in a rural town. The small firm may also find there are, in the area, a number of other similar firms, which together create external benefits such as having a financial sector accustomed to particular dealing with specific industries or with skilled labour being available without having to be trained.

The hypothesis that inner city areas would be fertile incubators for new firms was first proposed by Hoover and Vernon (1960) in their examination of New York. They suggested that small firms in certain industries would find it advantageous to locate in high density metropolitan areas. They identified ladies clothing, printing, toys and jewellery as industries where the inner city firm may have advantages since these trades carry low inventories and require low mechanisation because of the fluctuations of fashion. Such firms attempt to minimise risk by restricting overheads, but in doing so have to remain very small. Once the firm developed and grew it was, according to Hoover and Vernon, likely to encounter constraints, notably the difficulty of securing suitable premises in the inner areas, and was likely to move to a surburban or rural location. The hypothesis that the inner areas were attractive to new firms – and that the more successful firms subsequently moved out of the area, remained essentially untested, despite popular accept- ance, until Leone and Struyk (1976) published their work on five US cities. They found some evidence that the central area of New York had a relatively high proportion of new start-up industries but the evidence for other central areas was weak. Leone and Struyk could find very little evidence for the hypothesis that inner city firms wishing to expand, subsequently moved to a more suburban location. In fact they found that such firms normally moved to an alternative location within the inner area.

Further research by Nicholson, Brinkley and Evans (1981) and by Cameron (1980) has also questioned the validity of the 'incubator' hypothesis. Nicholson *et al.* examined new firms in London, but could find no evidence that firms found the inner city a particularly favour- able location. Firms indicated that the reason for locating in these areas was because of the benefits of being close to markets, rather than lower costs of production. Perhaps the only support for an incubator hypothesis was that Nicholson *et al.* support the observation made by Fagg (1980) that new firms tend to locate in old premises – whether in the inner or outer areas – and that since the inner city has a greater concentration of old premises it is likely to be attractive to the new firm.

Cameron (1980) examined the differential location patterns of firms in the inner and outer areas of Glasgow. He found that the birth-*rate* of new firms in the inner city area was approximately two-thirds of that of the conurbation as a whole. Interestingly neither Nicholson *et al.* nor Cameron find any support for the assertion that firms which are born in the inner areas subsequently move out of the area once they expand, although both studies find that inner area firms are very mobile. Most moves are usually of short distances to other parts of the inner area.

If small firms were particularly suited to the inner areas it would be expected that they could be creating more new jobs, or losing jobs less rapidly than large firms. We have already seen that large manufac- turing firms, as a group in the UK, are losing jobs rapidly but there is no evidence that the growth of small firms is concentrated in the inner areas. If anything, the evidence suggests that the shift into the rural areas of population has been accompanied by the creation of new firms which have subsequently shown high rates of employment growth.

Fothergill and Gudgin (1982) suggest, in contrast to Falk, that the inner area is a particularly unattractive location for a firm which intends to grow since there is a shortage of space for expansion.

Although certain classic inner city industries may find the central areas attractive, these tend not to be industries which subsequently grow and create large numbers of jobs. Such firms maintain their position by not growing since size reduces their capacity to react to fluctuations in demand. On the other hand, those industries likely to grow are ones with high skill content and, as is shown in Chapter 4, are likely to be established by entrepreneurs with high educational qualifications. Such an individual will wish to minimise the distance from home to work as shown by Cooper (1973) and is more likely to live in the suburbs than in urban areas. These factors, together with the entrepreneur's preference, noted by Nicholson and Brinkley (1979), to locate in a 'green field' area suggest that a rural town, rather than an inner area, is likely to host the location of those new industries likely to show permanent substantial employment growth.

The Inner London Borough of Tower Hamlets, studied by Howick and Key (1980a) clearly illustrates these problems. In the borough very small industry is significantly more important than in the UK as a whole since 42.7 per cent of employment is in establishments employing less than 50 people, compared with a UK average of 16 per cent. This high proportion of employment in small establishments has not prevented a massive turnover of firms and net job losses. Between 1973 and 1976 manufacturing employment in the borough fell from 28,024 to 20,910, even though 2,780 new jobs were created. Howick and Key (1980b) questioned these small manufacturers (dominated by the textile and food and drink trades) on the perceived advantages of an inner city location. Proximity to customers and suppliers was frequently mentioned, but Howick and Key make an interesting distinction between traditional inner city industries such as textiles, printing, furniture, etc. and those industries attracted to the area by the existence of the docks. The former are satisfied with their location in the inner area, with their precise location being determined by the availability of suitable (cheap) premises. Industries initially attracted by the docks (engineering, metal working, timber and food), however, showed greater dissatisfaction with the area since during this period dock-related activity declined sharply. These industries also create relatively few jobs per square foot of working space and are more likely to be constrained by the shortage of space in most inner city premises.

The inner city, although it has a higher proportion of employment in small firms, has not prospered. Keeble (1978) showed that for the seven major conurbations in Britain, those which had the largest mean factory size in 1972 were the only ones whose employment in manufacturing had increased between 1959 and 1971. A Spearmans Rank co-efficient of $r = 0.92$, significant at the 0.01 level was obtained from correlating mean factory size and manufacturing employment change.[3] It is unlikely that large numbers of manufacturing jobs will return to such areas by embracing a small firms policy since the main cause of manufacturing job loss has been the closure of large plants and the failure of medium sized plants to grow.

(g) The Small Firm and Technological Change

Although it has proved difficult to measure its contribution precisely, it must be true that technical progress has made a significant contribution to the economic growth of all nations. Improved technology has enabled existing products to be produced with fewer inputs, which can then be used elsewhere in the economy to produce more or different goods. Technology has also enabled wholly new products to be manufactured. Structural problems have, however, occurred in all economies in transferring resources from the declining to the growing industries.

The role which small firms have played, and could play in the future, in stimulating technical change is open to debate. For example a case can be made that in favourable circumstances the small firm could make a major contribution to both technological advance and the creation of new wealth. There are a number of instances where individual firms have succeeded in what appear, otherwise, to be unfavourable environments. Probably the best known examples of geographical areas where small and new firms have made a major impact is Santa Clara County in California (Silicon Valley) and alongside Route 128 in Boston, Massachusetts. According to Little (1977) there were, in 1974, approximately 800 new technology-based firms in Silicon Valley and over 400 in the Route 128 area of Boston, most of them in electrical, instrumentation and information technology. Little also shows that in the United Kingdom in 1976 there were probably less than 200 such firms – of which approximately one-half were too small to be identified. Little suggests that the number of new technology-based firms (NTBF) in the Federal Republic of Germany is, if anything, even smaller.

The importance of small firms in this sector cannot be underestimated. They represent the cutting edge of new technology, they can create jobs, wealth and make a major contribution to exports. For example seven technology-based companies in the USA, founded between 1900 and 1935 had, by 1974, combined sales of $26 billion and employed a total of 764,000 people. Such firms not only grow rapidly but also have a lower failure rate than other types of firm. Roberts and Wainer (1968) found that only 20 per cent of science-based firms established by ex-Massachusetts Institute of Technology staff failed within the first five years, compared to an average US failure rate of 50 per cent. Some equally impressive growth rates have been shown by two NTBFs in Europe. Racal Electronics, founded in 1951 had, by 1975, sales totalling £50 million and employed more than 4,000 people. Nixdorf Computer AG, in the Federal Republic of Germany, also showed remarkable growth over a similar period having sales in 1975 of DM633 million and employing 7,600 people.

These firms remain very much the exception in Europe, even amongst high technology firms. In other sectors, studies of the contribution to technological development of small and large firms have encountered a number of measurement difficulties. The first is that it is unclear whether to compare small firms' contribution to technical development with their proportion of expenditure on research and development or with their proportion of total output or employment. Using the former index, Ray (1979) quotes the work of Freeman (1971) showing that small British firms contributed approximately ten per cent of all post-war innovations – markedly *more* than small firms' share of R & D spending. From this he suggests that the relative absence of small firms in the UK is an important limiting factor upon the ability of the economy to develop and that their spending is highly productive. Ray does not mention, as Freeman does, that whilst small firms contributed ten per cent of all innovations they, over the same period, produced more than 20 per cent of net output and employed more than 20 per cent of the manufacturing labour force. Thus small firms would appear to produce more innovations per £ of research expenditure – but produce slightly less innovations per £ of output or per employee.

Secondly, it is unclear what index of technical output should be used. Freeman and Ray referred to post-war innovations but innovations are not homogeneous – some are major developments whilst others are merely minor modifications to existing practices. The use of an innovations index may also tend to underestimate the importance of the small firm since, as Jewkes, Sawyers and Stillerman (1969) point out, development tends to be ,undertaken by the large firm, whereas inventions are more likely to emerge from the unstructured small firm environment. Jewkes *et al.* showed the majority of the 70 major post-war inventions derived either from universities, private inventors or from small firms. It then required the access to funds available to the larger firm before commercial exploitation of the invention became feasible and it is this interdependence, in matters of technological development, between large and small which is stressed by Bolton.

The small firm is less likely to engage in R & D than the large firm. Johns, Dunlop and Sheehan (1978) show that approximately four per cent of Australian enterprises employing less than 150 people were engaged in R & D compared with 90 per cent of enterprises employing more than 1,500. They also quote Japanese data for 1973 which shows that, in each industry, firms with less than 300 employees were less likely to have an R & D programme, than were firms of a larger size. In their study, Rothwell and Zegveld (1978) show that most of the innovative ideas for the small firm come from within – normally from the founder himself. They show that 70 per cent of innovative ideas in the small firm are 'in house', compared with only 49 per cent for firms employing more than 1,000. Cox (1971) in a study for the Bolton Committee showed that although small firms in the survey provided 31 per cent of total employment, they provided only 15.5 per cent of employment for qualified scientists and engineers (QSE). Only in electronics did small firms employ a higher proportion of QSEs than their share of total employment.

The relatively low proportion of QSEs employed by small firms is reflected in more recent results provided by Oakey (1979) who examines the innovations data originally used by Freeman, together with data on the Queens Award to Industry – the latter being a scheme launched in 1965 to recognise outstanding achievement by British industrial firms in either exports or technological development. Oakey contacted 323 firms who had either received the award or who had, according to Freeman, made a significant innovation. He found that an establishment with more than 1,000 employees was ten times more likely to have developed and implemented a significant innovation than an establishment employing between 100 and 999 people, thus supporting the original data presented by Freeman. Oakey also showed that there were significant regional differences, especially in establishments employing less than 100 people. In the prosperous regions of the UK – the south-east and the West Midlands – there was one innovating plant for every 540 establishments, whereas in the development regions there was one innovating plant for every 1,300 establishments. No account was taken, however, of the structure of industry in the two groups of areas.

Small firms as a group also spend less on R & D per employee than large firms and they produce fewer innovations than large firms. On the other hand, they produce more innovations per £ of expenditure on R & D and almost certainly produce more major inventions than large firms. Their unique contribution to technological change is that they are willing, often at the risk of failure, to develop products which the large firm feels will sell in insufficient quantities, or which the large firm may wish to suppress for fear of competition with existing profitable lines of business. The establishment of a small firm offers an opportunity for a technologist to develop his scientific expertise and to demonstrate the viability of his idea to his former employers. Large firms are now becoming more aware of the effects of losses of good quality staff and are making a greater effort to direct the energies of entrepreneurial scientists into areas which benefit the parent company — see Rothwell (1975).

For every Racal, Sinclair, etc. there are probably several thousand small firms who have no wish to innovate, and a good deal more who are incapable of so doing. In this, as in many other respects, the small firm in the electronics or instrumentation industry bears no resemblance to a firm of similar size in the furniture, printing, food processing or dressmaking industry.[4] The grouping of firms, on the basis of size, is probably less meaningful in terms of innovation than any other aspect of the debate over the merits of small and large firms. The problems which the NTBF faces differ markedly from that of similar sized firms in more conservative industries. Finally, the importance for technical change of the link between the large and the small enterprise has to be stressed — a link which can be of mutual benefit. The small firm may generate an idea and then require assistance to develop it. This may be provided by the larger firm either through a licensing system or by the acquisition of all or part of the small firm. On the other hand, many ideas developed in the research laboratories of large firms are, from its viewpoint, not exploitable on a sufficiently large scale to merit further development. These may either be developed by an existing small firm, or by the research staff setting up on their own.

2.4 Birth and Death Rates

One of Alfred Marshall's best known analogies was between the stock of firms in an economy and trees in a forest. At a single point in time, Marshall argued, there were large trees and small trees with the two apparently living side-by-side in harmony. However, some of the small trees are growing rapidly, others are stagnating and others declining. Some small trees would eventually grow so rapidly as to replace the larger trees, with the forest constantly evolving and changing, partly in response to outside circumstances. In the same way, groups of firms in an economy are also subject to change. There is substantial turnover of firms, with many being born, living for only a few years and subsequently dying, but a very few eventually reaching the commanding heights of the economy. For the majority of new firms neither of these extremes are reached. Instead, perhaps for the lifetime of the entrepreneur, the firm continues in a small way, possibly being acquired by a large group, once it has an established track record.

These general patterns seem to vary relatively little between countries. In the United States data are available on birth and death rates of the business population from 1900 onwards where births include transfers of ownership and changes in legal organisation. Kaplan (1948), reviewing the data for this period up until 1941, showed that in the years 1920 and 1921 the existing stock of businesses was added to by one-quarter, and in all years a minimum of 15 per cent addition to the business stock was made according to this very wide definition of births. Death rates of listed companies also averaged around 20 per cent per year – although there appears, during this period, to be markedly less annual fluctuation in the death rates than in birth rates.

Data on company incorporations and business names registered for Great Britain are shown in Figure 2.3. Company incorporations reached virtually 25,000 in 1948 with many individuals starting business after the war, but by 1952 this had fallen to approximately 12,000. From 1952 the numbers of companies rose in virtually all years to a peak of 47,000 in 1964 but then fell sharply until 1968, peaking in 1973, falling sharply in 1974 and then rising in all subsequent years.

Table 2.11 shows data for both company incorporations and business names registered for each five year period since 1950 in England. It shows that for each quinquennium the number of business names registered has increased, with the 1966-70 period showing the greatest annual increase of 63 per cent, over the previous period. For other periods, the increase varies between 18 and 32 per cent.

Figure 2.3: Companies Registered in Great Britain 1945-79

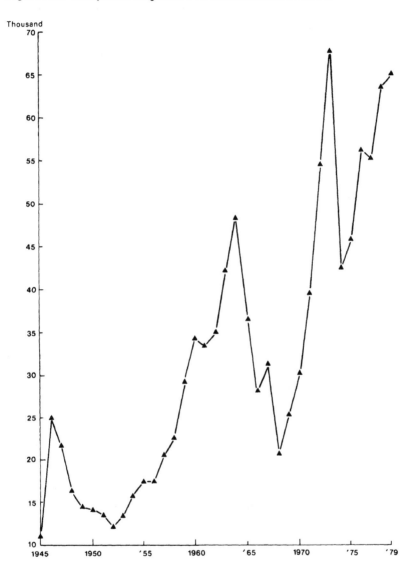

Table 2.11: New Firm Formations in England (Annual Average)

	Incorporated Companies	% Change	Business Names Registered	% Change
1950-5	13,773		27,939	+17.9
1956-60	23,873	+73.3	32,930	+25.5
1961-5	37,661	+57.8	41,326	+20.3
1966-70	26,065	−30.8	67,378	+63.0
1971-5	47,704	+83.0	89,256	+32.4
1976-9	57,565	+22.3	116,731	+30.7

The data for company incorporations also shows a marked upward trend over the period since 1950, with only the 1966-70 period showing a fall. Neither of these data sets are wholly satisfactory in describing the number of businesses which actually started operations in that year. A business may be registered but as Scott (1980) shows, up to one-quarter never actually trade. Existing companies or individuals may register a business in anticipation of trading but then never exercise that option. The data on company incorporations is also to be qualified since it cannot be inferred that a company which becomes incorporated in a given year began in business in that year. It may have existed for many years as an unincorporated company. Despite these deficiencies it is clear that, in the UK, new firm formation rates appear to have been increasing fairly continuously since 1950.

There are major difficulties in comparing the extent to which variations in birth rates between countries 'explain' differences in the stock of small firms. Bolton only made comparisons between new firm formation in the USA and UK, but even this has been shown to present difficulties. Bolton argued that in 1968, the most recent year for which data were available, 0.4 new companies were registered in Britain per thousand population compared with 1.4 per thousand in the USA. From this and other evidence on the average age of firms, Bolton inferred that low birth rates rather than high death rates were the prime cause of a smaller stock of small firms in Britain than in the USA. Bolton was unfortunate, as Storey (1980c) pointed out, in selecting 1968 as the year to make comparisons, since as Figure 2.3 shows UK company incorporations were the lowest for ten years and have never since fallen to this level. Had Bolton picked other years the UK/USA differential would have been markedly less. Bannock (1980), in correspondence on this matter, showed that the UK rates of company incorporation per head were about 33 per cent of that of the USA in

1968 but rose to 75 per cent that of the USA rates in 1973, and in all intervening years exceeded 50 per cent.

Interpretation of statistics on death rates, particularly between countries, is also difficult. For example a distinction has to be made between companies which disappear through being taken-over, those which go into liquidation, those which are bankrupt and those which never start in business. Dun and Bradstreet records for the United States are probably the best available and selected records are reproduced in Table 2.12. It shows a substantial variation over time in failure rates, which were particularly high in 1930. In fact they reached a peak of 154 failures per 10,000 concerns in 1932 and then fell continuously until after the Second World War. The late 1950s saw an increase in failure rates but these fell in the 1970s.

Table 2.12: Failures of United States Businesses Since 1920

Year	Number of Failures	Failure Rate per 10,000 Listed Concerns
1920	8,881	48
1930	26,355	122
1940	13,619	63
1950	9,162	34
1960	15,445	57
1970	10,748	44
1978	6,619	24

The characteristics of failed businesses in both Britain and the United States have been extensively studied. In essence, the research shows that the majority of failures are of very new businesses and that most fail because of managerial deficiencies. Betty Churchill (1955) in a survey of firms in the United States found that the probability of a newly formed business surviving its first year of operations was less than 0.7, and the probability of it surviving its first five years was less than 0.5. Dun and Bradstreet data confirms these results. They show that 47.8 per cent of all failed businesses were less than five years old.

There are marked variations in failure rates according to industry. Somewhat surprisingly Churchill showed from her data that new firms in the wholesale trade were, in all years, significantly more likely to survive the first two years than the average for all industries, so that 31 per cent of new wholesaling firms survived for ten years or more, compared to the average for all industries of 19 per cent. By far the highest death rates, according to Churchill, were found in the construction industry, although deaths were also high in the retail trades.

The causes of death have also been investigated. Brough (1970) in a study of 100 private companies wound up compulsorily under English law in 1965, contrasts the reasons given for failure by the official receiver and by the directors of the company. His results are reproduced in Table 2.13 which illustrates the differences in views of failure held by those operating the business and those of an outsider. The receiver's view is overwhelmingly that most failures are due to mismanagement or to gross mismanagement. Not surprisingly this is not the view of the directors who never identify this as a cause. No doubt those directors whom the official receiver regarded as mismanaging the company chose to blame ill-health, poor quality of labour or, of course, the English weather! Directors and the official receiver do seem to agree on the importance of having sufficient capital and sufficient working capital – although it is not clear from Brough's study whether both parties agreed that these were the causes of failure or whether different diagnoses were made of the same firms.

Table 2.13: Causes of Failure of Companies

Principal Causes of Failure in the Opinion of the Official Receivers		Principal Causes of Failure in the the Opinion of the Directors	
1.Mismanagement	67	Insufficient working capital	28
2.Insufficient capital	31	Insufficient capital	23
3.Insufficient working capital	20	Bad debts	18
4.Excessive remuneration paid to directors	7	Inexperience	10
5.Inadequate accounting	5	Poor labour and poor supervision	10
6.Inexperience	5	Keen competition	9
7.Gross mismanagement	4	Ill health	9
8.Bad debts	4	Underestimating	7
9.Underestimating	4	Expansion too rapid	6
10.Pilfering or fraud	4	Shortage of materials	4
11.Overtrading and expanding too quickly	3	Bad weather	4
12.Increasing overheads	3	Pilfering and fraud	4
		Inadequate accounting	3
		Increasing overheads	3
		Others	6

Source: Brough (1970).

The role of previous business experience noted by both directors and the official receiver is identified in a review of US studies of business failures by Dickerson and Kawaja (1967). They say 'it was found that inexperienced and uneducated managers were the least likely to succeed, whereas educated and experienced managers have the highest success rate'.

Similar findings were also made by Barbee (1941) who found that 80 to 90 per cent of failures are directly attributable to the personal quality of the man who fails, although in many cases ill health or family circumstances can be an important cause of failure. Woodruff and Alexander (1958) in their examination of successful and unsuccessful companies make frequent references to the personal characteristics of the man who runs the business, with college graduates performing significantly better than those without this level of education. Clearly, then, starting a business is very risky, especially for those who are inexperienced in management. This point is underlined in the programmes of training for the entrepreneur which are now provided by the US Small Business Administration. Solomon and Whiting (1977/9) estimate that approximately half the annual 400,000 business failures could be saved by appropriate management training for founders before their position had become hopeless. They also suggest that up to 800,000 small businesses which are currently struggling could also benefit from a programme of training for their founder. For the new firm founder, it may be some consolation that Scott's work on newly incorporated companies in Scotland in the 1970s showed that many such companies were remarkably resilient. Of 935 companies registered in Scotland in 1969 he was able to identify 43 per cent who had traded for between five and seven years and 17 per cent who had traded for eight years. Since there were 23 per cent of the population which were untraced the proportion of 'successes' could have been even higher.

The stock of firms in an economy continues to be dominated by relatively old firms. It takes a considerable period for the saplings to make a major impact upon the type of trees which dominate the forest. Even in the Australian economy only eleven per cent of manufacturing firms were less than five years old and, in terms of their effect in total output or employment, the impact of most new firms is negligible for up to a decade.

2.5 Conclusion

In the 1960s it became part of popular folklore to attribute slow growth in certain developed economies to the use of outdated technology in small scale plants, in back-street locations. Such enterprises were contrasted with large firms, able to reap scale economies, who were using modern technology and were located in accessible rural/suburban areas. The UK, in particular, embraced this explanation of its poor economic performance and the period saw a massive increase in industrial concentration. The impact upon UK growth rate was at best negligible and at worst negative.

Towards the end of the 1970s such ideas had become discredited. The small firm, ignored by government for generations, was suddenly presented as an economic saviour and many extravagant claims have been made for its potential to create wealth, employment, etc.

This chapter has soberly reviewed the evidence on the extent to which small firms in practice justify these claims. It presents data on new firms, and assesses the extent to which a high birth rate of firms is associated with high rates of economic growth in the national economy. The review is heavily weighted towards the well-researched manufacturing sector, even though it contains under 20 per cent of small firms in developed countries, and the sector itself employs a decreasing proportion of the labour force.

Acknowledging this major reservation the results suggest that small firms' role and contribution to development is more complex than many commentators have suggested. For example, whilst there may be an association between the rate of economic growth of national economies and the importance of small firms, it is unclear whether rapid growth causes opportunities for small firms, or whether it is the small firms that cause the economic growth. Comparative work is hampered by lack of consistent definitions of small firms.

It is frequently proposed that the major economic role for small firms is to act as a source of competition to larger firms, so reducing the latter's ability to raise prices. The small firm must be either an actual, or a potential, threat, yet in Japan where the small firms sector is probably larger than anywhere else in the developed world, most such firms are complementary to, rather than competitive with, the large firm. They are, in Lydall's terms, 'jobbers' rather than 'marketeers'. The Japanese example illustrates that a small firm sector which competes with large corporations is neither a necessary nor sufficient condition for economic growth in a country.

The small firm has recently been hailed as a major source of new jobs both in specific areas such as the inner cities, and in developed countries as a whole. The absence of data on non-manufacturing small firms, except for the USA, makes testing of this hypothesis difficult but several points are clear. First, even in the United States, the majority of new jobs are created in large firms (as are the majority of jobs lost). Secondly, although small manufacturing firms as a group have been producing an increasing proportion of total manufacturing output, this may be due more to factors causing a decline in demand for the products of the large firm than to an increased demand for the products of small firms. The fact that an increase in the share of manufacturing output produced by small firms last occurred in the 1930s suggests that such trends are characteristic of a period of depression, and perhaps restructuring. The wisdom of assuming either that small firms can recreate economic growth, or will prosper once such growth is resumed would appear to be an act of faith.

The extent to which small firms provide a conflict-free working environment is also open to question. The evidence available suggests that the probability of conflict between two individuals in a large establishment is no higher than in a small establishment. This is partly due to differences in the motivations of the workforce; in the small firm there may be a greater sense of responsibility, whereas in the large firm the risk of financial loss through conflicts, absenteeism, etc. ensures that conflict is minimised.

Whilst many claims for the small firm remain unproven it does seem clear that such firms continue to be an important source of employment, even in the most advanced economies. They do provide, in certain industries, a disproportionate number of inventions and a high proportion of innovations. The fact that most small firms will show minimal levels of growth, and that the majority disappear within five years of establishment, does not detract from the fact that a handful show rapid growth and will be major producers and employers within two decades of start-up.

A more meaningful distinction is not between small and large firms, but rather between old and new firms. The new firm tends to be more dynamic, more innovative and also more likely to die than a long established firm of similar size. The United Kingdom's poor economic performance since 1945 is perhaps more likely to be attributable to the relatively low birth rate of new firms than to the existing stock of small firms — although both could be symptomatic, rather than causes, of poor performance.

There is then considerable justification for considering the contribution which the new firm can make to the local, regional and national economy. It is important to consider the extent to which social barriers exist limiting the willingness of individuals to consider starting their own firm. Differences certainly exist between the USA and the

UK on the extent to which the standing in society of those who are declared bankrupt are held by their peers. Differences exist in cultural attitudes, and differences exist in terms of market opportunities. For the remainder of this book attention will be directed towards the most volatile section of the small firm population – the new firm.

Notes

1. This section closely follows Storey (1980a).

2. These very general trends occur whether arithmetic or geometric means are used to describe growth rates.

3. It is unfortunate, of course, that Keeble chose to relate average firm size at the *end* rather than the beginning of the period to employment change.

4. It is not suggested that innovation is absent from these industries – but merely that the pace of development is somewhat slower.

PART TWO

NEW FIRM FORMATION: THE THEORY

3   THE NEW FIRM: AN ECONOMIC PERSPECTIVE

3.1 Introduction

The new firm has a central place in economics. It represents a real or imagined threat to firms currently producing goods and services within a given industry. According to economic theory, perfect and imperfect competitive markets have substantial numbers of potential producers patiently waiting for prices in that industry persistently to exceed long run average costs. Once this happens new firms will enter the market and produce output as technically efficiently as existing firms. This threat disciplines firms currently in the industry to produce output in the most technically efficient manner, and to sell it at a price which in perfect competition will yield only normal profits in the long run.

The new firm in its early years is normally either a partnership or a sole proprietorship. It combines the characteristics of the classic entrepreneurial enterprise, whereby individuals as capitalist-employers bear the risk of producing goods and employing others. J.S. Mill, and a number of other nineteenth-century European economists distinguished between risk taking, which they regarded as 'pure' entrepreneurship, and the management of enterprises. Gradually, however, the term 'entrepreneurship' was widened until it included risk-bearing, innovation as well as the organisation and management of a business enterprise; and in this latter sense it covered established as well as new firms.

In this chapter the writings of economists, economic historians and philosophers on the subject of 'entrepreneurship' are reviewed. Coverage is inevitably incomplete and the reader interested in pursuing these matters is encouraged to consult the references given in the text. The purpose of this review is to illustrate how the subject of entrepreunership has been variously observed throughout history, mainly by those whose actual contact with men of industry was very limited. The writings of economists are designed to provide a contrast with those of non-economists and to form a background to the detailed empirical work found in Part Three of this book.

In reviewing the economic approach to new firms the inevitable starting point is the static perfect competition model. Here the new firm mechanistically enters those markets where prices persistently exceed long run average cost. The effect of this entry is to increase the welfare of the community through price reduction due to increased supply. In imperfect markets, however, although super-normal profits are being made, entry either does not take place, or takes place on too limited a scale, either because of the existence of natural barriers or because existing firms threaten to or do prohibit entry.

In static models of perfect and imperfect competition the new firm founder is assumed to respond immediately to the signals of the market place. He has no 'discretionary' role, since it is assumed that profit maximisation is his sole objective. This passive role for the entrepreneur, reacting efficiently to changes in relative prices outside his control, is central to the modern theory of the firm, yet is in sharp contrast with casual observation and with the writings of previous generations of economists. Indeed the emphasis currently placed by governments upon encouraging indigenous enterprise in less developed countries suggests that at least development economists have a healthy disregard for the modern theory of the firm.

The only 'school' of modern economists who have provided any sound theoretical basis for a role for the entrepreneur is the Austrian school. They regard the emphasis in neo-classical economics upon states of equilibrium in markets as misleading, and suggest that it is movements towards a position of equilibrium that require greater explanation. The Austrian school take imperfect rather than perfect knowledge as the norm. Here there are opportunities for the entrepreneur to exploit for a gain of pure profit. If he is able to purchase goods from individual i at a price less than individual j is prepared to pay, and cover his own costs, then pure profit may be made. The entrepreneur by purchasing from one group and selling to another, therefore, moves the market towards a state of equilibrium whereby, at the single price, buyers and sellers are satisfied. This opportunity for pure profit is reduced where producers and consumers are assumed to have perfect knowledge. Unfortunately whilst this approach is descriptively much richer it leads to relatively few testable hypotheses.

Static economic theory, on the other hand, whilst it can and does provide testable hypotheses, has a very mixed record in terms of predictive performance. Doubts have been expressed, for example, over whether statistical associations between high profit and market concentration in the United States were merely temporary and would be eroded away by the entry of new firms, or whether they were real barriers behind which firms could continue to make high profits in the long run. Doubts over the predictive performance of entry theory are also expressed at the level of the casual observation that the highest number of new enterprises were in industries which had the lowest, rather than the highest, rates of profit. Finally, it is often suggested that expected profit is only one of a large number of variables which affect the choice by an individual of whether or not to start in business.

At the end of the chapter an attempt is made to provide a synthesis, which has its roots in economics, yet attempts to accommodate these diverse strands. It is intended to offer an insight into differences in new firm formation rates both between industries and over time. It distinguishes between existing established firms moving from one industry to another, and an individual establishing a firm for the first time. The assumption, derived from the job search literature, is that an individual chooses between unemployment, self-employment and paid salaried employment according to their relative prices. There seems to be some reason to believe that such an approach will prove to be a better predictor of new firm formation rates than the examination of industrial profits and entry barriers.

3.2 The Perfect Competition Model

Perfect competition has traditionally been the starting point for discussions on the theory of the firm. Here the consumer has full knowledge of the single product on offer, and the many sellers in the market are unwilling to set a price which exceeds average costs, either because the existing firms in the industry will undersell them at that price, and/or because such a policy will induce the entry of firms willing and able to sell at average cost. This concept of a queue of entrepreneurs, standing outside industry i, waiting for price persistently to exceed long run average costs is one which, although faintly ludicrous, recurs continuously throughout-economic theory. In this context the firm is said to be a 'price-taker' since it cannot, by its own actions, alter the price either at which it sells its output, or at which it purchases its inputs. The consumers of the product produced by this mythical firm have perfect knowledge so the firm cannot sell its product for a price higher than that of its competitors. All it can do is to produce its output in the most technically efficient manner possible and sell it at the going price. Under this system the 'discretion' which the firm can exercise is nil − other than that of going out of business.

Perfect competition in the product market is a necessary, but not a sufficient, condition for welfare in an economy to be maximised. Welfare maximisation is said to occur when it is not possible, by re-arranging the resources within society, to make one person better off without making at least one person worse off, such that the gainer cannot compensate the loser and still be better off. Once the opportunities for mutually beneficial trade have been exhausted the allocation of goods and services in the economy is said to be Pareto Optimal and this remains the prime objective of economic policy in a static world. For Pareto Optimality to be achieved three main conditions have to be satisfied:

(i) The marginal utilities of all the consumers must be equalised, i.e. consumers must not find it beneficial, at the prevailing level of prices and incomes, to reduce consumption of good x and increase their consumption of good y. The ratio of the marginal utilities of each consumer for the two goods is called the marginal rate of substitution (MRS) and it defines the willingness of the individual to forego one good to obtain more of the other. The equality condition guarantees that individuals do not find it worthwhile to trade with one another, so as to make anyone better off and the others at least no worse off.

(ii) The second condition is that of technical efficiency. This requires that a given output of goods be produced by the minimum combination of inputs, i.e. the marginal physical product (MPP) of any two inputs is identical, so that it is not possible for there to be a net gain by taking away input i from producing good x and transferring it to producing good y.

(iii) For overall efficiency in the economy the third condition is that MRS = MRT, where MRT is the marginal rate of transformation and is the quantity of x in the economy that has to be foregone in order to produce an additional unit of y, when the economy is fully employed and output is produced in a technically efficient manner.

The presence of universal competition is normally regarded as sufficient to guarantee Pareto Optimality, since all three conditions are satisfied. Each consumer has the same MRS since each equates his own marginal utility to the price of the goods, which in perfect competition is identical for all consumers. Perfect competition also guarantees that output is produced in a technically efficient manner since otherwise the more efficient firms would take the markets of the less efficient. Hence the second condition is satisfied. The third condition is satisfied through the simultaneous achievement of conditions (i) and (ii).

The above sections have been stripped of many of the qualifications found in the specialist literature on this topic. For current purposes it is at least sufficient for the reader to appreciate that an understanding of perfect competition is the cornerstone of any assessment of changes in an economy. Nevertheless, it would be unwise to infer that economists are unaware of the limitations of the static analysis. For example, whilst perfect competition satisfies the conditions required for a Pareto Optimal distribution of resources, these conditions might equally be matched by a perfectly informed government acting as a *deus ex machina*. The analysis itself assumes the absence of non-priced external effects, and that goods are perfectly divisible. Most importantly, the aggregate demand for certain goods will depend upon the existing distribution of income. Second order conditions in framing maximisation conditions are assumed to be satisfied, whilst 'second best' effects are ignored. This static analysis which ignores technical change, risk and uncertainty also requires acceptance of the fundamental Paretian value judgement that individuals are the best judges of their own welfare. In short, there are a number of aspects of the Paretian approach which give rise to concern, and the reader interested in pursuing these matters further should consult Bator (1968), Rowley and Peacock (1975) or Henderson and Quandt (1971).

3.3 Imperfect Markets: The Welfare Loss

Although economists frequently express reservations over the concept of Pareto Optimality, they continue to regard deviations from the perfect competition model with suspicion, if not antagonism. In essence the most important difference between a perfect and an imperfect market is that the pricing policy in the latter is likely to be influenced by the threat, or actual entry, of new firms. New firm formation and/or cross-entry are major factors influencing prices. The firm in a perfectly competitive market, by altering its output, cannot alter either the price which it pays for its inputs or the price at which it sells its output. It accepts a fixed price (p) for its output, but its costs depend directly upon the quantity produced, together with a fixed cost element. The perfectly competitive firm sets its marginal cost, equal to the price of the output. This contrasts with the position of the monopolist who is unable to sell all his output at the single price. As he increases his sales, the unit price for his output falls so that to maximise profits the monopolist sets marginal revenue, equal to marginal cost. Providing second order conditions are satisfied the output of the profit maximising monopolist will always be less, and the price higher than for the perfectly competitive firm, if their underlying cost conditions are the same.

Since there are at least, in theory, benefits to be obtained in introducing competition into imperfectly competitive markets we can see that new firms have a central role in breaking down the position of the monopolist. It is then important to assess the value of new firms and be able to measure the welfare losses associated with monopoly, since the prime function of new firms is to act as a competitive force in monopolistic industries.

The welfare losses associated with monopoly are normally divided into three categories: (1) the deadweight triangle losses; (2) losses associated with attempting to acquire monopoly power; and (3) X-inefficiency. The deadweight loss has been the most extensively documented and estimated. It occurs because the profit maximising monopolist finds it worthwhile to restrict output (hence driving up the price) to less than that which would be produced by the perfectly competitive firm. Figure 3.1 shows that the perfectly competitive profit-maximising firm will produce Q_c and the profit-maximising monopolist will produce Q_m on the assumption that their production costs are identical. The consumer surplus in the economy (the amount people are willing to pay for a good minus the amount they actually have to pay), will fall from ACP_c under perfect competition, to AP_mB under monopoly, i.e. a loss of P_mBCP_c. This, however, is not a total loss to society since the profits of the production sector will rise by P_mBDP_c, as a result of the reduced output. Hence there is only a loss to society as a whole of BCD. This is known as the deadweight triangle, or allocative loss. The size of the triangle therefore clearly depends upon the slope of the demand curve for the product.

A number of estimates of allocative welfare loss have been made by Harberger (1954), Kamerschen (1964) and Worcester (1973). Although there is still some debate on the correct way of estimating this triangle, in practice, it seems clear that the losses in GNP, certainly in US manufacturing are not high. The highest value was obtained by Kamerschen — who estimated losses in GNP could be up to eight per cent, but more recent work by Worcester confirmed earlier results by Harberger that losses were unlikely to exceed one per cent.

The above studies assumed the cost curve of the monopolist was identical to the firm in perfect competition — see Figure 3.1. There may, however, be reasons why the cost curve of the monopolist is above that of the perfectly competitive firm.

Figure 3.1

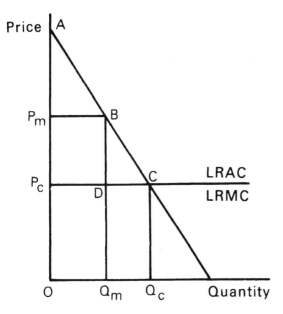

This aspect of technical or X-inefficiency was developed originally by Commanor and Liebenstein (1969). They argued that the monopolist does not have the same incentive as a firm in perfect competition to combine capital and labour in the most technically efficient manner. The firm in perfect competition knows that unless production costs are minimised it will fail to sell its output but the monopolist has some discretion. Workers and managers may have objectives which are not necessarily compatible with profit maximisation. This is often linked to the separation of ownership from control in major corporations where managers have an objective of maximising their own salaries, status, etc. The owners (shareholders) of the firm, on the other hand, have insufficient knowledge and day-to-day control of management. Hence, providing the company is making a return which satisfies the minimum requirements of the shareholders then management, protected from outside competition, may be able to pursue non-profit maximising objectives.

Stigler (1976) and Parish and Ng (1972) question whether X-inefficiency is truly a welfare loss. These authors argue that it is a direct transfer of utility from the producer to the consumer sector since the extra utility derived by the manager at work in a monopoly is exactly offset by the increased production costs. Hence there is no nett loss to society, but it seems unlikely that, even in a general equilibrium context, their X-inefficiency represents an efficient use of management resources.

To conclude this section we remind the reader (yet again) that this is a purely static analysis, and it is an assumption that costs of production in perfect competition are lower than in monopoly. When account is taken of economies of scale, of technical change and the creation of knowledge the assumption may be unjustified.

3.4 Barriers to Entry

If the entry of new firms into a market is the prime difference between perfect and imperfectly competitive markets, can it be assumed that price exceeding long run average cost occurs only in the short run? The work of Bain (1956) suggested there were reasons why, in certain industries, 'established sellers can persistently raise their prices above a competitive level without attracting new firms to enter the industry'. These reasons he called barriers to entry. In discussing the role of entry into markets we are identifying the major economic function of new firms in economics, i.e. to act as an actual or potential threat to firms currently producing in industry i.

According to Bain, entry took place by the combination of two events: (1) the establishment of an independent legal entity, new to the industry; and (2) the concurrent building or introduction by the new firm of physical production capacity, not used for production in the industry prior to the establishment of the new firm. This definition excludes acquisition of one firm by another, and expansion by existing firms within an industry. As was pointed out by Andrews (1964), it also excluded firms already established elsewhere (in industry j) moving into the industry (into i).

Let us assume, however, that the decision which faces the firm currently in j, or the individual, is whether or not to start business in industry i. Theory suggests the result depends upon two factors — the reaction of the firms already in the industry, as perceived by the potential entrant, and the costs of production once inside the market. If the firm in j expects to make at least normal profits at the post-entry price, then entry into i is assumed to take place. The entrant's expectation of the reaction of existing firms to a new producer is assumed to conform to the so-called 'Sylos Postulate'. Sylos-Labini (1962) argued that entrants behaved as if they expected existing firms to maintain pre-entry output, and that this expectation is realised. The effect of entry is therefore to increase the output of the industry and hence to reduce the price at which output is sold. Whether this expected post-entry price will induce entry depends upon the costs of production to the potential entrant. If a discrepancy continues to exist between price and the long run average cost of the existing producers, i.e. abnormal profits continue to be made in the long run, then barriers to entry are said to exist.

These barriers, according to Bain, were of three main forms. The first two are characterised by cost advantages, whilst the third is reflected through the demand for the product. The first cost advantage is that of an absolute difference in costs between two producers. Here, because of superior production techniques (possibly through patents), access to a unique input, etc., the existing firm can produce its output at a lower unit cost than the entrant. The second cost advantage is that of economies of scale, whereby the higher levels of output of the existing producer, over that of the entrant, mean the former's unit cost of production is lower. A third major entry barrier may be effective product differentiation. Here, although the entrant can produce a product which is as cheap as that of existing firms, in the minds of the consumer it is not a comparable (i.e. an inferior) product.

Bain undertook considerable empirical work estimating both the height and the effect of entry barriers. He classified industries according to whether they had 'very high', 'substantial' or 'moderate to low' barriers to entry, defined according to the extent of economies of scale and absolute cost advantage. He then examined whether profit rates were higher in industries with different entry barrier height, but similar levels of seller concentration, and found that industries with 'very high' entry barriers had significantly higher profits than those with 'substantial' or 'moderate to low' barriers. Verification of these results was provided by Mann (1966).

Two major criticisms have been levelled at this approach. The first is that estimating the height of barriers to entry by reference only to absolute cost advantage and the existence of scale economies ignores the expectations of potential entrants on how existing firms will react to their entry. Only if the Sylos-Postulate is assumed to hold in all circumstances can reaction be ignored. Where the postulate is non-operational the expected reaction of existing producers could be as effective a barrier to entry as economies of scale or absolute cost advantage. The testing of such expectations, of course, presents major difficulties.

A second criticism concerns whether the relationship between profitability and seller concentration reflects a state of equilibrium or disequilibrium in these industries. If there are real and permanent barriers to entry then it is reasonable to believe that high profits will continue in the absence of changes in demand or supply conditions. But if high profits reflect merely temporary disequilibrium in the market then they will be transitory and are likely to be eroded away by entrants. Brozon (1971) provides evidence for the former hypothesis by showing that the rate of return on net worth of the 19 industries examined between 1950-60 by Mann fell significantly between 1960 and 1966. This was true for all industries, irrespective of the height of entry barriers.

3.5 A Role for Entrepreneurship in Economic Models

The above brief survey of current economic models of markets and firms has ignored a specific and unique role for the entrepreneur. The models are framed in terms of entrants and existing firms, and no distinction is made between firms which are wholly new, and existing firms which are moving into a different industry, even though the two groups may react differently to incentives. In a static world, capital and labour, in perfect markets, are optimally combined to produce output in a technically efficient manner. The firm mechanistically accepts the price which it pays for its inputs and the price at which it sells its outputs. In this situation 'entrepreneurial gain' (spotting a gap in the market), etc. are irrelevant. In Baumol's (1968) words:

> the firm is assumed to perform a mathematical calculation which yields optimal (i.e. profit maximising) values for all its decision variables . . . There matters rest, forever or until exogenous forces lead to an autonomous change in the environment. Until there is such a shift in one of the relationships that define the problem the firm is taken to replicate precisely its previous decisions, day after day, year after year.

Baumol was not confident that modern economics could offer a useful insight with entrepreneurship. He felt that the emphasis upon maximisation and minimisation within the subject, by definition, excluded a role for the entrepreneur in economics, although he recognised that useful insights could be provided by other disciplines. Domar (1968) in discussing Baumol's paper, suggested however that the latter was in danger of repeating a tautology.

> If the entrepreneur is defined as an exceptional person who sees into the future what other people do not see then he obviously cannot fit into economic models. If he behaved according to a model then Baumol would demote him from the position of an entrepreneur to that of a manager, or even make him a common maximiser operating within known, at least in some probability sense, inputs and outputs.

This modern view of entrepreneurship differs from those of at least two important other schools of economic thought. The first is that of nineteenth- and early twentieth-century economists who viewed the entrepreneur as central to the promotion of economic development. The second is the modern Austrian school of economists who see static market equilibrium models as irrelevant to explaining behaviour since there are constant shifts in, and movements along, the demand and supply functions. The Austrians view the entrepreneur as an individual who whilst pursuing his own self interest eases the market towards an equilibrium position. The Austrians recognise, however, that other factors will intervene before the market actually reaches a state of equilibrium.

The nineteenth- and early twentieth-century view of the entrepreneur was (of course) summarised by Marshall (1961).

> But in the greater part of the business of the modern world the task of so directing production that a given effort may be most effective in supplying human wants has to be broken up and given into the hands of a specialised body of employers, or to use the general term, of businessmen. They 'adventure' or 'undertake' its risks; they bring together the labour and capital required for the work, they arrange or 'engineer' its general plan, and superintend its minor details. Looking at businessmen from one point of view we may regard them as a highly skilled industrial grade, from another as middlemen intervening between the manual worker and the consumer.' (p. 293)

As Harbison (1956) points out economists have traditionally stressed that the entrepreneur has three major functions: (1) the bearing of risk and uncertainty; (2) innovation; and (3) the organisation and management of a business enterprise. The risk bearing hypothesis was developed by Knight (1921) who argued that the entrepreneur entered into fixed price agreements with labour and with material suppliers, and that profit was a residual available after output had been sold and all fixed price agreements had been met. The actual level of profit obtained by the entrepreneur depends on his ability to anticipate the price at which the final product will be sold, which in turn may depend upon his own ability, the actions of others and upon good fortune. Knight's entrepreneur had control over his enterprise, and in return for taking the responsibility for producing a product, i.e. bearing uncertainty, he obtained profit. One result of the Knight approach is the notion that changes in relative prices can induce individuals either to become an entrepreneur for an uncertain return or to become labourers at a fixed but certain wage rate.

> The labourer asks what he thinks the entrepreneur will be able to pay, and in any case will not accept less than he can get from some other entrepreneur, or by turning entrepreneur himself. In the same way the entrepreneur offers to any labourer what he thinks he must in order to secure his services and in any case will not offer more than he thinks the labour will be worth to him, keeping in mind what he can get by turning labourer himself. (pp. 273-4)

The above quotation from Knight is reproduced by Kihlstrom and Laffont (1979) who use the Knight framework to provide a general equilibrium model of new firm formation. They assume the function of the entrepreneur is to provide his own inputs to the production process and to bear the risks associated with production. The model postulates that, at a given wage rate, an individual agent chooses between the uncertain profit of being an entrepreneur or the certain wage rate. They show that, assuming all individuals are equal in their ability to switch between entrepreneurial and labouring functions, there is a single equilibrium position in the labour and product markets, with the more risk-averse induced to become workers at lower wage rates than other agents.

In short Knight, and the models which derive directly from his work, distinguish the entrepreneur as the individual who decides whether a business shall exist, chooses the field of the business and determines the way in which the business is to run. On the other hand the employee, whether he is a labourer or an executive, is subject to the overall direction of the entrepreneur. The work of the employee, says Knight, is a routine task of exercising his best judgement and leaving the consequences to others.

In addition to bearing risk the entrepreneur is also characterised as an innovator. This role was clearly expounded by Schumpeter (1934). The innovative entrepreneur jolted the economic system out of a state of equilibrium by introducing a new product, or new production process. Schumpeter's entrepreneur had the foresight to see that by such action he could increase the pure profits of his firm, but the length of time that these profits continued depended upon the reaction of rivals, and the nature of the innovation. Samuelson (1975) described this process vividly.

> The violin string is plucked by innovation, without innovation it dies down to stationariness, but then along comes a new innovation and plucks it back into dynamic motion again. So it is with the profit rate in economic life.

We have seen above that Marshall saw a major function of the entrepreneur as being to organise and manage his business — 'to superintend its minor details' — but that Marshall's description was more 'all embracing' than that provided either by Knight, or by Schumpeter. It is now clear that Marshall in his description was remaining within what, by that time, had become the British tradition of viewing entrepreneurship as intimately associated with the bearing of personal risk in the event of failure. Originally Adam Smith (1776) did, contrary to the assertions of Kirzner (1980), distinguish the role of the capitalist from that of the entrepreneur but by Marshall's time this distinction was no longer drawn. Consequently the distinction between income received from interest and pure profit was rarely made and it was assumed that without capital an individual could not exercise entrepreneurship. Ownership of capital was a necessary condition for entrepreneurship, and since ownership and management were, at least until the mid-nineteenth century in Britain, normally embodied in the same individual, it was quite natural for the entrepreneur to be the manager of the enterprise. Only with the development of the joint stock principle did ownership and control become divorced.

3.6 Economics and Entrepreneurship: An Alternative View

The role of the entrepreneur had not excited much interest amongst economists for virtually half a century, until the important work by Kirzner (1973). The Baumol view that the entrepreneur had been eliminated, by the nature of the subject, from the study of markets was accepted by all but a few dissidents within the profession.

Kirzner offered the first challenge to the hegemony of the Baumol position, by questioning whether it was appropriate to examine only equilibrium levels of prices and output. In Kirzner's view economists' interest should be in the processes by which movements were made towards an equilibrium position rather than in the equilibrium position itself. In the Austrians' view the entrepreneur does not necessarily own or manage a business, incurs only the opportunity cost of his time, takes no risk and offers no innovation. Indeed the characteristic of the 'entrepreneur' in this Austrian sense is that he is just as likely to be an individual as a businessman. The individual who recognises that the market for a good or a service is out of equilibrium will exploit this position. Where there is excess demand for a good at a given price, an individual may purchase goods at the prevailing price and sell to those who are prepared to buy at the higher price. The entrepreneur encourages the markets' movement towards a state of equilibrium, there being greater opportunities for such actions under conditions of imperfect knowledge. He is alert to opportunities not recognised by others and it is this awareness which is defined as pure entrepreneurship.

The distinguishing characteristic of the entrepreneur, in Austrian terms, is the ability, in a world of imperfect knowledge, to recognise the opportunity for profit. This is quite separate from the ownership of resources. The 'Austrian' entrepreneur reduces disequilibrium in the market, and in this sense differs fundamentally from the role presented earlier by Schumpeter. In the Austrian context the market is assumed to be in a state of disequilibrium and the entrepreneur reacts to these prices, and brings about movements towards equilibrium. In the Schumpeter model the entrepreneur deliberately brings about movements *from* an assumed state of equilibrium – he 'disturbs the circular flow'.

There can be little doubt that the Austrian view of the entrepreneur has a number of attractions. It discusses the process of price setting in markets without having to rely on the assumption of perfect knowledge, and individuals being price-takers. It accords with the layman's concept of the entrepreneur as someone who identifies a 'gap in the market'.

Finally, it provides an alternative for theoreticians dissatisfied at the lack of realism of models which examine shifts from one equilibrium position to another. Nevertheless, despite this descriptive richness, the Austrian approach may present even greater problems to 'positive' economists than the approaches which it criticises. Difficulties of deriving testable hypotheses have inhibited developments of the theory and it may be that the Austrians' greatest contribution has been to encourage 'mainstream' economists to delve back into their bag of tricks to obtain a new economic view of entrepreneurship. The Austrians, by their emphasis upon imperfect knowledge, have stimulated economists to model the effect of a given stock of knowledge upon entrepreneurship. For example, Calvo and Wellisz (1980) show that where the stock of knowledge is increasing rapidly, but where the distribution of abilities amongst the population remain unchanged, the entrepreneur needs to be more exceptional. This, in turn, may lead to new firms growing very quickly in such industries — an obvious example being micro-circuitry. Calvo and Wellisz also show formally that rapidly advancing technologies tend to attract younger entrepreneurs.

It may be that although at present this type of work is able only to derive fairly self-evident results, the models of Calvo and Wellisz and those of Lucas (1978) offer a real promise for development since they are orientated towards the derivation of empirically testable hypotheses.

3.7 Towards a Synthesis: Theory and Practice

Having briefly outlined the various approaches to entrepreneurship which have been made by economists, with specific reference to new firm formation, we now turn to the predictions and testing of hypotheses found in the literature. A reviewer cannot fail to be struck by the absence of empirical studies of new firm formation, despite its central place in economics. There are, as observed above, a vast number of studies linking industrial structure to economic performance, particularly as measured by profitability. Such studies assume that an increase in the rate of profit in industry i will induce entry into that industry.

$$E_i = E_i(\Pi_i) \tag{3.1}$$

where $\quad E_i$ = entry of firms into the ith industry

$\quad\quad\quad \Pi_i$ = ratio of profit in the ith industry to that in all other industries

and $\quad \dfrac{dE_i}{d\Pi_i} > 0$

Such studies, however, recognise that entry into some industries is substantially more difficult than into others. The height of entry barriers will deter some potential entrants. The barriers may be due to the absolute cost advantages of existing firms, or to scale economies, or to some form of product differentiation within the market, or to the absolute costs of starting in business.

$$E_i = E_i(\Pi_i, C_i) \tag{3.2}$$

where $\quad C_i$ = investment required to establish a firm of minimum efficient size in the ith industry

and $\quad \dfrac{\partial E_i}{\partial C_i} < 0$

Equation (3.2) is used by Mansfield (1962) in a major empirical work, relating profit change in industry i to actual number of entrants. He defines E_i as the number of new owners of productive facilities becoming established in an industry in a given period, and surviving to the end of the period, divided by the stock of firms at the beginning of the period. The concept is therefore one of 'gross' entry, rather than changes in the stock of firms (i.e. entry minus exits). In many respects it does not correspond to Bain's definition of entry cited on p. 54. Bain's definitions included firms that entered the industry but which perished before the end of the period. Bain also specifically excluded establishments which changed ownership without adding to productive capacity. Mansfield was forced to include such firms because the data did not enable them to be eliminated. Mansfield also encountered major problems over his definition of C_i. In practice he merely updated Bain's estimate of minimum efficient size (even though productive patterns had almost certainly changed during the war). He also recognised that many entrants were, in practice, below the minimum efficient size and could not be expected to earn profits

Despite these reservations (mainly consigned to appendices and foot-notes) Mansfield proposed that the effects of the variables in equation (3.2) were likely to be multiplicative and using data for several indus-tries for a number of time periods, he derived the results shown in equation (3.3).

$$L_n E_{it} = 0.49 + 1.15 L_n \Pi_{it} - 0.27 L_n C_{it} \qquad (3.3)$$
$$\qquad\qquad (0.43) \qquad\quad (0.14)$$

(standard errors in parenthesis)

The equation shows that entry rates are higher when relative profits in industry i increase and are lower when capital requirements rise, as would be predicted from basic theory.

Apart from Mansfield's study there have been few attempts to relate actual entry of firms to changes in profitability. The lack of follow-up studies is due to the absence of suitable data on new firms. This is very unfortunate since there are grounds for believing that the model presen-ted by Mansfield is incomplete and could be misleading.

To develop a more robust model of entry we need to distinguish between new firm formation and transfers.

$$E_i = NF_i + TR_{ji} \qquad (3.4)$$
$$NF_i = \text{wholly new firms in industry i}$$
$$TR_{ji} = \text{transfers from industry j to i}$$

Transfers occur where a firm currently in industry j decides to move into i. Legally this may take the form either of purchasing an interest in an existing firm (i.e. not adding directly to the capacity of the indus-try) or creating a new establishment in i whilst continuing to produce in j. Finally it will include reductions in productive capacity in j and trans-fers to i.

$$TR_{ji} = f(\Pi_j/\Pi_i; C_i) \qquad (3.5)$$

In the case of transfers it is likely that the Mansfield model will be valid since the firm will consider the relative rates of profit in the two indus-tries concerned. The firm will also look more favourably upon indus-tries where entry barriers are lower, and will pay particular attention to the expected reaction of firms currently producing within i. It will also be more likely to expand into those industries of which it has knowledge such as those which it supplies, or which supply it.

Wholly new firms are less likely to respond in the ways predicted. Equation (3.6) outlines some factors which, in theory, might be expected to influence the number of wholly new firms in industry i.

$$NF_i = f(G_i, C_i, U_i, S_i) \qquad (3.6)$$

G_i = growth in employment in industry i

S_i = proportion of total employment in industry i in firms with employment of less than 100

U_i = unemployment rate in i

We shall discuss each of the arguments in the function separately but we begin by noting that the concept of profit is not directly included, even though we are in sympathy with Knight's approach of viewing entrepreneurship as a choice between paid employment and self-employment. These options, as we shall see, are included in both the G_i and the U_i variables.

Equation (3.6) explains the rate of new firm formation in industry i in a given time period. This is measured as the number of wholly new firms entering that industry as a proportion of the total stock of firms, although in practice measurement would probably be of new firms which survived until the end of the period, rather than total entrants. It is not, as in earlier equations, the total number of (surviving) entrants.

The G_i variable reflects the positive attractions of the industry to an entrepreneur. If he sees that a number of his former colleagues have established their own firms, and have succeeded, this is likely to stimulate him to follow suit. A measure of G_i would be the number of surviving new firms in a previous period (NF_i^{t-1}) or the total employment growth of the industry during the same time period.

The capital requirements for an operation of minimum efficient size must remain a significant barrier to entry, so that the C_i variable is retained. Its retention in practice, of course, continues to present the same definitional and measurement problems which Mansfield encountered.

We have seen that Knight argued that everyone with work experience is a potential entrepreneur. The individual is assumed to choose rationally between paid salaried employment, self-employment and unemployment. Similar notions are found in Oxenfeldt (1943).

The reasons for establishing a business vary widely. The selection of entrepreneurship may be in preference to employment with others; in preference to unemployment; or in an effort to exploit the most profitable opportunities in the economy.

Oxenfeldt discusses most of the factors identified in equation (3.6). He argues that because there are 'search costs' individuals do not necessarily choose to start businesses in the industries where profitability is highest. 'Instead he is likely to select for the establishment of the new firm the industry which is most accessible and to which his prior business experience is related.' If the individual is currently employed he may start in business for three major reasons: first, he may find his current employment situation unsatisfactory because of a sense of frustration with missed promotion, or personality clashes with his boss or because of fear of redundancy. Secondly, he may start his own business when his training/apprenticeship is complete and when he has saved sufficient capital. Thirdly, he may see an opportunity to make a profit, not recognised by his fellows. In the first case it is likely that he will remain in the same industry since that is where his main expertise lies. In the second case he will start in business in the industry where he served his apprenticeship, whilst in the third case the chances are higher that he will observe the opportunity for profit in an industry where he has experience than in one with which he is unfamiliar.

These hypotheses have been tested by Johnson and Cathcart (1979b). They found that of 115 founders of manufacturing businesses in the northern region, 57 per cent established their firm in the same industrial 'order' in which they were formerly an employee, with over 40 per cent of new firm founders remaining within the same Minimum List Heading (MLH). These support Oxenfeldt's own results obtained by investigating the background of entrepreneurs in the shoe industry: 98 per cent of those who became manufacturers and 97 per cent of those becoming retailers were previously employed in that industry. Of those investigated, 90 per cent were employed in the same branch of the industry. He also found that of those engaged in wholesaling, 43 per cent had previously been a business owner. Even in manufacturing the proportion was 30 per cent.

Gudgin (1978) obtained similar results in a survey of new firm founders in the East Midlands. He found that 85 per cent claimed to have experience in the industry in which they established their firm. Gudgin, however, pointed out that there were considerable variations in this rate by geographical area. For example, only 47 per cent of respondents in Newark and 50 per cent in Erewash Valley had experience of their trade, whereas the proportion was 96 per cent in Wellingborough. Gudgin explains these differences in terms of the industrial structure of the locality, suggesting that single industry towns offer less opportunity for a local entrepreneur to move into different industrial sectors.

Equation (3.6) also proposes that the entry rate of wholly new firms into industry i is related to the number of small firms in that industry. It suggests that an operational definition for this might be the proportion of total employment in industry i in small (defined as less than 200 employees) firms.

Several commentators have suggested that the existing sizes of enterprises are a major factor determining new firm formation rates. The man who works in a small firm is trained for entrepreneurship, since it is more likely that he will have to be involved with all aspects of the production process. The manager of a small firm, for example, although probably paid a salary substantially less than a lower-middle manager in a larger firm, has to be conversant with all aspects of managing the business. On the other hand, managers in the large firms who have specialised in certain areas – production, marketing, etc. – have tended to lose the 'all round' experience of managing a firm. The experience of the small firm employee is likely to give him greater confidence that he can successfully begin business on his own, primarily because he will have been in a position, as an employee, particularly if he was in a managerial position, to see and understand the operations of all parts of the firm. On the other hand, the Bolton Committee (1971) and Boswell (1972) have argued that the quality of management is lower in small than in large firms, suggesting that this confidence may be misplaced, at least in the case of large numbers of individuals.

Empirically, it is difficult to identify a variable which captures the greater willingness of individuals who have previously worked in small firms to form their own firm, yet which is uncorrelated with a barriers to entry variable. The entry barriers literature suggests that new firm formation is higher in industries with a high proportion of small firms since the latter reflects low capital requirements and the absence of scale economies. Taken with the observation that, irrespective of industry, most individuals form a firm in the industries in which they were formerly employed, it is clear that from a random selection of new firm founders, those previously working in small firms are likely to be 'over' represented.

Not surprisingly, empirical investigations have, with one major exception, shown that new firm founders are more likely to come from a small than from a large firm background.

Table 3.1 shows that the probability of an employee working in a firm employing less than ten people, forming his own firm, is substantially higher than that for an employee working in a firm employing more than 250. This is documented in four separate studies for different time periods, for three countries, and for very different types of entrepreneur. In the North American case the entrepreneurs are in science-based industries whereas in the British studies a variety of industries are examined. Without exception they all show that the very small firm is a much more fertile incubator than the large.

Table 3.1: New Firm Formation Rates, Classified According to Size of Incubator Plants

	England East Midlands[1]	Northern[2]	North America[3]	Scotland[4],[a]
Size of Previous Employer				
1-10	11.9	14.25		7.37
11-99	4.0	7.25	9.7	2.26
100-499	2.8	2.75		1.02
500+	1.0	1.0	1.0	1.00

Note: a. The size band of previous employer for Scotland area: 1-25, 26-100, 101-250, 251+.
Source: 1. Gudgin *et al* (1979); 2. Johnson and Cathcart (1979b); 3. Cooper (1973); 4. Cross (1981).

This analysis has been criticised by the present author (1981b) for failing to distinguish between barriers to entry and the small firm *per se*. The studies cited above take no account of industrial structure of the sample of new firms. If, for example, most of the new firms in the sample were in the timber and food industries where barriers to entry are low, the fact that many new firm founders came from a small firm background is only to be expected since this is a reflection of industrial structure. It does not provide any evidence that the small firm within a given industry generates a greater willingness amongst its workforce to establish their own enterprises. Since, as we have shown, there is a high probability that an individual will form a firm in the industry in which he was formerly an employee, the opportunities for the workforce in shipbuilding or on a petrochemical complex are more limited than those in joinery or baking. Local Authority Planning Officers do not take kindly to proposals to establish ethylene crackers or blast furnaces at the end of gardens in residential areas! The local bank manager will also take rather more convincing that an individual who has worked as a riveter in a shipyard has sufficient business acumen to successfully establish his own ship repair yard, than he will that an individual who has worked as a carpenter could establish a joinery business. In short, the option of entrepreneurship is much easier to exercise for those working in industries where the minimum efficient size is small than where it is large.

Hence in comparing small and large firms as 'incubators' account must be taken of industrial structure. This author compares new firm formation rates in Cleveland and the East Midlands and shows there is a positive correlation between those industries in which Cleveland has a higher proportion of its workforce in small firms, and those having a higher rate of new firm formation. This suggests that, even taking account of industrial structure, i.e. barriers to entry, the small firm in industry i is a more fertile incubator than the larger firm in that industry.

Not all empirical studies support this conclusion, with the pioneering work in Britain on new firm formation by Beesley (1955) suggesting the opposite. Beesley was interested in explaining differences in the economic performance of the north-west and south-west zones of the West Midlands. He found the north-west zone performed significantly better than the south-west zone, in the sense that it had a higher ratio of 'surviving' entrants in the total population of establishments. Beesley attributed the superior performances of the NW partly to the larger size of establishments in that area, although he was not championing size *per se*. Rather he suggested that the integrated steel finishing trades required a high degree of variety in metal working skills, leading to product innovation and development. His comment that: 'For example, the fact that there were proportionately more larger establishments in the north west zone's metal industries than in the south west zone's may have given the zone as a whole more experience of management techniques' is prefaced by the acknowledgement that this was one of many other possible contributory factors in explaining performance – the majority of Beesley's explanations being devoted to the industrial structure and social history of the area.

Johnson and Cathcart (1979a) and Gudgin (1978) have postulated that the more rapidly growing industries are more likely to attract entrants, and the contracting industries less likely to attract entrants. Gudgin states that an increase in growth in an industry may be regarded by an external potential entrepreneur as an indication that there is a potentially satisfactory (post-entry) level of profit to be made within the industry.

The best equation derived by Gudgin in support of this hypothesis is shown as equation (3.7).

$$E_i = 0.011 \underset{(0.002)}{X_{2i}} - \underset{(0.008)}{0.048 X_{3i}} - 0.320 \quad R^2 = 0.59 \qquad (3.7)$$

E_i = entry rate of firms into industry i, 1947-55, surviving until 1967

X_{2i} = percentage of plants employing less than 20 people in 1955 in the ith industry

X_{3i} = growth in total employment 1947-67 in the ith industry

(standard errors in parenthesis)

Gudgin's reaction to the absence of a profit term in this equation is to suggest that expected profits are of relatively low significance for the entrepreneur, and that the desire for independence is of relatively greater importance.

Johnson and Cathcart also perform a similar analysis of new firm founders in the north. Their equation is reproduced below as equation (3.8).

$$E_i = -37.3 + \underset{(2.8)}{0.36} EMP_i + \underset{(3.9)}{0.06} G_i + \underset{(1.11)}{0.45} S_i \quad R^2 = 0.69 \qquad (3.8)$$

EMP_i = employment in industry i

G_i = growth in employment in industry i 1965-75

S_i = percentage of plants in industry i employing under 100 employees 1972

('t' values in parenthesis)

Equations (3.7) and (3.8) seem to be mutually supportive, suggesting that whilst industry size may be important in 'explaining' inter-industry entry rates, variations in growth rates are of less significance. Johnson and Cathcart speculate that the insignificance of a growth term may be due to the myopic view of the potential entrepreneur, who is primarily concerned with assessing *his* prospects in the industry which *he* knows. This suggests that over time new firm formation rates in industry i will be affected not only by expected profits of forming a firm in industry i, but in comparison with the alternatives of paid employment, or unemployment. The likelihood of an individual currently employed in j starting a firm in industry i, however, will depend upon the height of entry barriers in i, expected profits and differences in the attitudes of the workforce in the two industries.

Shortage of data makes the testing of these hypotheses extremely difficult. Both Gudgin and Johnson and Cathcart acknowledge that profits are a factor influencing the choice of whether or not to enter an industry, yet no profit term appears in their equations, because of the technical difficulty of obtaining suitable data. For example, to test the above hypotheses, data would be required on rates of profit which an individual entering that industry, in that locality, could be expected to make, i.e. an ex-ante measure. In practice the only generally available data are in the *Census of Production*. This will be an average, over the whole country, of establishments and firms of all sizes. It does not offer a comprehensive coverage of the very small firm sector into which the new firm founder will enter. Finally, it represents actual, ex-post fact, as opposed to the entrepreneur's expectations.

The role of unemployment in inducing entrepreneurship and new firm formation has been discussed extensively. As in many other respects, Oxenfeldt offers perhaps the most coherent account.

> If an individual is involuntarily unemployed, whether as a result of a general economic depression, technological advance, sickness or old age, his need for a new source of income is generally much greater than that of employed persons. If he is able to establish a business, he requires little inducement to do so. Most unemployed persons would probably be willing to take great risks for a chance to secure a small income and to erase the stigma associated with unemployment. It is not irrational – or unusual – for an individual who is unemployed to set up a business even if the chances of succeeding are small. (p. 120)

If there is nothing to be lost by setting up a business then it is clear that unemployment, actual or even threatened redundancy, may be sufficient to induce an individual to form his own firm. We should recognise, however, that there is a greater stigma associated with bankruptcy in the UK than in the society which Oxenfeldt described.

Nevertheless, unemployment or threatened redundancy can act as a spur to those individuals who have thought about starting their own business. The majority threatened by, or actually laid off, will continue to look for paid work, but even these are likely to look more favourably upon offers of partnerships than when they were in paid employment.

If unemployment and new firm formation are causally linked then more new firms will be formed when profits in an industry fall, or at least when demand for labour falls. Since it has been shown that the new firm founder looks to form his own firm in the industry in which he was an employee, a reduction in the demand for labour is likely, *ceteris paribus*, to increase the number of entrants to that industry.

No empirical work has been conducted in Britain in relating profitability to new firm formation at the industry level but Johnson (1980) has shown that there is a statistical association, at an aggregate level, between new firm formations and unemployment.

$$FR_t = -0.19 + 0.33U_{t-1} + 0.91FR_{t-1} \quad R^2 = 0.97 \qquad (3.9)$$
$$ (0.16) \quad (0.11) \qquad (0.07)$$

FR = formation rate: new business names ÷
     male working population $_t$.

U = unemployment rates

t, t-1 = time periods

(standard errors in parenthesis)

This is shown in equation (3.9) above, using data on business names registrations and national rates of unemployment. It shows there is an association between the rate of new firm formation and the rate of unemployment one year previously.

Unfortunately, the inferences which can be made from these results are less clear. First, in theory, it is the relative profits in industry i that determine entry into that industry. The association in equation (3.9) between formation rates and unemployment may hide a more important association. For example, Morley (1979) has shown the existence of a strong relation between unemployment and profit, reproduced as equation (3.10).

$$U_t = 14.54 - 0.70\Pi_{t-1} \quad R^2 = 0.88 \qquad (3.10)$$
$$ (15.0) \quad (12.8) \qquad DW = 1.96$$

He argues that a fall in profit induces an increase in unemployment. According to Johnson this will then induce an increase in the rate of new firm formation. This might suggest the existence of a self-correcting mechanism in the economy, with new firms springing up to take the place of those whose profits had declined, but it is unlikely. New firm formations may be concentrated in industries which are easy to enter, but all too easy to leave. Many of the entrants 'marching stolidly into the ambush' do not have sufficient managerial or personal skills to enter an industry and compete successfully. Oxenfeldt argues that those who are unemployed are the least likely to form a successful business, and suggests that in most cases they are forced to enter industries where capital requirements are lowest, since the financial institutions are unlikely to lend to an unemployed individual without a job or experience of running a business. The financial institutions may also lend to certain types of industries and not to others. For example, they may look more favourably upon entrepreneurs starting in wholesaling where the majority of the cost is in purchasing stock which can be easily realised by the bank in the event of failure whereas investing in highly specific capital equipment may be considered too risky. Hence the industries which are easiest to enter are likely to be the most competitive, where the risk of failure is highest.

We now return to equation (3.4) reproduced below.

$$E_i \quad \equiv \quad NF_i + TR_{ji} \tag{3.4}$$

We have argued that entries into i are defined to be identical to wholly new firms NF_i, plus firms which have switched from industry j to industry i, either by taking over plant and equipment owned by a firm moving out of i, or by adding directly to the productive capacity of the industry.

Throughout the discussion a number of variables have been identified as significantly influencing entry rates, notably expected profits, minimum efficient size and the growth rate of the industry. It should now be clear that the effect on E_i of changes in profitability depend on the relative strength of two influences. A decrease in profitability in industry i may encourage firms currently in that industry to shift resources to j, which is now relatively more attractive. Gross entry from established firms is likely to be reduced and net entry from established firms is likely to fall. If, however, the fall in profits of firms currently within i, is reflected in a reduced demand for labour within these same firms, then there is likely to be a net increase in the pool of unemployed labour in that industry. When the labour market in general is tight, many of these individuals with transferable skills will find employment in other industries, but even in those conditions a number will conclude that forming their own firm is more attractive than either unemployment or paid employment in industry j.

The net effect of a reduction in profitability in i on entry will depend on the strength of these two influences, one serving to raise entry rate through new firm formation and the other to decrease it. In aggregate it is unclear which of these effects are greater, although it is likely that firms transferring from industry j to industry i will be somewhat larger than the wholly new firm. The effect of a decrease in profit in industry i will therefore have an indeterminate effect on the total number of firms in that industry, and may change the size distribution of such firms by increasing the number of very small firms, many of whom will be recent entrants, and decreasing the number of larger firms.

2.8 Conclusion

In this chapter the writings of economists on the subject of entrepreneurship and new firm formation have been briefly reviewed. In static economic theory the prime purpose of the new firm is to act as a real or potential threat to firms currently producing in industry i. The new firm, in perfect competition, will move into industry i once price persistently exceeds long run average costs and, by doing so, reduce the 'excess' profit in that industry to a normal level.

New firm formation, in static economic theory, is framed in the context of competition, such that firms formed by individuals are seen to be mechanistically responding to the signals of the market. There is no 'spotting a gap in the market', no exercise of initiative. These characteristics of entrepreneurship are specifically excluded from the model. Instead it is assumed that all individuals have the same information and that the appropriate number form their own firms and enter industry i, where price currently exceeds long run average costs, so as to return that market to a state of equilibrium. If perfect competition did not have such elegant properties such hypotheses would have been dismissed long ago, but they continue to hold sway.

The logical inconsistencies of the perfectly competitive market adjustment process pointed out by the Austrian school of economists have failed to dislodge 'equilibrium' from the centre of the stage in economics. The emphasis placed by the Austrians in understanding the mechanism by which prices adjust in a market, and specifically in recreating a role for the entrepreneur, have received polite applause but added little by way of framing of testable hypotheses.

It now seems that only through detailed empirical work on the predictions of the traditional market models will the static economic approach be modified. It is, for example, unlikely to be true that alterations in the relative or absolute levels of profit in industry i will more than partly explain new firm formation rates in i. The hypothesis presented originally by Knight, that an individual chooses between being a labourer and being his own boss, deserves wider consideration. In addition it is unreasonable to assume that each individual is equally suited to entrepreneurship, even taking account of different attitudes to risk. Some individuals may be satisfied with a given level of means and prefer to spend their time in leisure pursuits. Some may be more motivated by a desire for independence than for money. In some geographical areas social norms, such as a preference for collective action, may militate against entrepreneurship. The size of firm in which an individual works also may influence his confidence in becoming his own boss. This confidence may also be affected by his level of education such that he may be unwilling to compete directly against 'clever' people.

In short, whilst the concept of an entrepreneur responding automatically to market signals is useful it is not a comprehensive explanation of new firm formation.

4 NEW FIRM FORMATION: SOME NON-ECONOMIC APPROACHES

4.1 Introduction

The previous chapter showed that economists have, as central to their discipline, theories of new firm formation or entrepreneurship. These theories are based primarily upon factors which influence the slope and position of the demand curve for entrepreneurship, such as changes in demand for the final product, or in the relative costs of inputs. The supply curve of entrepreneurship, on the other hand, is assumed by economists to be invariant or, where movements do occur, their explanation is regarded as beyond the discipline of economics.

Kihlstrom and Laffont (1979) typify this approach. They assume each individual faces a choice between working for himself or being a wage earner, and that he is able to move freely between these two states. Actual movement is assumed to be induced by changes in relative prices. Barriers to entry into entrepreneurship in the form of inadequate knowledge, limited motivation or cultural prejudices are excluded on the grounds that they can be 'handled' through postulating the existence of a utility function, one argument in which is the desire for money, wealth, etc., whilst non-monetary values such as independence are incorporated in a separate term.

Sociologists, psychologists, economic historians and even economists interested in development in the Third World, argue that the 'supply-side' cannot be dismissed as purely passive. Their research suggests these factors are more important in explaining economic development than changes in relative prices, since the latter merely create the opportunity for entrepreneurship. The extent to which this opportunity is seized locally, or by outsiders, or allowed to slip away entirely, is directly dependent upon psychological and motivational influences in the local economy. To raise new firm formation in country X or region Y it may be more cost-effective for government to isolate, on psychological grounds, individuals who are suited to entrepreneurship and to encourage their aspirations, rather than attempt to create a climate for economic opportunity through demand management policies. These observations are supported by the limited power of changes in capital and labour in 'explaining' different economic growth rates between countries and over time.

In this chapter several socio-psychological characteristics of the entrepreneur are identified. In some societies, regions and at certain points in time, individuals embodying these characteristics seem to be more abundant than at others, so that advantage is taken of the opportunities available. At other times, new markets become available, only for these to be eagerly grasped by foreigners. Native industry appears to be moribund.

Offering a reasoned account of such developments is frustrating for those social scientists accustomed to analysing 'hard' data, since inference is often based upon non-random observations such as biographies of successful entrepreneurs. In eighteenth- and nineteenth-century Britain, for example, whilst the personal and social characteristics of the Arkwrights, Owens and Wedgwoods are well documented, much less is known of the 'plodding men of business'. Studies of entrepreneurs, in different countries and over different time periods, further complicate the task of identifying common threads, so that whilst it is interesting to speculate for example on how the eighteenth-century British entrepreneur would have coped with late-nineteenth-century conditions, argument does tend, at best, to be inconclusive.

Payne (1978) in a scholarly account of Britain's entrepreneurs, whilst lamenting the absence of biographies of those industrialists of less than front rank, suggests that the problems facing Britain's industrialists at the end of the nineteenth century were substantially greater than those of their forebears at the beginning of the century. The inference from Payne is that perhaps Arkwright *et al*. might not have coped too well in late-nineteenth-century Britain.

Difficulties of applying statistically rigorous testing to hypotheses have resulted in extravagant claims of generality amongst the theories. Even amongst those who lay claim to statistical testing, the evidence presented has not always proved robust under detailed scrutiny — Schatz (1965).

In presenting evidence on the 'supply-side' of entrepreneurship this chapter identifies several themes which occur consistently throughout the literature. It begins with a discussion on the role of the family, childhood experiences and the role of education. Closely related to this is the role of class divisions in the many societies in which entrepreneurship is studied. It then examines the psychological motivation and personality of new firm founders, followed by a discussion of religious beliefs. Finally, it discusses the work-experience factors influencing the individual's choice to start in business, but throughout the interrelationship between all these factors is emphasised. Class, religious beliefs, education, family structure are however so closely linked that it is rarely possible to identify one as *the* single significant variable.

4.2 The Role of Class Divisions and Education

Social class differences amongst entrepreneurs are often invoked to explain variations in the frequencies with which businesses are established and their subsequent performance. Class affects an individual's perception of social reality — the lower class position being associated with an uncertainty over events. In contrast, those reared into the upper classes believe that they can, by their own actions, influence events — Kohn (1977). The uncertainty of the lower classes' position is argued to encourage conformity and, in this context, a reluctance to undertake the additional uncertainties of entrepreneurship.

In the early stages of industrial change in Britain however the highly successful new firm founders seem to have come from a considerable variety of backgrounds (Ashton (1948)), although it would seem that there was an emphasis upon the lower-middle class, especially those with mercantile connections. The suggestion, by Samuel Smiles, that anyone prepared to apply himself to making money would be successful was something of an overstatement, if only because access to capital was limited to those with wealth. Marshall argued that the capital market worked perfectly and that finance could always be found for projects which offered a good prospect of a return, but it seems clear that the opportunities for obtaining funding increase with greater resources.

Dahmen (1970), for example, in his study of industrial change in Sweden, found the majority of first generation, i.e. pre-1914, Swedish industrialists were from the upper or upper-middle classes. He attributes this to easier access to capital, and notes that only when wages rise, and income in Sweden becomes more evenly distributed does the second generation of Swedish entrepreneurs come from a wider mix of social backgrounds.

Before 1914, and especially in the earliest decades of industrialisation of Sweden, the new firms, particularly in certain industries, were both founded and financed by persons who either were active in commerce, especially in wholesaling, or else had many ties to commercial activity . . . The majority of the firms started between the wars and had workers, or persons of similar status, as founders. About 80% of them started in the community where the founder happened to have his residence. (p. 415)

Dahmen argued that in the early stages of industrialisation, when there were few firms, the potential entrepreneurial base was narrow but that once more firms became established and grew the manufacturing workforce increased. Workers then gained expertise in production giving them sufficient confidence to start their own firms. Nevertheless, firms founded by those of lower social origins performed less well than those owned by individuals in higher social groupings. As reported in Chapter 3, Oxenfeldt shows that many firms established by workers are the result either of actual or threatened redundancy. Such firms represent to their owner an attractive alternative to unemployment, provided they offer the likelihood of income higher than that available to the unemployed. Individuals of higher social origins will only enter 'trade' if the expected returns, *ceteris paribus*, exceed that which could be obtained from alternative employment, which is assumed to be at a higher wage rate than that of the unemployed. There is no immediately obvious reason why non-monetary influences such as the desire for independence should vary between classes, so that purely 'economic' reasons may 'explain' the differing performance of firms founded by different social groupings.

Both Dahmen and Oxenfeldt find evidence to support this hypothesis. Both show the entrepreneur coming from a low social class, on average, founds a firm in an industry in which he was previously employed. The performance of the firm in terms of growth of output, profitability and employment is generally lower than that of otherwise similar firms established by an individual in higher social groupings.

Dahmen refers to those firms started by founders as an alternative to unemployment as begun on the 'livelihood principle'. He argues that in many respects these firms are not truly entrepreneurial, in the sense of risk-bearing, since the founder is taking no greater risk in being self-employed than he was as an employee. In the case of the new firm founder the objective of establishing the firm is to obtain a similar standard of living to that which he would have obtained as an employee, but with the benefit of greater independence. In the economists' terms the objective of the 'livelihood' founder is to maximise personal independence subject to an income constraint, whereas the entrepreneur will maximise income subject to an independence constraint. In this case it is not surprising that 'livelihood' firms fail to grow in economic terms since material reward is not the objective of the founder. Indeed, it would be contrary to the objective of achieving a given level of independence, since if the firm grew it might become a potentially attractive acquisition for a larger firm.

Similar conclusions are reached by Oxenfeldt, who demonstrates that the unemployed, who represent a larger proportion of the lower income groupings, are more likely to enter trades where capital requirements are low and competition is fierce. Hence they are also more likely to fail in their chosen trade, or at least find it difficult to grow substantially, in part because the optimum size of firm in that industry is small.

It is, of course, difficult to examine the effect of social class on new firm formation in isolation, since the former is strongly correlated with education levels and with wealth. The entrepreneur from the upper-middle class is more likely to be better educated and more wealthy. The benefits of education, in this context, are that they ensure he has greater choice both of initial occupation and of industry. The well educated potential entrepreneur is more likely to obtain some managerial experience prior to establishing his firm. Higher standards of basic education also tend to give the individual greater confidence to begin his enterprise. In the more sophisticated and technically advanced industries, only those with the highest educational qualifications could consider establishing firms. The development of computer technology, semi-conductors and micro-processors requires new firm founders to understand fully the technology involved. New firms in these industries have often been associated with institutes of advanced education such as universities, illustrated by the link between the Massachusetts Institute of Technology and the science industries of Boston which developed along Route 128. Cooper (1973) shows that a number of new firms were established by university academics, either in their spare time, or in conjunction with a full-time partner. He shows also that a number of these employed local science graduates who, in turn, after several years' experience developed their own expertise and subsequently established their own firms.

In many respects the availability of universal education, at least in the developing countries, should enable a greater diversity of social groups to take advantage of opportunities in industry, but in practice there continues to be a strong emphasis upon the middle and upper-middle classes making the greater use of such facilities. Even the British Open University, designed to assist those whose formal education had stopped prior to obtaining a degree, seems to attract as students a high proportion from the middle classes — often those with a degree in another subject.

Education should improve managerial performance and give greater occupational choice to individuals, but in practice the major 'consumers' of education are often the middle and upper-middle classes. Hence workers may be excluded from employment in certain industries by the barrier of inadequate education. The education system in Britain, however, has been identified as an important cause of the country's relatively poor economic performance since 1870. Aldcroft (1975), for example, suggests that science was of secondary importance in the hierarchy of education skills taught in British schools and colleges at a time when other European and North American countries held scientific education in much greater esteem. In Britain, the arts and classics continued to cream-off talents which elsewhere might have been directed towards science and engineering. In addition, the education system in Britain has never, in the view of many, given sufficient encouragement to those wishing to enter industry. Too frequently the brighter pupils have entered commerce and the public service, occupations which the educators have believed, rightly or wrongly, to be more prestigious. Industry has been left with the residual.

A number of studies have examined the relationship between social class, education and entrepreneurship. Goldthorpe *et al.* (1968) examined the aspirations and motivations of a relatively affluent group of workers in Luton, England, in 1962. They found that amongst the manual workers 25 per cent claimed to have thought seriously about owning their own business — and that this was, if anything higher than a comparable study by Chinoy (1955) of United States automobile workers. Goldthorpe *et al.* also found that this route to 'improvement' was seriously considered by a higher proportion of respondents than promotion from within the firm to a position of foreman. Nevertheless, the authors of this study felt that only a minority of affluent workers had, in their view, seriously considered entrepreneurship and they conclude:

Basically we would suggest that these 'ways ahead' are primarily for other people; for those with education and qualifications who could look forward to a genuine career within their employing organisations, or for those with the financial backing to give a business venture a fair chance of success. They were not regarded as offering generally realistic opportunities for rank and file workers.

Other studies have examined relationships between educational levels of founders and the performance of new firms. Gudgin, Brunskill and Fothergill (1979) in a study of new manufacturing firms in the East Midlands of England showed that firms founded and managed by those with degrees or equivalent qualifications perform significantly better than those of non-graduates. Their results are reproduced as Table 4.1 and show that these differences are not 'explained' by factors such as the age of the firm. The authors do not discuss the role of inter-industry differences, nor do they discuss the sensitivity of their results to the inclusion of extreme points, but given the small sample size it is doubtful whether account could have been taken of such factors.

Table 4.1: Performance of New Firms in the East Midlands

Background of Founder	No. of Firms	Average Initial Capital (1976) £	Average Annual Turnover 1978-9 £	Average Employment
Graduates, etc.	13	21,600	591,000	25.9
Other white collar workers	11	12,100	169,600	11.5
Commercial	7	10,500	295,600	21.4
Manual	16	3,800	192,800	17.6

Other studies of entrepreneurs are less clear on the role of education in both influencing the willingness of an individual to establish a firm and affecting his ultimate success. Roberts and Wainer (1968) in a study of entrepreneurs establishing technically-based firms along Route 128 in Boston found that those with Masters Degrees were, in general, more successful than those with PhDs. Nicholson and Brinkley (1979) show from a study of new manufacturing firms in south-west London that out of 74 such firms established since 1965, only 15 were founded by graduates, and only seven by individuals whose parents had been in business as owners.

Boswell (1972) studied surviving founders of small firms in the mechanical and electrical engineering and the hosiery and knitwear industries. In total he interviewed 64 firms, and was able to speak to the founder in 30 cases. Table 4.2 shows the educational and family background of those founders where this is known. It also shows the most common type of new firm founders in this sample, i.e. the skilled manual worker who attended an elementary/secondary modern school and obtained a technical or craft qualification. Nevertheless, bearing in mind the distribution of education and qualifications in the community, those with degrees (and even those from public schools!) are substantially overrepresented whilst the unskilled manual worker is underrepresented. In these aspects, though again the sample is small, and significance tests are not undertaken, the results do not obviously contradict the hypotheses outlined that those with higher educational (social) skills are more likely to form their own firm, and once in business to be more successful, than those with a lower educational attainment.

The diversity of backgrounds is also reflected in the work of Scase and Goffee (1980) who report their discussions with 96 active proprietors in the personal services sector. This sector was chosen for investigation because of its low entry barriers so as to maximise the representation amongst those of working-class origins (although many had become 'middle class' due to their business success). Few had any formal educational qualifications. Nevertheless, several controlled enterprises with an annual turnover in excess of £1 million, although there is no formal attempt in the research to link educational qualifications to the performance of the firms.

Table 4.2: Family Background, Education and Qualifications of Founders of Manufacturing Establishments

Father's Occupation	Unskilled Manual Worker	Skilled Manual Worker	White Collar/ Supervisory	Business	Professional
	2	11	10	6	1

Education	Elementary/ Sec. Modern	Grammar	Public School	Not known	
	13	11	3	3	

Qualifications	None	Craft	Technical	Degree	Not known
	2	11	12	4	1

Scase and Goffee's most pertinent observations relate not to the number of entrepreneurs from working-class backgrounds, but to the extent that, even after their 'promotion' they remained, almost fiercely, working class in outlook. Class differences documented by Goldthorpe (1980), which remain in Brtain despite a quarter of a century of unprecedented economic progress and supposed equalisation of opportunities for industrial and social mobility, are likely to continue to influence the supply of entrepreneurs for the foreseeable future.

4.3 Family Background and Enterpreneurial Personality

The associations between social class and education are not independent of family background. A number of hypotheses have been proposed on the influence which an individual's family has on his willingness to enter business, and his likelihood of success once in business. For example, Lees (1952) suggested that eldest children, because responsibility is imposed upon them at an early age, tend to show more enterprise and initiative than their younger brothers and sisters. The roles of father and mother are often regarded as central in influencing the motivations and aspirations of children. McClelland (1961) observes that development in societies was often immediately preceded by a reduction in the dominant role of the father within the family. This may occur because of the absence of the father from home, either temporarily or permanently, or because of the nature of the father's job which takes him away from home, e.g. soldiers, sailors, etc. Finally, the father himself may be self-employed and, because of the demands of the business, spends long periods away from home. In this situation the mother turns to the child who is expected at an early, but not too early an age, to accept responsibility for decisions of the household.

Even where the father is present the mother continues to be a central figure. The need for achievement (n-achievement) is central, according to McClelland, to achieving success in business and it can be inculcated into the child early in life. Here the mother performs the central role of encouraging and rewarding the child for achievement; she is supportive without being protective, persistent without being demanding. Excessive protection by the mother can lead to a discouragement of initiative by the child who, when allowed freedom to exercise his own judgement, is unaware of the risks associated with various forms of action. McClelland quotes the work of Winterbottom (1958):

The mothers of sons with high n-Achievement tended to expect 'self-reliant mastery' at earlier ages than sons of mothers with low n-Achievement. They also placed fewer restrictions on their sons than did the mothers of the 'lows', but the restrictions they did insist on were to be observed at an earlier age. Even so, the self-reliance training was expected still earlier by the others . . . In a word, the sons of the 'lows' remain more dependent on adults both for achievement help and for restrictions, for a longer period of time.

In many respects unstructured interviews with entrepreneurs offer support for more formal psychological analysis. Collins and Moore's (1964) survey of entrepreneurs suggested that two-thirds claimed to have suffered a difficult childhood and had learnt to struggle at an early age. Similar observations were made by Boswell (1972) even though the latter did not specifically question entrepreneurs about their childhood experiences, other than to ask about father's occupation and the entrepreneur's own educational qualifications. Boswell notes rather sardonically that since 14 of his founders had been brought up in working-class homes in either the early 1900s or in the Depression years, stories of childhood difficulties were not wholly unexpected. Of those entrepreneurs from outside the working class, just over half also mentioned family difficulties such as divorce or death of a father.

Collins and Moore (1970) show that 25 per cent of entrepreneurs had fathers who themselves were small businessmen, compared with only 17 per cent in a sample of senior executives of large companies. They also show that 30 per cent of entrepreneurs had fathers who were labourers, either skilled or unskilled, compared with 15 per cent amongst executives. This combination of relative poverty and frequently the absence of father from home is assumed to exert an important influence upon the child and upon his subsequent development.

Kets de Vries (1970) has attempted to identify these complex family forces acting upon the entrepreneurial personality, and they are shown in Figure 4.1.

Figure 4.1: Psychodynamic Forces Influencing the Entrepreneurial Personality

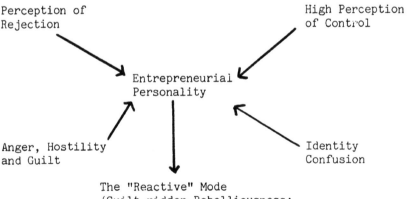

This shows that entrepreneurs frequently regard themselves as having been rejected as a child and it is this perception of rejection which subsequently influences their personality. The rejection is normally from the father, but entrepreneurs who grew up in conditions of extreme poverty also saw themselves as being rejected by society in general.

Psychologically the absence of the father has a number of effects. The first is to raise the importance of the son, particularly the first born son, within the family. In the absence of the father he becomes the head of the household, and even if he is not required to obtain money to maintain the family, is likely to be involved in decision making within the household. As he matures greater responsibility will be imposed upon him, so that he will become used to making decisions and learning from mistakes. This perception of rejection by the father parallels the increased control of the family affairs, thus encouraging leadership traits.

Having to lead a fatherless household can often lead to a sense of anger and hostility towards those in positions of authority. Psychologically the absent father is often equated with adult figures in later life, over whom the entrepreneur feels the need to triumph. In school days this is reflected in a rebelliousness towards teachers. The child may prove to be 'difficult' at school which, in turn, may lead to poor academic performance, leading to a heightening of hostility towards the world in general. The failure to perform well academically leads to a reduction in available job options with traditional careers closing their doors. Hence he may, after a period of drifting, find that the best available work option is to start in business. In some cases this realisation may lead to reunification with the father, with son taking over the business. In other cases, the fierce independence from father is maintained and son starts his own business, often along similar, but rarely identical, lines to the father.

Nicholson and Brinkley (1979) offer some empirical support for this sketchy hypothesis. They show that seven out of the 74 new firm founders had fathers who were in business themselves. Interestingly, only one of that seven had undergone sufficient formal education to obtain a degree. In Boswell's survey six out of a total of 30 founders had fathers who had been in business, but it is not possible to determine the number who obtained degrees. Of the 26 inheritors, four had degrees.

The non-acceptance of socialised behaviour which Kets de Vries notes in his diagram is a reflection of the entrepreneur equating, in his mind, the raw deal dealt him by his father. Throughout life his dealings are characterised by a feeling that other individuals are attempting to 'rip him off', and this aggression may be directed, at various points in time, towards the bank manager, an old boss or a partner.

The wicked absent father contrasts with the caring mother who is often found to be a dominant figure in families producing entrepreneurs. The mother symbolises the stability which the entrepreneur is striving to attain, yet in which he is frustrated by authoritative individuals. These influences partly explain major themes in his interpersonal relations. For example, as an employee the individual rejects the authority of his employer but, having started his own business, he is likely to take a paternalistic attitude towards his staff. He protects the weak, in the same way as he protected his mother at home, but he will not accept any diminution of his own authority and will react angrily to any real or perceived threat from other groups or individuals. This is reflected in the unwillingness of small firm founders to 'groom' a successor for fear of compromising their own position.

Collins and Moore (1970) summarise the position well:

> Entrepreneurship is patterned by modes which are learnt in early childhood. Many times we will find these men caught in situations of insecurity symbolically similar to those they knew in childhood. (p. 38)

In discussing the personality of the entrepreneurs emphasis has been placed upon the role of parents, but the effect of social norms and ethics are also important. Virtually all entrepreneurs are characterised by an exceptional capacity for hard work yet, particularly in Britain, a reluctance to move up the social hierarchy even once substantial wealth has been accumulated. The motivation for achievement may in some cases be financial, but it is rarely social, so that ostentatious shows of wealth are rare, and where they do occur, appear to be deliberately 'tasteless' in order to demonstrate wealth rather than class. For example, Scase and Goffee's respondents when asked about the personal characteristics required to be a successful small businessman stressed the need both for exceptionally hard work, but also to make profits, almost for their own sake. Scase and Goffee state:

> Turning to styles of life we found that, in general, the proprietors we interviewed lived rather modestly, primarily because they give priority to the business . . . their standard of living is not unusually high and can best be described as 'low middle class' for the owners

of smaller enterprises and 'upper middle class' for the owners of large concerns. Furnishings are functional rather than decorate (even) amongst the owners of larger enterprises styles of living are more luxurious but less so than might be expected . . . Business owners tend to lead very private lives . . . they are too affluent to be working class, but lacking in the cultural skills to be 'middle class'.

Even Bannock (1981a) in describing a typical small businessman says:

He was a big man with a shock of black hair, an old oil stained blazer, with leather round the cuffs. His fingers were nicotine stained. John had never taken any exams, but had served an apprenticeship with a heavy diesel manufacturer and had two years with REME at the end of the war. He was not very good at getting on with theoreticians.

These cultural distinctions have been formalised by Smith (1967) who identifies the craftsman and the opportunist type of entrepreneur. The craftsman entrepreneur (C-E) normally comes from a blue collar background, having had limited education but once at work has considerable technical success. Smith then relates this upbringing and experience to the type of company which the C-E forms and shows these tend to be paternalistically organised, with little forward planning. Management is characterised by a reluctance to use outside finance and an emphasis upon reputation rather than sophisticated marketing. In terms of social behaviour the C-E remains faithful to his class roots, even though he often has accumulated sufficient wealth to move into more sophisticated circles. Smith contrasts this type of social behaviour and type of enterprise established with that of the opportunist entrepreneur (O-E), coming from a middle-class background. The O-E normally has a well rounded education and moved on to a generally successful but normally varied working career. He obtains managerial experience, often at quite a senior level, and then establishes his company. He does not, like the C-E, identify with the workers so employee relations are less paternalistic. The major difference between the O-E and the C-E occurs in terms of the types and performance of companies which they establish. The O-E founded firm is managed so as not to involve the founder in the detailed, day-to-day running of the firm, but leaving him free to concentrate on strategic matters. The O-E shows a willingness to utilise outside sources of capital and is not subject to fears of control loss. Marketing is approached actively and given a high priority. Life style is more upper class than that of the C-E, with a more diversified social life.

Smith developed a scoring system which quantified these personal characteristics and then related these to the type of firm which the entrepreneur established. He found there was some evidence to support the hypothesis that C-E produced more rigid firms characterised by unwillingness or inability to change and develop, whereas the O-E was more likely to produce an adaptive firm which was constantly evolving, reacting to, and occasionally imposing its own will upon, its business environment.

Using Smith's scoring system, Nicholson and Brinkley have shown that there is also some evidence that the O-E tends to found firms which grow faster in terms of output, employment and profitability than those founded by C-E, but their sample is small. Even so there does seem to be some evidence suggesting that education/family background play a role in influencing the type of company established – and possibly the success and development of that company.

4.4 The Role of Minority Groups and the Protestant Ethic

The development of industry in most societies has tended to be uneven. Some social classes or groupings are more influential than others, with new forms of economic development being initiated by well defined groups. In Britain Nonconformists were strongly represented amongst the early industrial entrepreneurs, whilst Protestant groupings in Germany were also prominent in shaping the development of industry. The existence of a link between the Protestant faith and its secular values, on the one hand, and economic development on the other, has been raised by a number of social historians and philosophers.

Weber (1904) was able to produce a number of quotations from Calvin suggesting that the concept of predestination in religious beliefs and those personal characteristics of successful industrialists were causally linked. Of these Weber writes:

> The Elected Christian is in this world only to increase the Glory of God by fulfilling His commandments to the best of his ability. But God requires social achievement of the Christian because He wills that social achievement shall be organised to His commandments, in accordance with that purpose. (p. 108)

individuals who were demonstrably willing and able to start their own businesses. Where the individual was prepared to start his business in an area of high unemployment, such as north-east England, he was positively welcomed. The Commissioners for the Special Areas were able to provide government-built factories for rent for the first time in Britain in Team Valley, Gateshead in 1937, and refugees who were thought to have good commercial prospects were offered access to capital by the Home Office.

By 1938 about 11,000 Jewish refugees from Germany, Czechoslovakia and Hungary had been admitted to Britain in the previous five years, yet they had formed 250 enterprises which employed approximately 15,000 people. By 1939, 55,000 adult German and Austrian refugees were in Britain of whom there were up to 5,000 manufacturers, although many of these were subsequently interned for a substantial period during the war. After the war these enterprises flourished and Loebl estimated that in the northern region alone 54 manufacturing enterprises were started by refugees and that by 1974 these employed 16,932 people, providing a vital element of diversification to the northern economy.

Britain's policy towards those refugees displaced by Nazi Germany, whilst partly humanitarian, was also highly discriminating with a strong emphasis upon allowing only those individuals with commercial experience to enter the country. Virtually all of Loebl's 54 manufacturing firms were founded by refugees who had either run a business themselves or whose families had been in business. No data are given of those individuals who were unable to obtain a permit to enter Britain because they had no experience in trade! The Jews who came to Britain may therefore have been more enterprising and intelligent than a truly representative sample of European Jews in the 1930s.

The observation that enterprise and entrepreneurship is not exclusively linked to the Protestant ethic is also illustrated by Benjamin's studies of firms in the Seychelles reported in Greenfield, Strickton and Aubey (1979). He contrasts the longevity and prosperity of Chinese and Indian firms with those of the native Creoles. In many respects the differences between the groups encapsulate with one exception the social and motivational factors identified in this chapter. The exception is that Chinese and Indian families show a close interaction between father and son with the father regulating all aspects of the son's life, whereas in the Creole culture the male is peripheral. Education is however given priority by the Indians and Chinese but ignored by the Creoles. The Indian and Chinese families are close-knit, so that help in running the business may always be obtained. Similar family assistance is not available to the Creole entrepreneur. In short, the Indian and Chinese family structure is orientated towards business development. The opposite is true for the Creoles.

Some support for the hypothesis that immigrant groups are 'forced' into enterprise through blocks being imposed on their progress in the 'host' society is also provided by Aldrich (1980) in his study of Asian shopkeepers, in Wandsworth, London.[2] He finds that they are significantly better educated than white shopkeepers in the area, with 22 per cent of Asians having college degrees compared to only three per cent of white shopkeepers, and attributes this to barriers to entry to managerial jobs. Aldrich notes, however, that this does not explain why shopkeeping should be so attractive to Asians, yet have such a low representation amongst those of West Indian origin. This lack of a tradition of enterprise amongst Negroes has also been remarked upon by Frazier (1957) in his studies of blacks in the United States, but there seems to have been little attempt to explain the underlying causes of these clear differences between ethnic groups.

4.5 Aspirations and Motivation: Firm Size

Throughout this chapter there has been a clear recognition that the aspirations and motivation of individuals differs between socio-economic groupings, religions, nationalities, etc. In the previous chapter it was shown that large firms were significantly less fertile as incubators than small firms, but no motivational explanation was developed. Cross (1981) has compared the reasons given by entrepreneurs, coming from a large firm background, for forming their own firms, with those from small firms. This is reproduced as Table 4.3. It shows that only one-quarter of large firm employees gave 'advancement' as the major reason, whereas frustration with the type of work undertaken and its bureaucratic structure was given in 45 per cent of all cases. Frustration was much less apparent as a motivating factor amongst those working in small firms, with advancement being mentioned by 61 per cent of respondents as a prime incentive.

The frustration of working in a large company and the role which it plays in encouraging entrepreneurship is clearly not independent of other factors such as the previous experiences of new firm founders. Cross shows that of his 29 founders from medium/large organisations, 27 gave their previous employment position as manager and/or director.

Table 4.3: Reasons Given by Founders for Leaving Their Previous Employer Immediately Prior to Setting up a New Manufacturing Enterprise in Scotland, 1968-77

Reason	Size of Incubator Organisation				
	Medium-Large	%	Small-Other	%	Total
Advancement	7	24.14	94	61.44	101
Nationalisation	2	6.89	0	—	2
Take-over	3	10.34	5	3.27	8
Closure	1	3.45	18	11.76	19
Frustration	13	44.83	20	13.07	33
Greater financial reward	0	—	10	6.54	10
Return to Scotland	3	10.34	2	1.31	5
Made redundant	0	—	3	1.96	3
Retirement	0	—	1	0.65	1
Total	29		153		182

Only one founder would have been weekly paid, or blue-collar. This contrasts with the entrepreneurs from a small firm background. Here 43 per cent gave manager and/or director as previous occupation, whereas over 30 per cent would have been weekly paid. Since the grading of the new firm founder from a small firm is likely to be lower than that of the large firm founder, it is hardly surprising that the former is more strongly motivated by the desire for advancement.

It is important to isolate those features of size which make the large firm a less fertile incubator for entrepreneurship than small firms, since there may be ways in which to raise their fertility. This question was, in fact, raised by Lord Vaizey when the author was questioned by the House of Lords Select Committee on Unemployment:

Lord Vaizey: You say that in certain parts of the country there may be a climate which is favourable to small firms. Professor G.C. Allen said that in his PhD thesis 50 or 60 years ago in his study of Birmingham and the Black County. From your work could you go into a little more detail about what it is that you think lies behind this?

Storey: If you work in a relatively small firm employing, let us say, less than ten people, the probability is that if you have enough managerial talent you will see the whole operation through from the beginning to the end; in other words, you will sweep the floor, you will do the accounts, you will do the buying, you will do the company marketing, public relations and might even

> lend a hand on the production side. That means you are in a much better position, you are better trained, to establish your own firm, because you have seen the job through as a comprehensive exercise. If, however, you work at Doxford Engines in Sunderland as a riveter or a plater, you have probably always worked as a riveter or plater. You may have interesting hobbies such as wood-carving at home, but the transferability of your skills is much less than the small firm employee.

In the smaller firm each employee is required to undertake a greater variety of tasks than the worker in a larger firm. He will be encouraged to adopt a flexible approach to work and, providing he does not appear to threaten the power position of the owner/manager, indications of initiative are likely to be rewarded. Experience of all aspects of running the business are likely to be available to him, and the individual may judge that he may as well run a business for himself as for somebody else.

A more 'economic' view of this decision derives from the fact that employment in a small firm is less secure than in a large firm and that, on average, wage rates are also lower. Hence it is not surprising that individuals, with ability, are more likely to consider entrepreneurship since this is probably only marginally more risky than working for an existing small firm. To some extent a sample of small firm employees is self-selecting if individuals who have a preference for risk gravitate towards the smaller firm. In this case it is also not surprising that such individuals will be more prepared to begin in business than their more risk-averse colleagues in larger firms.

4.6 Conclusion

Readers who are sympathetic to a behavioural approach as a means of explaining differences in growth rates between economies may feel that this chapter has adopted a somewhat nihilistic view of their subject matter. The intention is not to downgrade the role which psychological and sociological explanations provides, but rather to illustrate that it is not easy to identify a single causal explanation. The fact that a number of early entrepreneurs in Britain came from Nonconformist backgrounds could be related to their upbringing, their religion, their access to capital or to their social class. It is not clear which if any, or what combinations, of these factors is the cause of their being strongly represented amongst eighteenth- and nineteenth-century British industrialists.

The co-linearity between certain religions, parental roles, class, education, managerial experience and access to capital make it difficult to isolate the independent effect of a single influence upon economic development. The lack of statistical rigour in the testing of hypotheses, in part due to the nature of the topic, means that some complex, yet essentially unprovable, hypotheses are proposed.

The partial nature of these 'explanations' of spatial, cultural and temporal differences in entrepreneurship continue to frustrate major developments in the subject. It seems clear that many 'socially marginal'[3] groups and individuals, of which immigrants are a prime example, become entrepreneurs, but their social marginality fails to explain the frequency with which this role is accepted by many Asians but rejected by Negroes. It also fails to explain why certain individuals respond to what Bruce (1976) calls 'the determining event' — whether it is the death of a close family member, or redundancy or failure in an examination — by becoming an entrepreneur whilst others remain crushed.

The major exception to these statements concern McClelland's n-achievement hypothesis. He proposes that the outstanding economic development of certain groups or classes can be traced to a basic need for achievement. This need transcends religions, class and country. McClelland believes that if policy makers wish to increase the rate of development in an economy the most efficient strategy would be to increase the n-achievement levels in the population. This could be done by a specific programme of inculcating n-achievement motives into individuals. McClelland reports some success in raising the n-achievement scores of students subjected to counselling sessions, but whether a temporary raising of n-achievement scores of adults offers any long term benefit is open to doubt and has not been tested. The alternative, of attempting to raise the achievement motives of the very young,by for example, influencing the availability of children's reading material, is more likely to be effective, but risks charges of attempted brainwashing. The most significant criticism of introducing a programme to raise n-achievement levels is that it is unclear whether high scores on the index are the root psychological cause of a desire for development or whether they are merely symptomatic of such a cause. To infer it is the underlying explanation of differences in economic progress amongst groups, given the evidence currently available, would be unwise.

Despite this research on motivational aspects there appears to be little conclusive evidence that these theories offer a comprehensive explanation of economic development. The psychological and sociological characteristics of the new firm founder are fairly consistent across societies and time periods, but it is unclear whether it is possible to alter these in a given society so as to increase the rate of new firm formation. Even if they can be altered, it is likely to take at least 30 years for today's children to form their own firm. Equally, changes in education take many years before they are reflected in economic development.

There must also be some doubt about whether sociological explanations are merely reflecting variables which are essentially economic. For example, many founders of new firms who had previously worked in large firms said they found their previous employment frustrating. This is regarded as symptomatic of working in a large de-personalised establishment, with its lack of personal involvement in the decision making of monolithic corporations. Nevertheless, the 'economic' explanation that, since most new firm founders from a large firm background come from the upper managerial grades, there is no way that they could regard it initially as 'advancement' to start their own company with a few employees, may be equally valid. Since they have a relatively secure job and a relatively high income it is *only* frustration that could force them to start on their own. Precisely the opposite influences are at work with the founder who has previously worked in a small firm.

Whilst psychological and sociological explanations of entrepreneurial behaviour are valuable, their influence on the supply curve of new firm founders is likely to be effective only in the very long term. In addition it is not wholly clear which policies are likely to be effective. The policy maker is advised to tread warily in this area.

Notes

1. Lipman (1965) found in a study of Columbian businessmen that 41 per cent of his sample in Bogota were immigrants from other countries. In Chile, Briones found that 76 per cent of businessmen in firms with over 100 employees were of foreign origin, this result being reported by Derossi (1972).

2. Studies of small shopkeepers have been made by Bechhofer, Elliott and Rushford (1971). They conclude that the resilience of the sector, despite low profitability and unsocial hours, is due to ease of entry combined with an attraction for those wanting to be their own bosses.

3. Social marginality is defined to occur when there is a marked difference between the role or roles of an individual in society and the individual's view of his own personal qualities – see Stanworth and Curran (1973).

PART THREE

NEW FIRM FORMATION: SOME EMPIRICAL RESULTS

5 A SURVEY OF NEW FIRMS

5.1 Introduction

There have been many studies of small firms in Britain and the problems which they face — notably those by Boswell (1972), and the Research Reports which accompanied the Bolton Committee Report (1971), but relatively few on new firms. Although most new firms are small, most small firms are not new. Hence the new firm, which may have significantly different problems from the population of small firms, and is important in the long run diversification of the regional and national economy, is underrepresented in such work.

Those new firms which have been studied in Britain by Cross (1981), Gudgin (1978), Johnson and Cathcart (1979a,b) and Lloyd (1980) have been almost exclusively in the manufacturing sector. Virtually the only examination of the service sector was made by the Bolton Committee, but as noted earlier the emphasis was upon small as opposed to new firms.

There is, of course, no economic basis for regarding employment created in one sector, through the operation of the market mechanism, as in any way inferior to that created in any other sector. The service provided by the architect, the lorry driver or the footballer is paid for directly by the customer in the same way that manufactured goods are purchased. The prime justification for studying the service sector, however, is its rapid growth in employment since the mid 1960s, at a time when the manufacturing sector in Britain, and in a number of other 'advanced' countries, was in decline. Marquand (1979) shows that 56.4 per cent of all jobs were in the tertiary or service sector by 1975, but that in 1965 the manufacturing (secondary) sector had virtually as many jobs as services. The major cause of these changes has been the increase in the number of females at work, with most of these new jobs being created in the service sector.

These new jobs are created partly by the expansion of existing firms and partly by the creation of new firms, so it is important to identify the sectors in which firms are being created, so as to allow the policy makers to reach a balanced judgement on whether the public interest is well served by encouraging a higher rate of new firm formation in these industries. Unfortunately there are no national data available over time on the numbers of new firms in each industry even for the manufacturing sector, or any assessment of their contribution to jobs, investment, production, etc. To assess the contribution of new firms to employment and economic prosperity and to determine both the desirability and feasibility of raising the rate of new firm formation requires a clear definition of a new firm. It requires a distinction to be made between firms which are new to a given geographical area, which could be relocations of existing enterprises or new branches or subsidiaries of established companies, and wholly new firms which are created as independent companies with no previous trading record. It would then be valuable to know what proportion of wholly new firms created in time period t are no longer in existence in successive time periods, and whether this proportion varies according to the industry, location or subsequent ownership change. The contribution to employment, production, investment growth and the profitability of such enterprises could then be compared with that of other firms new to the area.

This chapter describes the general characteristics of a sample of 301 firms which were new to the county of Cleveland in north-east England. The survey includes both firms which were wholly new and firms which were previously established outside Cleveland, but which moved into the area after 1972. The survey includes all sectors of private industry with the exception of retailing.

5.2 Deriving a Sample of Firms New to Cleveland

A detailed description of the procedures used to derive a sample of firms new to Cleveland is available from the author. For most purposes it is sufficient to know that the Middlesbrough area telephone directories for 1973 and 1977 were compared. Business premises not in the 1973 directory but which were in the 1977 directory, except those in either retailing or the public sector were regarded as potentially new, and originally it was intended to interview 500 such firms.

Such a method of selecting new firms is crude but it illustrates the high death rates amongst new firms — a factor which has to be borne in mind when analysing the nature of responses. Out of 546 firms potentially new to Cleveland between 1971 and 1977, 132 had been lost to the local economy by 1979 — a failure rate of 24.3 per cent. This is probably an underestimate of the percentage failure rate for wholly new firms since the latter are more likely to die than firms new to the area.

5.3 Surveyed Firms: Some General Characteristics

In this section, the general characteristics of all firms new to Cleveland are identified. Of the 309 firms interviewed, four firms were found to have been in business in Cleveland, although not on their present site, before 1971 and these together with the four firms who had been on their current site before 1971 were excluded from further analysis. All subsequent tabulations are therefore provided on a maximum sample of 301 firms.

(a) Industrial and Organisational Structure of Firms New to Cleveland

There is a surprisingly high degree of uniformity both in the industrial sectors in which firms new to Cleveland are found, and in the organisational structure of new firms within these sectors. Firms new to Cleveland were evenly divided between industrial sectors, with manufacturing, construction and professional services each taking slightly more than 20 per cent. A somewhat lower proportion of firms new to Cleveland were found in the distributive sector, partly due to the exclusion of retailing. The greatest number of firms new to Cleveland were found in the 'other' category with transport undertakings and hairdressers being prominent.

Of these 301 firms new to Cleveland 58 per cent were single plant independent firms and 26 per cent subsidiaries. The organisational variation of construction firms new to Cleveland reflects almost exactly the pattern for the population of new firms as a whole, but the 'other' sector seems to include a higher than average proportion of independent firms, whereas there appear to be an above average proportion of subsidiaries in distribution.

Whilst these firms are new to Cleveland after 1971 they cannot all be described as wholly new firms since a number were in business elsewhere prior to that date. For a single plant independent firm to be classified as new to Cleveland, but not a wholly new firm, it must have closed its previous establishment outside the county and transferred the whole of its operations to Cleveland after 1971. The vast majority of new to Cleveland single plant independent firms, hereafter called independents, will therefore be wholly new firms. No other types of firm are classified as wholly new, even though a few could have been started as a single plant independent firm for the first time in Cleveland after 1971, yet at the time of the survey been either parents, branches or subsidiaries.

Of the total sample of 301 firms, 159 or 53 per cent were defined to be wholly new firms with their sectoral distribution not being significantly different from that of firms new to Cleveland, except that the wholly new firms were slightly more strongly represented in the 'other' sector and less well represented in manufacturing and distribution.

(b) Employment in Firms New to Cleveland

A total of 5,782 men and 1,663 women were employed in the 300 firms classified as being new to Cleveland.[1] Thirty-five per cent of the jobs at these establishments were classified as skilled manual, 25 per cent were unskilled and 14 per cent were classified as professional/managerial. The remainder were either clerical, semi-skilled, or were not classified.

A high proportion of these jobs were created in relatively few firms new to Cleveland. For example, the five largest employers of male labour provided 32 per cent of all male jobs, and the five largest employers of female labour provided 42 per cent of all new female jobs. Even greater disparities occur between employment of skilled and unskilled labour. The five largest employers of skilled labour provided 23 per cent of all skilled jobs, whereas the five largest employers of unskilled labour provided 69 per cent of all unskilled jobs. This suggests that making an impact upon the unemployment rates of underprivileged job groups such as the unskilled and women depend upon the ability of an area to attract large establishments rather than upon developing indigenous potential. This point is developed in Chapter 9.

Table 5.1 shows the employment size in 1979 of both firms new to Cleveland and of wholly new firms, subdivided according to industry. It shows that for those 228 new firms where complete information was available, 62 firms new to Cleveland (or 21 per cent) had by 1979 reached an employment in excess of 25, but that only eight per cent of wholly new firms had more than 25 employees. Alternatively, we can see that 175 (or 58 per cent) of all surviving firms new to Cleveland had an employment of ten or less in 1979, compared with 72 per cent of all wholly new firms. If account is taken of those who were 'born' after 1973, but who failed to survive until 1979, the data suggest that approximately 80 per cent of wholly new firms either fail to survive, or fail to grow beyond an employment of ten, up to six years later.

Table 5.1 also shows that employment size in 1979 is linked strongly to industry. For example, of the twelve wholly new firms in the survey having more than 25 employees by 1979, five were in the manufacturing sector whereas manufacturing firms accounted for under 20 per cent of all wholly new firms. Conversely, average employment size in the 'other'

Table 5.1: Industrial Distribution and Employment Size of Firms New to Cleveland

Industry[a]	Employment in 1979									
	1-4		5-10		11-24		25+		Total	
	Firms New to Cleveland	Wholly New Firms	Firms New to Cleveland	Wholly New Firms	Firms New to Cleveland	Wholly New Firms	Firms New to Cleveland	Wholly New Firms	Firms New to Cleveland	Wholly New Firms
Manufacturing	9 (0.15)[c]	7 (0.23)	15 (0.24)	8 (0.27)	16 (0.26)	10 (0.33)	22 (0.35)	5 (0.17)	62 (1.00)	30 (1.00)
Construction	13 (0.22)	13 (0.38)	20 (0.34)	13 (0.38)	11 (0.19)	4 (0.12)	15 (0.25)	4 (0.12)	59 (1.00)	34 (1.00)
Professional services	21 (0.33)	13 (0.40)	26 (0.41)	11 (0.33)	10 (0.16)	8 (0.24)	7 (0.11)	1 (0.03)	64 (1.00)	33 (1.00)
Distribution	12 (0.30)	6 (0.37)	13 (0.33)	6 (0.37)	8 (0.20)	3 (0.19)	7 (0.17)	1 (0.06)	40 (1.00)	16 (1.00)
Other	34 (0.46)	28 (0.61)	12 (0.16)	10 (0.22)	17 (0.23)	7 (0.15)	11 (0.15)	1 (0.02)	74 (1.00)	46 (1.00)
Total	89 (0.30)	67 (0.42)	86 (0.28)	48 (0.30)	62 (0.21)	32 (0.20)	62 (0.21)	12 (0.08)	299[b] (1.00)	159 (1.00)

Notes:
a. Manufacturing : Orders III to XIX.
   Construction : Order XX.
   Professional
   Services : Orders XXIV and XXV.
   Distribution : Order XXIII except MLH 820 and 821.
   Other : Orders I, II, XXII and XXVI (private sector only).
b. It was not possible in the case of two respondents to relate employment size and industrial group.
c. Proportions in parenthesis.

sector tends to be very small with 61 per cent of wholly new establishments having less than five employees.

(c) Employment Change

All firms new to Cleveland were asked to give their employment early in 1979 and, if they were in business, their average employment during the year 1978. In all, 101 firms increased their employment by at least one, 133 said they had not changed, and 51 reduced their workforce by at least one in these years.

Manufacturing had the largest proportion of establishments new to Cleveland showing a decline in employment, but also the second largest proportion of establishments showing an increase. This volatility is probably due to the generally larger size of manufacturing establishments. New construction firms have had similar experiences, but professional and other services have over half of the establishments showing no change in employment in these years. Wholly new firms in all sectors except professional services showed a greater tendency to retain the same level of employment between 1978 and 1979 than the population of firms new to Cleveland. Conversely, a small proportion of wholly new firms either increased or decreased their employment during these years.

(d) The New Firm's View of Future Prospects

Firms new to Cleveland who survived the critical first few years have prospered, and most of them in 1979 expected this to continue. Of those interviewed, 66 per cent thought they were likely to be employing more people in 1980 than they were currently employing, whilst only two per cent thought they would be employing less. In fact 105 firms had vacancies which they were unable to fill with, at that time, a total of 327 jobs on offer. These firms were also optimistic about their prospects for increasing their turnover during the following year. Only twelve per cent thought their turnover would be lower compared with 76 per cent who expected it to be higher. In no way can this level of optimism about future prospects be regarded as being representative of a cross section of all firms in Cleveland even in early 1979. These firms are more optimistic, and almost certainly more dynamic than an average of the total population of firms, or of the total population of small firms.

5.4 Conclusion

The general observations made in this chapter illustrate that although the number of jobs created by wholly new firms, in the short run, is not high, the jobs created by existing enterprises moving into the area is substantial. Both types of firms are optimistic about future prospects. It is also interesting to note that although the service sector has been expanding its employment considerably, at a time when manufacturing industry has been contracting, the latter still produced 19 per cent of all wholly new independent firms, and one-third of all wholly new firms with more than 25 employees. The manufacturing sector continues to be important in terms of creating jobs in wholly new firms.

Having derived this population of firms new to an area interest now turns to the characteristics of those individuals who have been prepared to start a wholly new firm and employ people in an area of high unemployment, in a country with supposedly penal tax rates and with restrictive labour laws. Who are they, why do they do it and what distinguishes those who succeed?

Note

1. One firm was unable to provide exact employment data.

6 THE PERSONAL CHARACTERISTICS OF NEW FIRM FOUNDERS

6.1 The Issues

Any justification for studying the personal characteristics of entre-preneurs implies a rejection of the view that new firms are formed in response to changes in relative prices. If, for example, Baumol's view of the entrepreneur is accepted, i.e. that of an automaton reacting passively to a change in the expected profits in industry i, then the characteristics of the entrepreneur, either as an individual or as a member of a group, become irrelevant. Once, however, it is shown that certain groups or types of individuals react differently to incentives the 'supply-side' of entrepreneurship becomes more important. If there are groups within society which require less stimulus to enter business then the higher the proportion of the population in this group the more responsive will society as a whole be to changes in the relative prices of self-employment, unemployment and paid employment. These groups may be characterised according to social class, religious affinity, education levels, etc.

There may also be groups who, once in business, are more likely to be successful. Chapters 3 and 4 reported that higher education levels were shown by Gudgin *et al.* to be associated with higher achievement levels in business, whilst McClelland hypothesised that certain societies were, at different times, more orientated towards achievement than others, and this 'explained' differences in economic performance.

This chapter examines whether the personal characteristics of Cleveland's entrepreneurs affect their likelihood of starting a new business, and once in business, make their firms more likely to succeed and grow. Each characteristic of the entrepreneur is discussed separa-tely, although it is recognised that a number are strongly associated. The conclusion attempts to derive a 'composite' picture.

6.2 Educational Qualifications

Gudgin *et al.* showed that firms established by graduates performed significantly better, in terms of turnover, than otherwise similar firms

106

established by non-graduates, whilst Smith in his study suggests that the nature of education is one factor distinguishing the craftsman-type entrepreneur from the opportunist. Many commentators, however, note that high academic qualifications are in some industries a necessary, but never a sufficient condition, for entrepreneurial success. The inventor besotted with his invention is rarely successful since frequently he assumes the rest of the world shares his opinion. Regrettably, for him, this is rarely the case. The process of invention is often lonely, so that many inventors are fiercely independent, but conversely poor communicators. The successful running of a business requires personal skills which are not necessarily associated with intellect.

The relationship between education and entrepreneurship will be examined in this section, where a distinction is made between an individual's propensity to start a business, and its subsequent development. Analysis is conducted upon wholly new firms, i.e. excluding firms which were established prior to 1971 outside Cleveland.

A total of 153[1] new firm founders had a total of 140 qualifications, with 49 having no qualifications. A total of ten new firm founders had degrees, 29 were time served tradesmen, whilst the remainder had miscellaneous qualifications such as hairdressing certificates, company training course certificates, as well as 'O' levels, HNC, etc.

New firm founders with a degree or a professional qualification were concentrated in professional services. No founder of a new manufacturing or construction firm in this sample had a degree, whereas 22 per cent and 33 per cent of founders in these industries were unqualified. The largest concentration of unqualified new firm founders were in the 'other' sector where just under half had no qualifications.

Three indices of the development of wholly new firms are used throughout this work, viz: employment in 1979, turnover and profitability in 1977-8. It is hypothesised that founders with formal educational qualifications will establish firms which will, *ceteris paribus*, be less likely to die, grow faster in terms of employment and have higher turnover profitability than those founded by unqualified entrepreneurs. In a sample of this size it is difficult to ensure that all variables are held constant. Nevertheless, the use of five industrial subsectors should allow for broad differences in industrial structure.

Table 6.1 compares new firm founders with and without qualifications according to the declared profitability of their enterprises in 1977-8. The table reports the replies received to questions on profitability so there is the possibility that not all individuals were truthful, or that despite the efforts of the interviewers different individuals had different views on the meaning of profitability.

Table 6.1: Profitability of Firms and Educational Qualifications of Founder

	Loss			Broke	Profit			
	More than 10%	5-9.9%	0-4.9%	Even	0-4.9%	5-9.9%	More than 10%	Total
With qualifications	1 (0.01)	4 (0.05)	4 (0.05)	2 (0.03)	19 (0.24)	17 (0.22)	31 (0.40)	78 (1.00)
Without qualifications	1 (0.03)	0 (0.00)	2 (0.06)	0 (0.00)	8 (0.23)	8 (0.23)	16 (0.45)	35 (1.00)

The table provides no evidence to support the hypothesis that educationally qualified founders are more likely to establish profitable firms. Forty-five per cent of founders without qualifications established firms which made a rate of profit in excess of ten per cent, compared to 40 per cent of those with qualifications. Nine per cent of firms founded by entrepreneurs without qualifications claimed to make a loss in the period, compared with eleven per cent founded by those with qualifications.

This lack of association may be due to the sampling process which resulted in an underrepresentation of unsuccessful new firms because these had disappeared by the time the survey took place. It is difficult to estimate the effect of this factor, but if the education levels of entrepreneurs are correlated with profits, most of the 'deaths' would have to have been of companies founded by individuals without formal qualifications.

A second factor is that a distinction between those with, and those without, qualifications is too crude. Instead any association may only be between founders with the highest academic qualifications and firm profitability. Even at this finer level, however, it is not apparent that those with higher qualifications either establish firms which subsequently have higher profits or are more likely to avoid losses. Of those founders providing profitability data and having a degree or professional qualifications, 23 per cent established firms which in 1977-8 failed to make a profit, compared with twelve per cent of founders with other qualifications. Of new firm founders with the highest educational qualifications approximately 40 per cent founded firms which in 1977-8 claimed to be making the highest rates of profit, compared with 42 per cent of firms founded by those with lower educational qualifications.

If profits were consistently higher in one type of industry, and if there is greater likelihood of unqualified new firm founders entering that industry, then cross tabulations of the type described may merely reflect industry differences. To identify the specific effect of educational qualifications requires comparison of single industry groupings.

Using a broad industry classification the numbers in each category are small, yet the results are interesting. In the manufacturing sector there were 22 respondents, eight of whom claimed to make a profit in excess of ten per cent. Seven of these also claimed to have educational qualifications, confirming previous work that in this sector there may be an association between the educational levels of the founder and subsequent performance of the firm. In none of the other sectors, however, was there any evidence of association.

Profitability in a single year is an imperfect guide to the performance of a new firm. A better index may be the employment of a new firm at the time of the survey since all wholly new firms will by definition have started with zero employment, not more than eight years previously. Even so, employment in 1979 is also an imperfect estimate of the growth of a new firm, since the optimal size of firms varies between industries.

Table 6.2 shows that, in aggregate, there is no association between whether or not the founder possesses educational qualifications, and the employment size of the firm. This is true even when account is taken of industrial structure.

Table 6.2: Firm Size, Industry and Founders Qualifications: Numbers of Respondents

Industry	1-4 Qual.	No Qual.	5-10 Qual.	No Qual.	11-24 Qual.	No Qual.	25+ Qual.	No Qual.	Total Qual.	No Qual
Manufacturing	5	2	8	0	7	2	2	2	22	6
Construction	10	3	8	5	2	2	3	1	23	11
Professional services	12	0	9	2	6	2	0	1	27	5
Distribution	4	2	5	1	1	1	0	0	10	4
Other	14	14	4	6	3	3	1	0	22	23
Total	45	21	34	14	19	10	6	4	104	49

Employment Size in 1979

A third index of new firm performance is that of turnover in 1977-8, shown in Table 6.3. The index is unsatisfactory because not all new firms provided turnover data and because, as with employment, it may not reflect the *growth* of the firm. Despite these limitations it provides an estimate of development of the new firm. Table 6.3 confirms previous results that no clear relationship exists between the entrepreneur's educational qualifications and the absolute level of turnover of his firm in 1977-8.

Table 6.3: Turnover, Industry and Founders' Qualifications: Numbers of Respondents

	Less than £20,000		£20,000-£49,999		£50,000-£99,999		£100,000-£499,999		Greater than £500,000		Total	
	Qual.	No Qual.	Qual.	No Qual.	Qual.	No Qual.	Qual.	No Qual.	Qual.	No Qual.	Qual.	No Qual.
Manufacturing	2	1	4	2	6	1	5	1	1	0	18	5
Construction	6	1	2	1	5	2	3	2	2	2	18	8
Professional services	9	0	5	0	6	2	1	0	0	2	21	4
Distribution	2	1	1	0	1	1	2	0	2	0	8	2
Others	4	6	2	1	2	2	2	2	1	2	11	13
Total	23	9	14	4	20	8	13	5	6	6	76	32

6.3 Motivations and Aspirations of Founders

The stated desire of individuals to make money and the observation that products or services could be supplied at a price which would yield a satisfactory rate of profit are the aspirations and motivations central to conventional economic theory. Here the entrepreneur is attracted by the opportunity or the 'pull' of perceived profit.

Studies of the entrepreneur have also shown that many are forced into entrepreneurship by frustration or despair caused by a lack of alternative employment opportunities. A third group of aspirations could be the desire for greater independence subject to maintaining a satisfactory level of income.

Differences in aspirations are important because the effectiveness of government policy instruments and incentives varies according to differences in motivation. At the simplest level, reduced rates of taxation for those in business will stimulate those whose motivation is purely financial. Such individuals may be more prepared to make their firms grow faster if the financial rewards are greater. For those motivated by a desire for independence subject to a minimum income constraint, however, it is unclear whether reduced tax rates for employers will induce greater output. Such individuals may instead work less hours and produce less output.

It is, in principle, possible to distinguish between those primarily forced into entrepreneurship, those motivated by a positive idea, and those who claimed to have specific knowledge of a market opportunity. These motivational categories are extremely broad so Table 6.4 shows typical responses which are incorporated into each of the motivational categories. They show considerable variety of responses in each general category and illustrate the difficulty of classifying responses.

Table 6.4: Classification of Motivations of New Firm Founders

Actual Reason Given	Classification
a. Made redundant	
b. Got the sack	
c. Closure of my employer	
d. Took early retirement	Forced into
e. Threat of redundancy	entrepreneurship
f. Unhappy with progress of previous employer	
g. Husband had accident, so set up this business in order to keep us	
a. I had the managerial ability	
b. Wanted to set up firm, work for myself	
c. Wanted to do better and make more money than the average person	Motivated by positive ideas
d. I like the work . . . it is my vocation	
e. Founder felt he could do better than his employer	
a. Founder had knowledge of work task as employee	
b. Founder had knowledge of local market	Knowledge of
c. Founder started supplying market 'freelance', or as hobby	specific market
d. Founder saw opportunity in the market	
a. Friend asked me to be his partner	
b. Chance event (e.g. 'Just happened to see this man and he said . . .')	Others
c. Suitable premises became vacant	
d. Encouraged to set up firm by relatives who provided money	

Although the motivational classification is crude it can be used to examine the performance of firms founded by individuals motivated by essentially negative responses such as redundancy, loss of a job or threatened job loss, or else frustration with existing work compared with those firms founded for more positive reasons. Table 6.5 shows that of those mentioning these essentially negative ideas, and who were subsequently classified as being 'forced' into entrepreneurship (who remained in business sufficiently long to be surveyed), 59 per cent placed themselves in the highest possible profitable category. This compares with 47 per cent of those motivated by positive ideas, and 43.5 per cent of those who claimed to have a knowledge of a specific market gap which their firm was established to fill. Thirty-six per cent of those in the most profitable category were motivated by 'other' reasons. This evidence provides no justification for assuming that those forced into entrepreneurship make less competent businessmen.

Table 6.5: Founders' Motivation and New Firm Profitability in 1977-8

Motivation	Loss or Break-even	Profit 0-4.9%	5-9.9%	More than 10%	Total
1. Forced into entrepreneurship	3	2	4	13	22
2. Motivated by positive ideas	0	13	5	16	34
3. Knowledge of specific markets	16	24	21	47	108
4. Other	10	22	19	29	80
Total responses	29	61	49	105	244
Total respondents	16	27	23	46	112

6.4 Characteristics of New Firm Founders

Research on new firm founders has identified a number of factors common to this group. This section tests whether these factors influence the types of business established and the ultimate success of the business. The first is that founders form their new businesses in the industries in which they were formerly employed. Secondly, a number of entrepreneurs begin their business on a part-time basis which enables them to assess the ultimate viability of the enterprise. Thirdly, unemployment can act as a positive incentive to start a business.

(a) Previous Employment

The survey identified the industry in which a business founder was formerly employed for 152 new firm founders. It shows that 91, or 60 per cent of the founders, remained in the same industrial order, and this data is shown in Table 6.6. Of the 31 founders of new manufacturing firms, 18 or 59 per cent, remained within the same manufacturing order, suggesting that the propensity for new firm founders to move industrial orders is not significantly different in the construction and service sector from the results obtained by studies of manufacturing entrepreneurs. Johnson and Cathcart (1979a), for example, found 50 per cent remained within the same manufacturing order, although Cross (1981) in his survey of 191 manufacturing firms in Scotland, found that only 75 founders remained within the same manufacturing order.

Both Cross, and Johnson and Cathcart, note the importance of the service sector in providing manufacturing entrepreneurs. Cross found 28 per cent of founders of new manufacturing firms were previously employed in the service sector, whereas Johnson and Cathcart found the proportion to be 22 per cent. Table 6.6 shows this proportion is somewhat lower at 16 per cent for the Cleveland sample.

The proportion of Cleveland's new firm founders moving from employment in the manufacturing sector to establish a service sector firm is 21 per cent and therefore not significantly different from the proportion of entrepreneurs moving in the other direction. Bearing in mind the increase in the proportion of total employment in the service sector in recent years, which presumably reflects the greater business opportunities in this sector, and the generally lower entry barriers in the form of start-up finance, this may seem a slightly surprising result.

Several explanations may be advanced. The first is that much of the increase in employment in the service sector has come, not in the private sector but in public and quasi-public organisations. Within the private sector the increase in jobs has been often for part-time female labour for which self-employment is an inadequate substitute. The increase in demand for private services which has taken place since the mid-1960s may therefore have been met more by expansions of existing, rather than by the creation of new firms. There may even be greater potential for the creation and growth of wholly new firms in the manufacturing than in the private service sector.

(b) The Role of Part-time and Previous Full-time Business Ownership

Thirty-four out of 156 founders claimed that their business had been a part-time activity before it became their full-time employment. The duration which founders spent in business on a part-time basis varies considerably. Fourteen part-time businesses were established for a

Table 6.6: Source and Destination of New Firm Founders

Founders' Business (Order): Destination

Founders' Business (Order): Source		1	2	3	4	5	6	7	8	9	10	11	12	13	14	15	16	17	18	19	20	21	22	23	24	25	26	27	Total
		Manufacturing																			Services								
Manufacturing	1	—	—	—	—	—	—	—	—	—	—	—	—	—	—	—	—	—	—	—	1	—	—	—	—	—	—	—	0
	2	—	1	—	—	—	—	—	—	—	—	—	—	—	—	—	—	—	—	—	—	—	—	—	—	—	—	—	1
	3	—	—	—	—	—	—	—	—	—	—	—	—	—	—	—	—	—	—	—	—	—	—	—	—	—	—	—	0
	4	—	—	—	—	—	1	—	—	—	—	—	—	—	—	—	—	1	—	—	—	—	2	1	—	1	1	—	9
	5	—	—	—	—	1	2	1	—	—	—	—	—	—	—	—	—	1	—	1	—	—	1	2	—	4	1	—	11
	6	—	—	—	—	—	—	7	—	—	—	—	—	—	—	—	—	3	—	—	—	—	1	1	2	3	1	—	15
	7	—	—	—	—	—	—	—	—	—	—	—	—	—	—	—	—	—	—	—	—	—	—	—	—	—	—	—	0
	8	—	—	—	—	—	—	—	—	2	—	—	—	—	—	—	—	—	—	—	—	—	1	—	—	—	—	—	3
	9	—	—	—	—	—	—	—	—	—	—	—	—	—	—	—	—	—	—	—	—	—	—	—	—	—	—	—	0
	10	—	—	—	—	—	—	—	—	—	—	—	—	—	—	—	—	—	—	—	—	—	—	—	—	—	—	—	0
	11	—	—	—	—	—	—	—	—	—	—	1	—	—	—	—	—	—	—	—	—	—	—	—	—	—	—	—	1
	12	—	—	—	—	—	—	—	—	—	—	—	—	—	—	—	—	—	—	—	—	—	—	—	—	—	—	—	0
	13	—	—	—	—	—	—	—	—	—	—	—	—	—	—	—	—	—	—	—	—	—	—	—	—	—	—	—	0
	14	—	—	—	—	—	—	—	—	—	—	—	—	—	—	1	—	—	—	—	—	—	1	—	—	—	—	—	1
	15	—	—	—	—	—	—	—	—	—	—	1	—	—	—	—	1	—	—	—	—	—	—	—	—	—	—	—	0
	16	—	—	—	—	—	—	—	—	—	—	—	1	—	—	—	1	—	—	—	—	—	—	—	—	—	—	—	1
	17	—	—	—	—	—	—	—	—	—	—	—	1	—	—	—	—	3	—	—	—	—	—	—	—	—	—	—	3
	18	—	—	—	—	—	—	—	—	—	—	—	—	—	—	—	—	—	1	1	1	—	—	—	—	—	—	—	4
	19	—	—	—	—	—	—	—	—	—	—	—	—	1	—	—	—	1	—	—	—	—	—	—	—	—	—	—	1
Services	20	—	—	—	—	—	—	—	—	—	—	—	—	—	—	—	1	—	1	—	25	—	1	1	—	3	—	—	32
	21	—	—	—	—	—	—	—	—	—	—	—	—	—	—	—	—	—	—	—	2	—	5	1	—	—	2	—	3
	22	—	—	—	—	—	—	—	—	—	—	—	—	1	—	—	—	—	—	1	1	—	1	7	1	—	—	—	9
	23	—	—	—	—	—	—	—	—	—	—	—	—	—	—	—	—	—	—	—	—	—	1	—	2	8	3	—	11
	24	—	—	—	—	—	—	—	—	—	—	—	—	—	—	—	—	—	—	—	2	—	1	—	1	1	20	—	7
	25	—	—	—	—	—	—	—	—	—	—	—	—	—	—	—	—	—	—	—	—	—	1	—	—	—	—	—	16
	26	—	—	—	—	—	—	—	—	—	—	—	—	—	—	—	—	—	—	—	—	—	1	—	—	—	—	—	21
	27	—	—	—	—	—	—	—	—	—	—	—	—	—	—	—	—	—	—	—	—	—	—	—	—	—	—	—	2
	Total	0	1	0	0	1	2	9	0	2	0	1	2	1	0	1	2	5	2	2	33	0	15	13	12	20	28	0	152

period of two years or less prior to starting full-time, although three had existed for five years or more.

The opportunity to start a part-time business, as Table 6.7 shows, varies with industry. Relatively few new firm founders in the construction industry started on a part-time basis, whereas approximately one-quarter in professional services, manufacturing and distribution had previous part-time experience as an owner.

Table 6.7: Part-time Business Ownership Experience Prior to Starting Current Business: Numbers of Respondents

Experience	Manufacturing	Construction	Professional Services	Distribution	Others	Total
Part-time	8	3	8	5	10	34
Not part-time	22	30	25	9	36	122
Total	30	33	33	14	46	156

Experience gained as a part-time business owner makes the individual more likely to be aware of the problems of developing the business yet enables him to demonstrate to finance houses that he has a 'track record'. It also gives a greater awareness of customers' requirements. Part-time experience can be a valuable apprenticeship for entrepreneurship, and is likely to be reflected in the superior performance of firms started on such a basis.

Table 6.8 shows that of the 15 wholly new businesses which claimed not to be making a profit in 1977-8 only one had been started on a part-time basis, compared to 20 per cent of all wholly new business. This contrasts with eleven new firm founders claiming to have had part-time experience, out of 47 who said they were obtaining the highest possible rate of profit. It suggests that part-time experience is associated with higher rates of profits in new businesses. These differences are only partly 'explained' by structural differences in profitability.

Table 6.8 suggests that in manufacturing, construction and 'other' industries those businesses started on a part-time basis are well represented amongst the businesses which in 1977-8 claimed to be very profitable. No such claim would be possible for new firms in professional services, whilst there are insufficient cases in the distribution sector to make any inference.

A similar analysis can be made of the role of previous business experience as a full-time owner upon firm performance. From the 153 usable replies to the question of previous business experience as an owner, 49 individuals claimed to have been in business before, with 33 claiming the business was either similar or identical to the one in which they were currently engaged. Two founders continued to take an active interest in their 'previous' firm. Five of the founders claimed there was some similarity between their current and previous business, but in the remainder there were no similarities. Previous business failures were attributed by founders to personal factors such as disagreements with their partner, although a variety of other factors such as shortage of suitable property, materials, etc., lack of finance, shortage of markets, etc. were mentioned.

Table 6.8: Part-time Business Ownership Experience and Profitability of Firm in 1977-8 by Industry: Number of Respondents

Industry	Loss or Break-even		Profit						Total	
			0-4.9%		5-9.9%		More than 10%			
	Part-time	Not Part-time	Part-time	Not Part-time	Part-time	Not Part-time	Part-time	Not Part-time	Part-time	Not Part-time
Manufacturing	0	5	1	1	2	6	4	4	7	16
Construction	0	2	0	7	1	6	2	12	3	27
Professional services	0	4	3	2	2	2	1	9	6	17
Distribution	1	1	0	2	0	0	1	3	2	6
Other	0	2	2	9	0	5	3	8	5	24
Total	1	14	6	21	5	19	11	36	23	90

An examination of the relationship between previous full-time ownership and profitability does not suggest any significant relationship. Founders with previous full-time business experience do not seem any more likely to establish very profitable new businesses than other types of new firm founders.

(c) Unemployment

Unemployment, or the threat of it, can act as a powerful stimulus to new firm formation. Dahmen (1970), Wendervang (1965) and Oxenfeldt (1943) have commented upon the importance of this influence, yet all have suggested that firms founded with the prime intention of maintaining the entrepreneur in work – the so-called 'livelihood principle' – are unlikely to be growth-orientated. Such firms contrast with those where the founder establishes the firm so as to raise his income, over and above that which it would have been had he remained in paid employment.

Table 6.9: Unemployment of Founder, Profitability and Industry of Firm: Number of Respondents

Industry	Loss or Break-even		0-4.9%		Profit 5-9.9%		More than 10%		Total	
	Un.	Not Un.	Un.	Not Un.	Un.	Not Un.	Un.	Not Un.	Un.	Not Un.
Manufacturing	2	3	0	2	1	7	4	4	7	16
Construction	1	1	3	4	3	5	4	10	11	20
Professional services	0	4	0	5	0	4	2	8	2	21
Distribution	1	1	0	2	0	0	0	4	1	7
Other	1	1	2	9	1	4	3	8	7	22
Total	5	10	5	22	5	20	13	34	28	86

Note: Un = unemployed immediately prior to starting business.

Table 6.9 examines profitability, by industry, according to whether or not the founder was unemployed immediately prior to starting in business. Profitability data are not available for all establishments, but 41 out of 156 new firm founders claimed to be unemployed immediately prior to starting their business. This 26 per cent rate compares with Cleveland's rates of male unemployment which in the 1970s were in the range of six to ten per cent. For at least one-quarter of the new firm founders in Cleveland, forming one's own firm was therefore a clear alternative to unemployment. Furthermore, this 26 per cent represents an underestimate of the impact of unemployment since it takes account of only those *actually* unemployed. The effect of unemployment will also be felt by those aware that they are *likely* to become unemployed in the future. Those not actually unemployed, however, were excluded from the analysis on the ground that they were included in tabulations on how and why the business was established.

Of those starting wholly new businesses in professional services, only three *claimed* to be unemployed immediately prior to starting the business, out of 33 new businesses in this sector. In all other sectors, however, virtually one-third of new firm founders claim to have been unemployed. Table 6.9 shows the profitability of new firms, by industry, according to whether or not the founder was unemployed. It does not suggest that firms founded by the unemployed are significantly less profitable than those founded by individuals in employment.

It was postulated earlier that firms established on the 'livelihood' principle would be expected to show low rates of growth. Table 6.10 shows that of ten new manufacturing firms founded by the unemployed, only one had, by 1979, more than 25 employees. Firms founded by the unemployed appear to be more concentrated in the lower size bands, with only two new firm founders who were unemployed, establishing firms which subsequently grew to 25 or more employees, yet they created 39 out of 144 firms in the smaller employment size categories.

Table 6.10: Unemployment of Founder, Firm Size and Industry: Number of Respondents

Industry	Employment in 1979									
	1-4		5-10		11-24		25+		Total	
	Un.	Not Un.	Un.	Not Un.	Un.	Not Un.	Un.	Not Un.	Un.	Not Un.
Manufacturing	3	4	3	5	3	7	1	4	10	20
Construction	4	9	4	9	2	2	1	3	11	23
Professional services	1	12	0	11	2	6	0	1	3	30
Distribution	4	1	0	6	0	2	0	1	4	10
Other	10	18	0	10	3	3	0	1	13	32
Total	22	44	7	41	10	20	2	10	41	115

| % of firms founded by individuals unemployed immediately prior to starting firm | 29% | | 17% | | 31% | | 13% | | | |

Relatively few new firms were founded in professional services by unemployed individuals. The sector also contains a high proportion of very small firms. The exclusion of professional services shows 55 per cent of firms founded by unemployed individuals were in the smallest size category of less than five employees, compared with 37 per cent of those founded by entrepreneurs who were in employment. Firms founded by the unemployed constituted only five per cent ot of firms in the highest employment size group, compared with eleven per cent of firms founded by those in employment. This suggests that the growth rates of firms founded by the unemployed are, *ceteris paribus*, somewhat lower than those of firms founded by employed entrepreneurs. It thus offers tentative support for the 'livelihood' hypothesis.

6.5 Conclusion

This chapter presents an elementary examination of hypotheses about entrepreneurs, the type of firms which they establish, and the performance of these new firms over time. The results presented are somewhat tentative partly because, although the sample was initially quite large, the failure of respondents to provide answers to all questions and holding variables such as industry constant, substantially eliminates degrees of freedom. Furthermore, the results presented, whilst representative of survivors, may not fully reflect all new firms.

Attention has been directed towards associations between the personal characteristics of entrepreneurs and performance of their firms. The measurement of performance presents difficulties, but three measures are used – the profitability of the firm in the financial year 1977-8, its turnover in that year and its employment size in 1979.

The tabulations provide at best general support for some of the hypotheses presented in Chapters 3 and 4. An examination of the previous employment of new firm founders suggests that in both manufacturing and in non-manufacturing the majority of founders establish a firm in the same industrial 'order' in which they were formerly employed.

Differences occur, however, between the current survey and previous work on the role of the founders' educational qualifications and the performance of his firm. This chapter suggests that although the two may be positively associated in manufacturing the association is weak, and possibly even negative, for other industrial sectors.

The motivations and aspirations of entrepreneurs are not easy to link to firm performance, due to difficulties of categorising responses. There is little evidence that new firm founders, who see themselves as being 'forced' into entrepreneurship, establish firms which subsequently perform poorly according to any indices. In part, this may be because the category also includes individuals 'forced' into entrepreneurship through frustration, and who might be expected to establish rapid growth firms. A second category of individuals 'forced' into entrepreneurship are those who were unemployed immediately prior to starting their business, and perhaps the most remarkable result in this chapter is that more than one-quarter of new firm founders claimed to have been in that position. The effect was particularly apparent amongst those founding manufacturing firms and in construction, but of negligible importance in professional services. The performance of these firms varied according to the criterion used but 'forced' founders appear to perform well in terms of profitability, but relatively poorly in terms of the employment size of their firms.

The effect of previous business ownership, either on a full-time or a part-time basis, was primarily to reduce the likelihood of subsequent loss-making — and presumably liquidation. Nevertheless, past experience, irrespective of industry, seemed a valuable attribute, although the proportion of founders obtaining this experience varied between industries.

The personal characteristics of the entrepreneur therefore seem to exert only the mildest influence upon the subsequent performance of his firm, although there is some general support for the hypothesis that wholly new manufacturing firms are more successful where these are founded by educated individuals with previous business experience.

Our failure to identify strong and consistent associations may be because the indices of subsequent firm performance are inadequate. These limitations are recognised, but the statistically insignificant associations suggest either the relationships really are weak, or that they are considerably more complex than can be highlighted by the simple testing undertaken in this chapter.

Note

1. Six founders refused to answer this question.

7 GETTING STARTED

7.1 Introduction

The decision, by an individual, in principle, to become an entrepreneur is substantially less complex than putting that decision into practice. Starting in business means appropriate premises have to be found, whether this involves converting the front room or the garden shed, or the purchasing or leasing of purpose-built accommodation. Finance may have to be negotiated with a bank, a finance company, or obtained from a friend or relative. A second mortgage on the individual's house may have to be arranged. Labour may have to be employed, potential customers identified, capital equipment and supplies purchased. There may also have to be discussions with local authority over the granting of planning permission, especially where this involves changing the use of an existing building, extending it or placing an advertising sign outside it. The Inland Revenue has to be consulted over the individual's tax position, and possibly other organisations such as the Health and Safety Inspectorate and the Regional Water Authority have to be informed. In most cases the Electricity Board will have to be contacted if power requirements are in any way unusual, and British Telecom notified if a telephone is to be installed. A suitable accountant has also to be found to advise the entrepreneur, not simply on matters of book keeping, but upon the management of the enterprise and the choice of an auditor.

This chapter examines two aspects of the process of starting in business — the search for premises and the role of publicly-funded agencies whose *raison d'être* is to encourage the birth and growth of new small businesses. Shortage of suitable cheap premises are frequently cited as a major constraint upon the development of small firms, by restricting the growth of existing small businesses and inhibiting the transition to entrepreneurship. This chapter assesses the evidence for such asertions. It also examines the role of agencies established to assist small firms. Are their services used? Are they valuable? Could they be improved? Section 7.5 of this chapter provides a consumer's viewpoint.

7.2 Premises for New Firms

Providing immediately available, cheap, yet appropriate, premises for industrial firms, especially in areas where firms would not, in the absence of such attractions, have chosen to locate, is a lesson which governments in Britain have learnt. The importance of such premises is underlined in virtually every survey of firms either considering relocating or having relocated. The availability of suitable sites and premises is consistently shown to be a major factor influencing location decisions (Townroe, 1979, Department of Trade and Industry, 1973).

As well as being an important factor in influencing the choice of location for existing firms moving between regions, the availability of suitable small cheap premises is also claimed to be important for those starting businesses for the first time. Falk (1978) claims the lack of availability of such premises, at a price which the budding entrepreneur can afford, is a major constraint on Britain's ability to spawn new firms. Segal (1981) goes further by stating:

> There is clear evidence that a lack of small premises has limited the formation and growth of small firms, and that where premises have been provided on suitable terms one of the effects has been to stimulate the formation of new firms and the growth of those already in existence.

Segal makes the same point in a report produced by Coopers and Lybrand (1980b), commissioned by the Department of Industry:

> The provision of premises on suitable terms has undoubtedly itself had the effect of stimulating the formation of new firms and the growth of existing small firms.

Planners are frequently blamed for the absence of such premises. The redevelopment of many city centres in the late 1960s and early 1970s, together with a devotion to eliminate 'non-conforming uses', has reduced the stock of small business premises in these areas.[1] Many small businesses are only able to operate in city centres, so that when the bulldozer was encouraged to run riot in Birmingham, Leeds and Newcastle-upon-Tyne, etc., not only were people moved out, but many small businesses were eliminated.

The concept of 'non-conforming uses' was applied to a number of areas where there existed a mixture of housing and industry. During the 1960s it was thought preferable to zone industry and housing since industry was frequently noisy and dirty and required increasingly heavy vehicles to transport goods and was the subject of considerable complaint from residents. On the other hand householders, parking their cars in narrow streets prevented access to factories, and complicated the operation of the businesses. Zoning seemed to be a classic Pareto improvement whereby both parties would benefit. Residents would gain through an improved environment, whilst the industry would benefit through easier, quicker and hence cheaper transport.

Whilst zoning was theoretically sound, its implementation raised several unforeseen problems. Redevelopment caused central areas, which had in the past provided suitable sites for wholly new businesses, to be denuded of such activity and to be left initially in a state of desolation proving a paradise for vandals. Eventually when redevelopment took place, the office accommodation which was often erected, frequently proved hard to let.

Yet it is easy to overdramatise the effect of redevelopment schemes upon the stock of small firms. Certainly a number of small city-centre-type industries such as printing, textiles, small toy and plastic good manufacturers were removed. Those studies which have tried to carefully document what actually happened (Chalkley, 1979), as opposed to those chronicling casual impressions, are more ambiguous. In general they show the major effect of urban redevelopment is upon the personal lives of families living in the areas — the uncertainty which it generates, together with dissatisfaction over the compensation payments received. Secondly, many businesses which did not relocate were coming to the end of their 'natural' life — through the ageing of the proprietor or his loss of interest. Their disappearance may have taken place irrespective of redevelopment. Thirdly, those businesses which relocated often performed well in their new location since this provided more space, enabling production to be planned more efficiently.

By the end of the 1970s, the demand for small business premises exceeded the available supply and this was not confined to one region or to urban areas. More important than demolition and redevelopment was absence of newly constructed premises suitable for the small firm. The private sector was reluctant, during the 1960s, to invest in such premises outside the south-east of England — and even here most of the investment was in the Greater London area. It was probably influenced by the prevailing philosophy of the 1960s and early 1970s that small firms were equated with technical and managerial backwardness and that this sector's demand for property could not be as buoyant as that of large enterprises. The industrial property market was orientated towards the provision of large premises suitable for the established expanding firms. By the end of the 1970s, when small firms were becoming more fashionable, constraints on the capital budgets of local authorities meant they were unable to make good this supply deficiency. These factors combined to raise the price of starter accommodation quite considerably and to 'choke off' demand which would have existed if prices had been lower. Furthermore, lags in the construction process meant that only in the early 1980s did an expansion in the construction of starter premises begin.

If, however, the property market works with even partial efficiency, such a state of affairs in only likely to be temporary. The private sector will observe these relatively high prices, due partly to demand-side factors, and will increase supply so that prices would be expected to fall from the level they would otherwise have reached. Clearly the price of starter property will be higher, even in real terms, than it was in the 1950s, but this cannot be regarded as a 'genuine shortage'.

If there are social benefits from people starting their own businesses and high rents discourage new firm formation then there is, at least, an *a priori* case for a public subsidy. This is particularly important since few new firm founders will move more than a short distance to establish their firm. Whether such a subsidy is an optimal use of public funds is more difficult. The next section is devoted to the search for premises conducted by both wholly new firms and all other firms new to Cleveland.

7.3 The Search for Sites and Premises in Cleveland

All establishments new to Cleveland (i.e. wholly new firms and firms new only to Cleveland) were asked about the search process (if any) they undertook before starting business on their current site. For 55 per cent of respondents, their current site was also their first site: other respondents were asked about the search which eventually led to their establishing in business on the site they occupied at the time of the interview.

The choice facing firms new to Cleveland may be summarised as follows:

(i) to set up an establishment in Cleveland or elsewhere;
(ii) to choose one site in preference to others within Cleveland;

(iii) to continue operating on the first site chosen or move to a more suitable site.

This section examines the decisions taken by respondents faced with these choices. All were asked whether areas other than Cleveland were seriously considered before establishing in the county. Only eleven per cent or 34 firms said they had seriously considered locating in another area. Of these firms, 23 mentioned areas elsewhere in the northern region, six said they had considered Scotland, one said Wales and one mentioned Northern Ireland. As many as 14 had considered areas elsewhere in the UK and one had thought about an overseas location. A number considered more than one area.

Those respondents who had seriously considered establishing in an area outside Cleveland were asked why Cleveland had been chosen. All 34 gave at least one reason and five gave three reasons. These are shown in Table 7.1. The small numbers mean the replies are only an approximate guide to the perceived advantages of Cleveland over other areas.

Table 7.1: Reasons for Choosing Cleveland Instead of Alternative Areas

Reason	No. of Replies		%
Operational or supply factors		14	24.1
Found suitable premises in Cleveland	4		
Good area for recruiting workers	3		
To be near suppliers	2		
Close to major road	2		
Others	3		
Product market factors		28	48.3
Knowledge of potential market	14		
Central to the area covered	6		
Customers were in Cleveland	5		
Lack of competition in Cleveland	3		
Personal association with Cleveland		8	13.8
'I lived locally'/local man	4		
Liked the area	3		
Had been working in Cleveland as employee	1		
Financial factors		5	8.6
Cheap office accommodation/premises	3		
Property available for purchase, not lease	1		
Availability of better grants	1		
Other reasons		3	5.2
Total responses		58	100.0

The most important group of factors leading respondents to choose Cleveland were the markets for the products or services provided by the firms. This contrasts with the results of other studies such as Department of Industry (1973) which emphasised the availability of skilled labour, and the role of suitable sites and premises. There are a number of possible explanations for these differences. The first could be that Cleveland has such poor sites that it is not surprising this reason is only rarely given as an important factor influencing decisions. This seems unlikely, since the county has always offered a variety of sites and premises which do not appear to be inferior to those of other assisted areas. A more likely explanation is that a high proportion of respondents were local people starting firms in the service sector selling into a local market. For this type of firm it is more important to know the locality, and be aware of the needs of customers, than it is for the manufacturing branch plants which were the subject of the Department of Industry investigation.

Once the decision to locate in Cleveland is made, the firm faces a choice of sites and premises. Each respondent was asked whether his firm had seriously considered any other sites in Cleveland before establishing on its current site. Of those able to answer the question, 43 per cent replied in the affirmative. *Thus, over half the firms appear not to have engaged in any site search and presumably accepted the first site offered or, perhaps, had decided to set up in business only when the opportunity of a site came to their attention.*

From Table 7.2 it can be seen that branch plants and subsidiary companies were more likely, compared with independent firms, to have looked at more than a single site before reaching their decision. This is predictable partly because such establishments are more likely to be influenced by concepts such as 'least cost siting', and partly because locational differences are genuinely more important for such firms. Furthermore, established firms are likely to have less information on the merits of sites than local firms.

The reasons given by respondents for rejecting sites are given in Table 7.3. Replies mentioning location relative to customers amount to only 1.7 per cent of responses; even if other replies mentioning location which may have included indirect references to customers are added (such as 'not central enough') the maximum aggregate possible is only 13.8 per cent. This is still less than the single most frequent reply of 'too expensive' (25.0 per cent) which, together with the other faults identified which are specific to the characteristics of the site or premises, amount to over two-fifths of all responses.

Table 7.2: Whether or Not Other Cleveland Sites were Examined: By Type of Firm

	Independent – One Site		Parent Plant		Branch Plant		Subsidiary		Total	
	No.	%	No.	%	No.	%	No.	%	No.	%
Other sites examined	64	(37)	5	(36)	14	(50)	36	(56)	119	(43)
Other sites not examined	108	(63)	9	(64)	14	(50)	28	(44)	159	(57)
Total	172	(100)	14	(100)	28	(100)	64	(100)	278	(100)

Within the miscellaneous group are statements such as the prevalence of vandalism in the area, or poor security. Also mentioned are the feeling amongst respondents that their type of firm would not be welcome in the area — either because of its environmental effect or because site owners would have to make too many modifications to buildings.

Table 7.3: Faults of Sites or Premises Rejected by Respondent Firms: Aggregated Replies

	No. of Replies	%
Transportation/Location aspects	19	8.2
Planning permission refused/might have been refused		
'Not central enough'	17	7.3
Competition around there	8	3.5
'Poor area'/'Didn't like the location', etc.	6	2.6
Too far from customers	4	1.7
Poor site access	3	1.3
Poor transportation facilities in general	3	1.3
Other general location faults	8	3.4
Sub-total	68	29.3
Characteristics of site/premises		
Too expensive	58	25.0
Lease/terms of lease not suitable	13	5.6
Site too small	11	4.7
Poor parking facilities	9	3.9
Too much modification needed	11	4.7
Too much delay in site/premises preparation	10	4.3
'In poor state of repair'	5	2.2
Premises too big	4	1.7
Other premises problems	14	6.1
Other miscellaneous site/premises problems	12	5.2
Sub-total	147	63.4
Other miscellaneous problems	17	7.3
Grand total	232	100.0
Respondents	108	

The search process for sites and premises by branches and subsidiaries of existing firms has been seen to be more comprehensive than that of single plant independent firms, most of which are newly created businesses. Table 7.4 shows a breakdown of the reasons given for rejecting sites both by wholly new firms and all other firms new to Cleveland. The industrial mix of the respondents is also shown.

A total of 58 new firm founders claimed to examine a site other than the one on which they started business, compared with 50 other firms new to Cleveland. The emphasis upon specific sites and premises problems, rather than transport or location aspects is again apparent — with the exception of those founding new businesses in 'other' services where High Street locations with adequate parking facilities are an important consideration.

7.4 The Role of Agencies in Assisting Industry

In recent years there has been a proliferation of the number of agencies, normally supported wholly or in part by public funds, whose task is to assist industry *to create jobs*. Local authorities, for example, have become increasingly interested in economic matters. In June. 1980, the Association of County Councils reported that of all Non-Metropolitan County Councils in England and Wales, 30 had an industrial development officer, ten had a nominated officer or contact and only seven had no specific arrangements for dealing with local economic development.

There has also been a sharp increase in the number of other publicly funded agencies, particularly in the assisted areas, whose functions are to assist potential entrepreneurs and small businesses in managing their business. Nevertheless, many small businessmen are unaware of the finance and facilities available. This, in turn is often regarded as a symptom of weak management, which many financial institutions cite as the main reason why they do not invest more in small firms. The Bolton Committee recognised this problem and as a result the Small Firms Information Centres (SFIC) were established in a number of regional centres. These were offices to which the small businessmen could turn in order to obtain information on accountancy, sales, employment, planning matters, etc. SFICs do not answer these questions themselves but direct the businessman, unaccustomed to dealing with such matters, to the relevant expert. This is referred to as a signposting function.

Table 7.4: Reasons Given by Firms for Rejecting Sites in Cleveland

Reasons	Manufacturing		Construction		Professional Services		Distribution		Other Services		Total	
	Wholly New	Others New to Cleveland	Wholly New	Others New to Cleveland	Wholly New	Others New to Cleveland	Wholly New	Others New to Cleveland	Wholly New	Others New to Cleveland	Wholly New	Others New to Cleveland
Transport and location problems	3	7	7	8	7	7	3	6	15	5	35	33
Site or premises problems	10	15	14	12	24	17	15	14	13	13	76	71
Miscellaneous	6	4	0	3	1	0	0	0	2	1	9	8
Total reasons	19	26	21	23	32	24	18	20	30	19	120	112
Total respondents	11	12	9	9	14	10	7	10	17	9	58	50

In addition to SFIC there are now a number of other agencies which offer this signposting function and more direct assistance. By 1980 within the county of Cleveland the entrepreneur could turn to at least 25 agencies within a 40-mile radius of Middlesbrough to obtain advice and assistance on matters such as premises, planning, finance, accountancy and management, etc. These agencies and their functions are listed in Storey (1981a). Few agencies offer a comprehensive service – all stress their own unique contribution by filling a specific need. The fact that most are supported by public funds and that there is apparently some overlap, suggests that an examination of their performance is worthwhile.

The paucity of published work on this topic is due to two factors. First, public organisations are unwilling to open themselves to full public scrutiny, yet without their co-operation any assessment is of limited value. Secondly, the criteria for evaluating the success of public agencies are not clear. Even if it were agreed that the objective is to create more employment in the locality, this is not a concept which can be easily 'operationalised'. Bringing new jobs to an area is, or at least should be, a team effort. In northern England enquiries for large sites are directed to the Department of Industry, English Industrial Estates Corporation (now English Industrial Estates), North of England Development Council and/or the County and District Councils. If the ultimate purpose of these bodies is to create jobs locally one measure of success might be the number of jobs created per £ of expenditure. It is however meaningless to evaluate agencies independently, since the performance of each is ultimately determined by that of other organisations.

Furthermore, a number of agencies see their primary role as providing advice to firms. If that advice is directed towards making the company more internally efficient this may be difficult to quantify in terms of direct employment created. The absence of clearly specified objectives makes evaluation of agency performance difficult. In addition, some agencies see themselves as less concerned with direct job creation, in the short term. Instead their efforts are directed towards selling an image of an area, and eliminating prejudices based on inadequate information. Indeed, some agencies argue this must be their role since it is impossible to link initiatives by the agency with economic development. Finally, it is difficult to assess the direct contribution which the agency made to the location. Would, in the absence of the agency, the firm have located in the area anyway? Despite the protestations of the agencies that their work cannot be evaluated in these simplistic terms some studies have been undertaken.

Coopers and Lybrand (1980a) examined the major agencies involved in job creation in northern England, but their assessment was based upon an inadequate number of agency clients. In fact one of the consultants' recommendations was that agencies should be continuously conducting their own performance evaluation by following up all enquiries to determine whether the firm expanded, contracted or went out of business.

A less subjective study was conducted by Howdle (1979) of the Small Firms Counselling Service (SFCS) in south-west England. He showed by interviewing SFCS clients that the service provided 'a valuable help to small firms . . . (and) is directly responsible for the survival of a considerable number of firms and has helped create many new businesses'. Storey and Robinson (1981), recognising these evaluation problems, examined the enquiries received by Cleveland County Council Industrial Promotion Department. They report that 'whilst the vast majority of the enquirers never relocate, 50 per cent of those who do shift, eventually relocate in Cleveland'. The paper also demonstrated that different definitions of the criteria for success in industrial promotion, produce markedly different results.

All the above studies ignore or assume away the interdependency of the agencies, and none shed any light on those firms/individuals who are potential rather than actual customers of the agency. This means a number of important questions are not being asked, viz.: what proportion of firms new to an area obtain advice or assistance from an agency? How can the agency make contact with the potential customers? What do those firms who use agencies think of the service they receive? How can it be improved? Are the clients of some agencies significantly more satisfied than the clients of others? It is towards a better understanding of these questions that the following sections are devoted.

7.5 The Propensity of Firms to Use an Agency Prior to Establishing in Cleveland

All 301 firms new to Cleveland were asked whether, prior to establishing their plant, they contacted any agencies: 138 or 45 per cent of all respondents claimed to visit an agency prior to establishing on their site (although only 122 or 40 per cent were able to identify the agency visited). These 122 respondents mentioned a total of 25 agencies, the most important of which are shown in Table 7.5 Since each respondent was able to mention up to four agencies a total of 217 'mentions' are shown in the table.

Table 7.5: Agencies Mentioned as Contacted

Agencies	Mentions		% of Users Finding Agency Helpful[a]	
	All Firms New to Cleveland No.	Wholly New Firms No.	All Firms New to Cleveland %	Wholly New Firms %
Cleveland County Council	52	18	66	47
Cleveland District Councils	43	22	61	50
Department of Industry	41	15	79	84
English Industrial Estates Corporation	29	11	75	70
Small Firms Information Centre	16	13	68	69
North of England Development Council	15	7	58	50
Others	21	9	60	44
Total	217	95		

Note: a. Some respondents were unable/unwilling to answer whether they found agencies helpful.

The agencies mentioned most frequently were Cleveland County Council (52 occasions) (Department of Industry (41) and English Industrial Estates Corporation (29) whilst the District Councils of Cleveland are mentioned in total 43 times. A number of agencies are not mentioned at all, despite having been established in the area before 1977. The propensity of the individual, starting his own firm, to contact an agency is less than that of the existing firm seeking a new location in Cleveland. Of the 122 respondents able to recall contacting a specific agency, 57 were new firm founders whereas 65 were existing firms. Thus 36 per cent of wholly new firms were able to identify an agency they had contacted prior to establishment compared with 46 per cent of firms moving into the area for the first time. There is of course a higher proportion of wholly new firms in the service sector where information may be less valuable (in the sense that grants and other financial assistance is often limited to manufacturing firms) and where average size of firm is lower. Thus 57 per cent of all wholly new manufacturing firms claimed to contact an agency prior to establishment, whereas the comparable figure for construction, professional services, distribution and 'other' were, 24, 33, 44 and 30 per cent respectively.

Variations in use of agencies by firms, according to industry, is also shown in Table 7.6, which shows that 39 respondents in manufacturing made contact with an agency, contacting a total of 84 agencies – a contact rate of 2.15. This rate is substantially higher than for firms in other sectors where in most cases it is well below 2.0, showing that not only do a higher proportion of manufacturing firms contact an agency, but that they also contact more agencies.

Table 7.6 also shows that Department of Industry, EIEC and NEDC deal primarily with manufacturing firms, whereas local authorities, the Small Firms Information Centre and 'others' deal with a much higher proportion of non-manufacturing firms. A distinction can also be made between agencies specialising primarily in wholly new firms and those appearing to deal more with established firms. The clearest example of the former type of agency is, as might be expected, the Small Firms Information Centre where 45 per cent of those using it were wholly new firms.

7.6 Reasons for Contacting an Agency

Table 7.7 shows the reasons which respondents gave for contacting an agency. By far the most important reason, both for all firms new to Cleveland and for wholly new firms, was to obtain details of available sites and premises. This alone contributed 28 per cent of all reasons for the sample as a whole, and 25 per cent for wholly new firms. The second most important set of reasons was financial – primarily checking on the availability of grants. Reasons B1, B2 and B3 when aggregated show that about 26 per cent of all enquiries from the sample as a whole and 31 per cent from wholly new firms were for these reasons. This appears to be high since only about 20 per cent of all respondents were manufacturing firms who were likely to have a good chance of obtaining grants, although during the 1970s construction firms were eligible for grants, and some service firms currently receive financial assistance. In addition, respondents could have contacted several agencies before realising that they were not eligible for aid. Of the remaining reasons for agency contact, planning matters, in total, contributed 18 per cent of all reasons for firms new to Cleveland and 16 per cent for wholly new firms. Within the 'other' reasons category there is a clear divide between wholly new firms and firms new to the area, so that the latter contacted agencies for information on services/conditions in the area, whereas wholly new firms wanted information on business practices.

Table 7.6: Use of Agencies by Industry

Agencies	Manufacturing		Construction		Professional Services		Distribution		Other Services		Total	
	All Firms New to Cleveland Firms	Wholly New Firms	All Firms New to Cleveland Firms	Wholly New Firms	All Firms New to Cleveland Firms	Wholly New Firms	All Firms New to Cleveland Firms	Wholly New Firms	All Firms New to Cleveland Firms	Wholly New Firms	All Firms New to Cleveland Firms	Wholly New Firms
Cleveland County Council	13	6	8	3	6	3	13	3	12	3	52	18
Cleveland Borough Councils	12	4	5	1	8	1	7	1	11	8	43	15
Department of Industry	25	7	6	3	5	3	3	2	2	0	41	15
English Industrial Estates Corporation	18	6	3	2	5	2	2	0	1	1	29	11
Small Firms Information Centre	4	3	4	3	4	3	2	2	2	2	16	13
North of England Development Council	5	2	3	1	4	2	2	2	1	0	15	7
Others	7	2	5	2	3	2	2	0	4	3	21	9
Total no. of contacts	84	30	34	15	35	16	31	10	33	17	217	88
Total no. of respondents contacting an agency	39	17	19	8	21	11	19	7	24	14	122	57

Table 7.7: Reasons for Contacting Agencies

	Firms New to Cleveland		Wholly New Firms	
A. Planning Reasons		43		18
1. For planning permission	21		8	
2. For planning permission for change of use	11		5	
3. Other planning reasons	11		5	
B. Financial reasons		73		33
1. To check on availability of grants	38		17	
2. To get financial assistance (no details specified)	12		7	
3. To obtain a development grant	12		6	
4. Other financial reasons	11		3	
C. Other reasons		125		59
1. To obtain details of available sites/premises	68		28	
2. Information on services/conditions in the area	13		2	
3. Hoping to get work from the agency	10		7	
4. General information on how to run the business	7		7	
5. Miscellaneous	27		15	

The data given in Table 7.5 to 7.7 reports only the information provided by the firms themselves. The new firm founder may, consciously or unconsciously, be less willing to remember seeking general business assistance — which he may equate with naivety on his part — than other aspects of the establishment process. Nevertheless, infrequent mentions of seeking advice from agencies and the very few mentions of certain agencies, especially those attached to academic institutions, suggest that only a very small proportion, even of wholly new firms in the 1971-8 period, actually used these advisory services. This in turn casts doubt on whether surveys by academics of their own clients are an unbiased sample of the local entrepreneurial population.

Further examination of the data showed that local authorities are an important source of information on premises and other information as well as being the major planning authority, but were an unimportant source of financial advice or other assistance, requests for which were directed towards Department of Industry, with the Small Firms Information Centre being the prime provider of this information for wholly new firms.

7.7 Satisfaction with the Agency

Two-thirds of respondents who visited an agency, prior to establishing their firms in Cleveland, found this helpful. Table 7.5 shows that Department of Industry was classified as helpful by 79 per cent of all new firms to Cleveland and 84 per cent of wholly new firms. In both cases it was the agency with the best 'rating'. The services provided by the Small Firms Information Centre also seem to be well received, as are those of English Industrial Estates Corporation. The Local Authorities are not as highly regarded as the above agencies, partly because their planning functions are seen as restrictive, compared to the positive roles of DI, EIEC and SFIC. The remaining agencies, although claiming to offer assistance, are also significantly less well received than the above group of three.

The table also shows that the satisfaction with agency performance expressed by wholly new firms is significantly less than that expressed by firms new to Cleveland. To examine whether this is associated with the size of the firm, Table 7.8 is constructed, which suggests that the smallest (in terms of employees) sized respondents tend to find the service provided by agencies less helpful. In table 7.8, for example, 32 per cent of all firms new to Cleveland and 41 per cent of wholly new firms found all agencies whom they contacted unhelpful. For firms employing four people or less in 1979 the comparable percentages were 42 and 52 per cent. This is supported by the comments received from a number of very small firms that, in their opinion, agency services are designed to assist larger firms. Nevertheless, it is curious that the highest level of satisfaction with agency services is found in firms employing between five and ten people in 1979, where only 26 per cent of all firms new to Cleveland expressed dissatisfaction. In part the distinction on the basis of size may also be due to a distinction between wholly new firms and those new to Cleveland. Table 7.8, however, shows that for each size band, new firms found agencies less helpful than the sample as a whole.

Size is also correlated with industry, since larger establishments are frequently in the manufacturing or distribution industries. An examination of the effect of industrial structure shows a major divide between manufacturing firms and all other sectors. Amongst manufacturing firms new to Cleveland only 24 per cent of contacts with agencies proved to be unhelpful compared with an average for other sectors of 38 per cent. The distinction is even more stark for wholly new firms where only 21 per cent of the agency contacts of wholly new manufac-

Table 7.8: Respondents Finding Agencies Helpful/Unhelpful: By Employment Size

	Employment Size in 1979									
	1-4		5-10		11-24		25+		Total	
	Firms New to Cleveland	Wholly New Firms	Firms New to Cleveland	Wholly New Firms	Firms New to Cleveland	Wholly New Firms	Firms New to Cleveland	Wholly New Firms	Firms New to Cleveland	Wholly New Firms
Helpful	19	10	39	22	31	12	44	9	133	53
Not helpful	14	11	14	11	18	10	18	5	64	37
% not helpful (mentions)	42%	52%	26%	33%	36%	45%	29%	36%	32%	41%
Total mentions	33	21	53	33	49	22	62	14	197	90
Total respondents	27	18	30	19	26	12	28	7	111	56

turing firms were unhelpful compared with 51 per cent for all other sectors.

Table 7.9: Details of Experience with Agencies

A. Comments on helpfulness	13
1. Department of Industry are perfect	
2. An EIEC official was very helpful	
B. Comments on unhelpfulness	17
1. Department of Industry wanted too many forms filled in	
2. The people at the Polytechnic were a complete waste of time	
C. Comments on eligibility	9
1. They were not interested because I wanted to manufacture and retail on an industrial estate	
2. Department of Industry could not help as we only bought second-hand equipment	
D. Comments on slowness	11
1. Took to long — I could not wait	
2. I have not received any money	
E. Other comments	31
1. They referred me elsewhere	
2. They only gave advice, but did not help in a practical way	
Total	81

The experience of respondents in dealing with agencies is shown with 'typical' replies being provided below the group heading in somewhat more detail in Table 7.9. Firms were questioned about the unhelpfulness of agencies, although several responded with comments even where they found an agency helpful, with nine of the 13 unsolicited comments on the helpfulness of agencies coming from manufacturing firms. The most typical comment was, however, that agency X was useless/a waste of time. Where these comments were developed they often referred to either the lack of eligibility of the firm for (normally financial) assistance, or the slowness of the agency in dealing with problems.

7.8 Ways of Improving the Service Provided by Agencies

Ninety-two replies were received on the question of whether there could be an improvement in the services provided by agencies. Fifty-five respondents thought improvements could be made, whereas 37 thought improvement was not possible. A total of 65 answers were

received on the question of how agency performance might be improved and these are grouped in Table 7.10 with 'typical' replies being
provided below the group heading. Most respondents thought the
services could be improved by making them available to a wider range
of industry groups. One-quarter of those suggesting ways of improving
the services felt additional services and assistance should be provided,
although this would have required changes in current statutory powers
of agencies. For example, a number felt grants should be paid not only
to manufacturers but to a wider range of service firms. Others felt
financial assistance should be provided for new companies by the
agency guaranteeing risk capital. This, it was felt, would make agencies
take the requirements of the small non-manufacturing firm more
seriously.

Table 7.10: Ways of Improving Agency Services

A. Planning	11
1. Better and swifter planning decisions needed	
2. Local authorities should be more flexible in giving planning permission for change of use of premises	
B. Red tape/bureaucracy	6
1. 'Agencies' have too much red tape/never cut corners	
2. Agencies should have a more flexible approach in dealing with firms	
C. Provision of information	8
1. More information should be provided through an advice bureau of some sort	
2. Agencies should make themselves better known	
D. Powers of agencies	14
1. Agencies should help service firms as well as manufacturing	
2. Agencies should give grants and loans to firms just starting	
E. Improve quality of service	14
1. Small Firms Information Centre should be closer	
2. 'Agencies should know about my line of business'	
F. Others	12
1. Agencies should take account of small firms	
2. Council should do repairs during warranty period	
Total	65

A number of respondents felt a greater variety of services could be
provided — some wanted a comprehensive accountancy service, whilst
others wanted to talk to individuals who had a detailed working knowledge of their industry — and were frustrated when those dealing with
their problems had only limited industrial experience.

Several respondents felt improvements could be made both in the dissemination of information and in better planning decisions. For example, it was felt that agencies should make themselves better known, and respondents indicated they would be happy to receive visits from agency staff and so become better informed about the availability of grants, etc. Indeed a number of respondents felt it should be the duty of the agency to inform the firms of available assistance rather than for the firm to have to seek out information. Planning matters were also the subject of some criticism, particularly the length of time taken to reach decisions.

Another source of complaint was that agencies were insufficiently flexible and responsive. A number of suggestions made were to reduce red tape and speed up the actions of the agency. Some respondents suggested that it should be made easier to find the appropriate individual to contact, although here there were conflicting requirements. Some wanted always to talk to a specialist, whilst others wanted only one individual to deal with their problem and not be continually passed from one official to another.

Finally, there were a set of miscellaneous suggestions ranging from helping taxi firms to suggesting that lists for Council tendering be updated more frequently.

7.9 Other Sources of Information

The infrequency with which firms new to Cleveland used agencies for information does not necessarily indicate that firms' location decisions were made in a state of ignorance. All firms were asked to identify the sources of information they used in selecting their site. The results are shown in Table 7.11.

Of all firms new to Cleveland, 32 per cent claimed not to use any source of information, whilst ten per cent claimed to be unable to answer the question. A total of 343 sources of information were identified by the remaining respondents with 57 per cent of firms new to Cleveland using at least one of the sources and 18 per cent using three or more services.

Table 7.11 refers to the number of times an individual source of information was mentioned. Thus of the 177 respondents new to Cleveland, and who collected any information, 124 made contact with estate agents and surveyors. This was by far the most important source of information on sites and premises, although 106 respondents visited the site/premises separately from the estate agents/surveyors. Only five respondents claimed to use specialist location consultants, although 34 carried out a detailed financial appraisal of alternative sites.

Table 7.11: Sources of Information on Sites and Premises

	All Firms New to Cleveland		Wholly New Firms	
	%	No.	%	No.
1. Contacted surveyors and estate agents	70.0	124	69.6	64
2. Made independent site visits	60.0	106	58.6	54
3. Made detailed internal costings of alternative sites	35.6	63	32.6	30
4. Contacted known local companies or individuals	19.2	34	20.6	19
5. Employed specialist consultants	2.8	5	2.2	2
6. Used 'the grapevine'	1.6	3	2.2	2
7. Others	4.5	8	7.6	7
Total mentions		343		178
Total respondents		177		92

Note: Percentages are of respondents.

There appears to be little difference between the sources of information used by all firms new to Cleveland and those used by wholly new firms, with, in both cases, 70 per cent of respondents using any sources of information turning to estate agents and 60 per cent making independent site visits. Similarly, approximately one-third of both groups of respondents claimed to have undertaken detailed costing of alternative sites. The only source of information which wholly new firms used more frequently than firms new to Cleveland was information sources such as 'the grapevine', 'keeping my eyes open' or 'using my own judgement' — i.e. other sources.

7.10 Conclusion

This chapter has examined the problems facing both existing firms relocating in a new area, and of individuals starting in business for the first time. It has concentrated upon two aspects — the difficulties of obtaining suitable premises and the role which public agencies play in assisting new firms.

The shortage of 'starter' premises has frequently been cited as a cause of the low rate of new firm formation in Britain, compared with other developed countries, but such a hypothesis is easier to state than to prove. The results in this chapter suggest that over half of all firms new to Cleveland, and over 60 per cent of wholly new firms undertook no search for premises — they accepted the first which they found to be available. This lack of a coherent search procedure could indicate either a shortage or a surfeit of premises. If there was a shortage then it might be quite rational for the entrepreneur to accept the first that became available, knowing that no others were on offer. On the other hand, if there are plenty of suitable premises, offering broadly similar facilities, then there is little point in conducting a detailed search.

High rents were the most frequent reasons given by firms/individuals for rejecting premises which they visited. This also might suggest that there is a 'shortage' of premises but it is unclear whether the property which the respondent occupied at the time of the interview was cheaper than that which he rejected earlier. Nevertheless, it seems likely that the supply of 'starter' premises has fallen over the past decade, partly through demolition, but primarily through relatively small additions to stock. It also seems likely that demand for such premises has risen throughout the 1970s because of the increased number of new firms which were founded, and hence the price of such premises has risen. It is less clear whether this represents a real barrier to the formation of new businesses, since so many new businesses fail in their early years (or months) or quickly outgrow their initial premises, so there is a rapid turnover of firms in such premises. For the individual wishing to start in business there should, therefore, be relatively few problems in obtaining starter premises, providing he can afford the rent.

If the rents of starter premises are high it is to be expected either that private capital will be attracted into their construction or, if there are social benefits associated with a higher rate of new firm formation, public finance might be used. There will inevitably be a lag between a building programme for small premises and an impact upon the stock of such properties but, given that the price elasticity of demand for small premises is inelastic (by reducing the price relatively few indivuals are attracted to become entrepreneurs), there is a real risk of excess supply in future.

The unwillingness of the individual starting in business to seek alternative sites is paralleled by his unwillingness to contact public agencies established to assist infant firms. Fifty-five per cent of all firms new to Cleveland said they visited no agencies prior to establishment, so there is clearly an opportunity for such agencies to extend their influence. The willingness of firms new to Cleveland to contact an agency depended upon whether or not it was a manufacturing firm. Such firms were more than twice as likely to contact agencies as were firms in the service or construction sectors. They were also much more likely to be satisfied with the services they received – presumably because of their greater likelihood of being eligible for financial assistance.

Despite this reluctance of the entrepreneur to contact agencies, and particularly the dissatisfaction expressed by the small newly established non-manufacturing firm, the number of agencies continues to multiply. It is increasingly important to identify criteria for determining the effectiveness of such agencies, bearing in mind that the entrepreneur is likely to be a character who cherishes his personal independence and ability to solve his own problems. He is frequently frustrated by what he sees as the slow process of bureaucracy in dealing with planning permissions and grants. This hostility to agencies has to be offset against the naivety of those entering into business, and the ignorance of those moving into new geographical areas for the first time.

Two criteria by which agency performance may be judged have been used in this chapter. The first is the proportion of new firm founders who used the agency, and secondly the proportion of customers who claimed to be satisfied with the services they received. According to such criteria Department of Industry, English Industrial Estates Corporation and the Small Firms Information Centre perform well. There are, however, a large number of other agencies who are not mentioned by firms in this sample and who seem to be offering broadly similar services. There surely is a need to reduce this duplication, if only to reduce the confusion amongst entrepreneurs over the variety of services provided.

Note

1. This reduction in city centre small businesses coincided with an increase in the proportion of total manufacturing output produced by small firms. It is therefore only true to say that the stock of small firms fell below that which it might otherwise have been. It is less clear whether there was any absolute reduction at a national level.

8 FINANCE FOR THE NEW FIRM

8.1 Introduction

The subject of finance for small firms has been vigorously debated for many years. The Macmillan Committee, reporting in 1931, argued that small companies had particular difficulty obtaining medium term finance in relatively small quantities. The Bolton Committee, 40 years later, in its review of small firms, devoted more space to the problems of finance than to any other single topic. It felt that despite the valuable work of the Industrial and Commercial Finance Corporation (ICFC), which was established to close the so-called 'Macmillan Gap', small firms continued to encounter genuine difficulties in obtaining finance from external sources, compared with larger enterprises. These difficulties were due to the extra cost to the banks of lending to small companies – the high cost of administration relative to the sums involved, and the higher risks of default on loans.

Bolton, whilst recognising that small firms incurred these penalties, did not recommend either the establishment of any new financial institution to lend to small firms or the provision of finance at subsidised rates. Instead the Committee believed small firms should have to compete for funds with all other sizes of enterprises and be put to the test of the market. The Wilson Committee (1979) again argued that, compared with large firms, small firms were at a considerable disadvantage in the financial markets, and recognised that this disadvantage was partly inevitable for the above reasons. Any unjustified bias against small companies in the costs of providing finance would, the Committee argued, be reflected either in higher profits of those institutions financing the small firm, or in the entry of new institutions to fill this profitable gap. The Committee could find no evidence for either. Nevertheless, it argued that existing institutions may subjectively overestimate the risk of lending to small firms, and particularly to new firms. For this reason the Committee supported the introduction of a loan guarantee scheme with a limited public subsidy, and with part of the risk being retained by the banks. They reasoned that competition between the clearing banks was insufficient to ensure viable small businesses could always obtain access to capital. In addition they suggested that there were clearly identifiable public benefits to aiding the small firm sector – notably the creation of jobs which were separate from, and additional to, the private benefits to the banks. Hence some public subsidy could be justified, and this argument was subsequently accepted by the government in earmarking funds for a loan guarantee scheme in its 1981 budget.

This argument is slightly curious, however, since the Committee recognised that no institution was either making excess profits from lending to small firms, or, having made such profits in the past, is now subject to more intense competition from entrants. Nevertheless, the Committee suggests that there are potentially viable small businesses unable to obtain funding because bankers are excessively risk-averse, yet if lending to small firms had become a highly profitable part of the business of finance houses then the clearing banks would surely have competed more actively for small and new firm customers. That they have not done so until recently to any great extent, or with any enthusiasm, suggests it is not for them a particularly profitable section of the lending market. Indeed it is frequently pointed out that the recent increase in lending to small firms by the clearing banks has coincided with generally higher levels of interest rates in the economy, with the consequent increase in bank profits, and a public clamour for these to be taxed.

Justification for a loan guarantee scheme, on the basis of the external benefits which the scheme generates in terms of jobs, also has to be carefully scrutinised. It is not sufficient to show there are identifiable public benefits and infer that some form of public subsidy is justified. Instead the provision of public funds requires first the identifiable public benefits to exceed the public funds injected. These benefits could be in terms of creating jobs for those who might otherwise be unemployed and who afterwards will contribute to public funds through taxation rather than by receiving financial assistance from the state. As shown in Chapter 2, the number of jobs created in new manufacturing firms is not high, and it needs to be shown that this is a more cost-effective use of public funds than maintaining or creating jobs in other types of enterprise. It also has to be shown that birth rates of firms can be raised and death rates reduced through the operation of a loan guarantee scheme. Finally the distributional consequences of the decision need to be considered. For example, will the majority of the jobs be created in areas which are currently prosperous? Is a loan guarantee scheme likely to result in relatively wealthy new firm founders obtaining the lion's share of the benefits of public expenditure?

It is not our purpose to try to answer all these questions in this chapter, nor to offer a comprehensive treatise on the subject of finance for the small firm. Instead the extent to which the new firm is a satisfactory client for the banks will be investigated using empirical data on new firms in Cleveland.

8.2 The Issues

The financial community has given the Wilson Committee recommendations on finance for small businesses a lukewarm response, primarily because it believed until very recently that the limited funds currently invested in small and new firms reflect the risky nature of such investment, and the absence of worthwhile investments. On the other hand, the small business lobby, and recently the government itself, seems to regard the inability of new and small firms to obtain suitable finance as a major constraint upon their development which, if relaxed, could stimulate development of this sector. Is it then a shortage of good investments, or the natural risk-aversion of bankers, that explains the relatively small volume of bank lending directed towards the small business?

As in most similar debates there is much to be said for both sides. Mitchell (1979) in her examination of the customers of ICFC for the Wilson Committee showed that, as a group, their performance was markedly superior to that of a typical cross section of new and small firms.

In the ten years 1967/8-1977/8 ICFC lent £16½ million to 277 firms to start-up (i.e. a business launch which was less than three years old). One-third of those start-ups subsequently failed, with ten per cent either having been taken over or ICFC having sold their interest. The remaining 57 per cent survived, with 44 per cent having become 'well established' firms. These firms alone had generated 5,400 jobs. Hence the arithmetic mean employment of a surviving ICFC customer is at least 34, and probably closer to 40 at the end of a decade. Chapter 2 showed that the typical new surviving manufacturing firm in those parts of Britain which have been studied, employed 14-16 people at the end of a decade. ICFC's customers are therefore far from typical of new small firms.

From a policy viewpoint this raises several issues. The first is whether ICFC's customers perform well because they have been carefully selected from amongst a large population of potential customers, the majority of whom would have gone into liquidation, even with finance from the Corporation. Alternatively is it the backing from ICFC which enables the company to expand, its creditors to have confidence that it is securely funded, as well as benefiting from the financial and managerial advice which the Corporation is able to provide?

If the explanation lies with ICFC's prudent selection policy, then the provision of additional funds to small firms through a loan guarantee scheme may create only temporary jobs because such firms may not be viable in the long run. Governments would therefore be supporting 'lame ducklings'.

There is also no certainty that a further investment of £16½ million over a decade would guarantee the creation of a further permanent 5,400 jobs. It is equally likely that ICFC has already 'creamed-off' the most profitable projects. New starts which are subsidised are arguably less likely, on average, to create jobs than those which the financial market chooses to support without a state subsidy. Alternatively, if there are a number of enterprises which, with financial backing, could be highly successful, then the modest sums earmarked by government to finance loan guarantee schemes could be well spent.

A second set of issues concerns the types of enterprise which the clearing banks, in particular, assist. For example the relatively large amounts of capital involved in establishing a manufacturing enterprise mean the bank plays a crucial role whereas, as we shall see, in the construction industry several companies claimed to have started without capital, existing on trade credit, etc. The fact that several enterprises began without the assistance of the financial sector does not necessarily mean this is the most effective way of conducting business. Should banks therefore make a more positive effort to interest the small businessman in the services and assistance which it can offer, or does such marketing involve a high chance of netting risky companies?

The banker's assessment of risk may be based upon the ability of the customer to present a cogent written proposal including previous accounts, financial projections, etc., which may be more related to education levels and business experience than business acumen. Those without formal managerial qualifications may be forced to look to the informal financial network for assistance, to pay higher rates, and hence raise the already high risk of failure. It is important to compare the characteristics of those who borrow from banks to start their business as opposed to those using other sources of finance. In the following sections these matters will be examined through a review of the financial development of new firms in the county of Cleveland.

8.3 Sources of Start-up Finance

Wholly new independent firms in Cleveland were asked for the sources of finance which founders used to begin their business — 152 firms provided usable answers with one-third using more than a single source. All mentioned sources are shown in Table 8.1, where responses are subdivided by industrial grouping. It shows that 52 per cent of all financial sources mentioned were personal savings,[1] with this proportion varying little between the industrial groupings. Where entrepreneurs used more than a single source of finance they were asked to identify the most important source. These figures are given in brackets. Personal savings were used by 75 respondents constituting the most important source for 56 per cent of respondents. Here an 'industry' effect was apparent with new manufacturing and distribution firm founders more frequently identifying personal savings as the most important source of initial start-up finance.

Loans and overdrafts from the clearing banks received 26 per cent of all 'mentions' as a source of finance, and were the 'most important' source of finance in 27 per cent of all cases. There appears to be no major industry effect amongst the borrowers, except possibly that those establishing in professional services seem rather more likely to use the clearing banks than other new starters.

Loans from friends and relatives received seven per cent of all mentions, house mortgages six per cent and loans from finance companies four per cent, where the latter were defined to be any formal financial institution which was not one of the major clearing banks. Included in the 'other' category were those who claimed to start without capital, those using government grants, trade credit, HP and leasing arrangement — but these were rarely the most important source of finance. There appears to be very little difference, by industry, in the proportion of businesses using more than a single source of funds, or in those using the 'other' category of funding.

These results can be compared with those obtained by IFT Marketing Ltd for the Wilson Committee (1979). Their survey of 96 firms which had been established in the previous five years in the service sector showed that 68 per cent of new firm founders claimed to use their own capital, 35 per cent used bank loans and overdrafts and ten per cent used family loans.[2] Their questions, however, do not relate to the start-up of the business, but rather to the current use of funds.

Bearing in mind that the present survey obtained 152 usable replies to this question, the comparable figures for initial capital financing in

Table 8.1: Mentions of Sources of Finance Used to Start a Wholly New Independent Business: by Industry

Source of Initial finance	Manufacturing		Construction		Professional Services		Distribution		Other		Total	
	No.	Prop.	No.	Prop.	No.	Prop.	No.	Prop.	No.	Prop.	No.	Prop.
1. Personal savings	20 (16)	0.53 (0.67)	24 (17)	0.54 (0.56)	20 (16)	0.48 (0.56)	12 (10)	0.63 (0.73)	28 (16)	0.48 (0.40)	104 (75)	0.52 (0.56)
2. House mortgage	3 (2)	0.08 (0.08)	4 (1)	0.09 (0.03)	4 (2)	0.10 (0.06)	0 (0)	0.00 (0.07)	1 (1)	0.02 (0.02)	12 (6)	0.06 (0.04)
3. Loans and gifts from friends or relations	2 (1)	0.05 (0.04)	5 (3)	0.11 (0.09)	0 (0)	0.00 (0.00)	0 (0)	0.00 (0.00)	8 (6)	0.14 (0.14)	15 (10)	0.07 (0.07)
4. Loans/overdraft from clearing banks	10 (5)	0.26 (0.21)	9 (8)	0.20 (0.26)	15 (11)	0.36 (0.35)	5 (2)	0.26 (0.20)	13 (10)	0.23 (0.32)	52 (36)	0.26 (0.27)
5. Loans from finance companies	0 (0)	0.00 (0.00)	2 (1)	0.04 (0.03)	1 (0)	0.02 (0.00)	0 (0)	0.00 (0.00)	5 (4)	0.09 (0.10)	8 (5)	0.04 (0.04)
6. Others	3 (0)	0.08 (0.00)	1 (1)	0.02 (0.03)	2 (1)	0.04 (0.03)	2 (0)	0.11 (0.00)	2 (1)	0.04 (0.02)	10 (3)	0.05 (0.02)
7. Total mentions	38 (24)	1.00 (1.00)	45 (31)	1.00 (1.00)	42 (30)	1.00 (1.00)	19 (12)	1.00 (1.00)	57 (38)	1.00 (1.00)	201 (135)	1.00 (1.00)
Total respondents	29		33		31		15		44		152	

Note: Not all respondents were able to identify the most important source of finance in starting their business.
Figures in brackets refer to 'most important sources'.

Cleveland were that 68 per cent of respondents used their own savings, 34 per cent used bank loans and overdrafts and ten per cent used loans and gifts from family and friends. The two surveys' results are similar in spite of the fact that the IFT survey did not include any firms in the northern region, and that it included retail establishments which were specifically excluded from the Cleveland survey.

Whilst there are strong similarities between the two studies there are also some contrasts. There appears to be a greater diversity of sources of finance in the Cleveland 'start-ups', with house mortgages, not mentioned in the IFT survey, being nearly as important as loans from friends and relations. The miscellaneous sources of trade credit, etc. also seem to be more significant, as do loans from finance companies.

IFT also note that the miscellaneous services and wholesale sectors are relatively intensive users of banks as a source of start-up capital, whereas the business services sector is less dependent upon the banks. This contrasts with the Cleveland results where the business services sector makes more use of the banks, with there being relatively little difference between the usage made by other sectors.

8.4 Sources of Initial Funding and Ultimate Success

The major question to which this chapter addresses itself is whether there is an association between the sources of initial funding of a business and its ultimate success. In this context success is measured by total employment in the year of the survey (1979), by expected employment change in the twelve months following the survey, by profit rates in years 1976/7 (where relevant) and 1977/8. The limitations of these indices of 'success' have already been discussed, but they are chosen because banks and financial institutions are interested in the current profitability of the enterprise, since this offers at least some guide to its long run viability.

Table 8.2 provides a cross tabulation between employment size in 1979 of wholly new firms and the source of capital used in establishing the business. The figures in brackets again identify the most important source of finance where more than a single source is mentioned. From an examination of 'mentions' it is difficult to derive any pattern which suggests an association between ultimate success in terms of employment size and either the use of personal savings, or access to clearing bank overdraft or loan facilities. Personal savings, for example, obtain 60 per cent of all 'mentions' by those establishing firms which

Table 8.2: Mentions of Sources of Finance Used to Start a Wholly New Independent Business: by Size

	Total Employment in mid-1979									
	1-4		5-10		11-24		25+		Total	
Source of Initial Finance	No.	Prop.	No.	Prop.	No.	Prop.	No.	Prop.	No.	Prop.
1. Personal savings	47 (37)	0.60 (0.64)	28 (21)	0.45 (0.49)	20 (12)	0.43 (0.46)	9 (5)	0.60 (0.63)	104 (75)	0.52 (0.56)
2. House mortgage	1 (1)	0.01 (0.02)	5 (3)	0.08 (0.07)	5 (2)	0.11 (0.08)	1 (0)	0.07 (0.00)	12 (6)	0.06 (0.04)
3. Loans and gifts from friends and relations	9 (6)	0.12 (0.01)	5 (4)	0.08 (0.09)	1 (0)	0.02 (0.00)	0 (0)	0.00 (0.00)	15 (10)	0.07 (0.07)
4. Loans/overdrafts from the clearing banks	15 (9)	0.19 (0.16)	21 (15)	0.35 (0.35)	12 (9)	0.26 (0.35)	4 (3)	0.26 (0.37)	52 (36)	0.26 (0.27)
5. Loans from finance companies	4 (4)	0.05 (0.07)	1 (0)	0.01 (0.00)	3 (1)	0.07 (0.04)	0 (0)	0.00 (0.00)	8 (5)	0.04 (0.04)
6. Other	2 (1)	0.03 (0.02)	2 (0)	0.03 (0.00)	5 (2)	0.11 (0.07)	1 (0)	0.07 (0.00)	10 (3)	0.05 (0.02)
7. Total mentions	78 (58)	1.00 (1.00)	62 (43)	1.00 (1.00)	46 (26)	1.00 (1.00)	15 (8)	1.00 (1.00)	201 (135)	1.00 (1.00)
Total respondents	65		47		30		10		152	

Note: Figures in brackets refer to 'most important sources'

subsequently grew to both the smallest and the largest employment at the time of the survey, but only about 45 per cent of mentions by those establishing firms which grew to either of the two intermediate sizes. Only one business initially using loans or gifts from relatives and friends had more than ten employees in 1979, whereas 'other' sources of finance were more frequently used for the establishment of businesses which subsequently grew to more than ten employees than for establishing businesses which remained very small.

Examination of the 'most important' sources of funds shows that loans/overdrafts from banks as a source of initial funding are associated with the firms with high employment in 1979. Thirty-seven per cent of respondents having an employment of 25 or more said the banks were the major source of funding in establishing their business, compared with only 16 per cent of respondents whose business currently employed less than five people. Personal savings continued to be the most important source of initial capital, where more than a single source was used, even for the new firms which, by 1979, had the highest levels of employment.

Perhaps the most surprising aspect of Table 8.2, however, is that businesses which in 1979 employed fewest people were more likely to begin with multiple sources of funding, whilst those that had the highest employment in 1979 were the most likely to have started with only a single source of funds – usually personal savings.

Financial institutions when considering investing in a new company will be less concerned about its employment growth than its current and expected future profitability. Respondents were therefore asked to specify whether or not their enterprise made a profit in 1977/8 and to give an approximate value to this figure. Naturally a number were either reluctant or unable to do so. In addition some may have deliberately misled the interviewer, whilst there may also have been a number of different concepts of profit in the mind of the respondent, i.e. pre-tax, post-tax, gross margin, return on capital, turnover, etc. In fact, the interviewer specified post-tax return on turnover but where this could not be easily converted from the available accounts an approximate figure was accepted. The main purpose of the question, as specified earlier, was to obtain a general impression of the financial performance of the business during the years in question. Noting these limitations, Table 8.3 gives profit rates for those 115 respondents who mentioned 158 sources of initial finance, classified according to the nature of the initial financing of the business.

There is no apparent relationship between mentions of sources of

Table 8.3: Mentions of Sources of Finance Used to Establish a New Business and its Profitability in 1977/8

Source of Initial Finance	Loss						Profit						Broke-even		Total mentions
	More than 10%		5-9.9%		0-4.9%		0-4.9%		5-9.9%		More than 10%				
	No.	Prop.	No.	Prop.	No.	Prop.	No.	Prop.	No.	Prop.	No.	Prop.	No.	Prop.	
1. Personal savings	1 (0)	0.33 (0.00)	5 (2)	0.63 (0.50)	6 (5)	0.67 (0.84)	16 (14)	0.50 (0.54)	16 (9)	0.45 (0.43)	33 (25)	0.50 (0.56)	2 (1)	0.50 (1.00)	79 (56)
2. House mortgage	1 (1)	0.33 (1.00)	0 (0)	0.00 (0.00)	0 (0)	0.00 (0.00)	2 (1)	0.06 (0.04)	4 (1)	0.11 (0.05)	4 (2)	0.06 (0.05)	0 (0)	0.00 (0.00)	11 (5)
3. Loans and gifts from friends or relations	0 (0)	0.00 (0.00)	0 (0)	0.00 (0.00)	0 (0)	0.00 (0.00)	2 (2)	0.06 (0.07)	3 (3)	0.08 (0.13)	6 (3)	0.09 (0.07)	0 (0)	0.00 (0.00)	11 (8)
4. Loans/overdrafts from clearing banks	0 (0)	0.00 (0.00)	3 (2)	0.37 (0.50)	2 (1)	0.22 (0.16)	10 (8)	0.32 (0.31)	8 (6)	0.22 (0.29)	16 (9)	0.24 (0.20)	1 (0)	0.25 (0.00)	40 (26)
5. Loans from finance companies	0 (0)	0.00 (0.00)	0 (0)	0.00 (0.00)	1 (0)	0.11 (0.00)	1 (1)	0.03 (0.04)	2 (1)	0.06 (0.05)	4 (3)	0.06 (0.07)	0 (0)	0.00 (0.00)	8 (5)
6. Other	1 (0)	0.33 (0.00)	0 (0)	0.11 (0.00)	0 (0)	0.00 (0.00)	1 (0)	0.03 (0.00)	3 (1)	0.08 (0.05)	3 (2)	0.05 (0.05)	1 (0)	0.25 (0.00)	9 (3)
7. Total mentions	3 (1)	1.00 (1.00)	8 (4)	1.00 (1.00)	9 (6)	1.00 (1.00)	32 (26)	1.00 (1.00)	36 (21)	1.00 (1.00)	66 (44)	1.00 (1.00)	4 (1)	1.00 (1.00)	158 (103)
Total respondents	2		5		6		27		25		47		3		115

Note: Some rounding of totals has taken place.

finance to start in business and financial success by 1977/8. There certainly does not appear to be any evidence to suggest that subsequently less successful, i.e. loss-making businesses relied heavily initially upon personal savings or other forms of non-bank credit. Of the 20 sources mentioned by loss-making respondents, five (25 per cent) used the banks for initial financing compared with 26 per cent for the whole population of start-ups. Those mentioning sources of funds, other than personal savings or loans from banks, also constituted four out of 20 loss-makers and 26 per cent of mentions by firms making the highest rates of profit in 1977-8, and 32 per cent of those firms who made the highest possible profit rates!

Examination of the 'most important' sources of finance also show few patterns. There is no evidence of the more profitable firms relying more heavily upon banks or upon personal savings during 'start-up' than the unprofitable.

In interpreting these tabulations it must continually be recalled that these results apply only to those firms who were sufficiently successful to be still in business in 1979. We have no data on the sources of finance used for those wholly new firms which established after 1971, but which had gone out of business by 1979. Nevertheless, the results of this section provide no evidence that the finance from the clearing banks figured prominently as a source of start-up capital for new businesses which subsequently became highly profitable. Perhaps more disconcerting is that the banks seem to be well represented as a source of initial capital for a number of new businesses which claimed to be making a trading loss, but this must again be qualified by recognising that there is a shortage of information about the new firms which failed before 1979.

This section suggests that, at least during this period, the clearing banks' selection of new businesses in which to invest was little better than a random sample (of survivors). We do not know the number of new firm founders who attempted to obtain a loan either from the finance companies or the clearing banks and who were rejected, but it is interesting to compare the personal characteristics of those who were successful in obtaining loan and overdraft facilities from the clearing banks, with those using less 'conventional' sources of finance.

8.5 Sources of Start-up Capital: The Personal Characteristics of Entrepreneurs

The performance of a new business is determined, to a large extent, by the personal characteristics of the founder.

In this section we examine the relationship between age, educational qualifications, local knowledge, previous experience, etc., the sources of capital used to start in business and ultimate success. Table 8.4 shows the probability that a new firm founder will make use either of personal savings, loans/overdrafts from the clearing banks and all other sources of loan capital. It cross-tabulates these sources of start-up finance with three social characteristics, viz.: whether or not the founder was employed, whether or not he is local (defined as being born and bred in Cleveland) and whether he has any previous business experience. The table shows that differences exist, in terms of these personal characteristics, although perhaps they are less marked than might have been expected. Nevertheless, they are compatible with previous studies of entrepreneurs.

Table 8.4: Personal Characteristics of Entrepreneurs and Uses of Start-up Finance

Personal Characteristics	Source of Capital (Probability of Individual Using Source j)			Total No. of New Firm Founders
	Bank Lending	Personal Savings	Other Sources	
1. Local founder	0.36	0.68	0.30	100
Non-local founder	0.33	0.67	0.30	48
2. Employed	0.35	0.68	0.27	40
Unemployed	0.30	0.65	0.40	110
3. Previous experience as an owner	0.35	0.71	0.35	48
No previous experience	0.32	0.67	0.29	100

Note: Not all new firm founders answered all questions. Hence the total numbers in the final column differ slightly according to the personal characteristics.

Table 8.4 shows that approximately 68 per cent of new firm founders drew upon personal savings in starting their business with the employed and previous owners, who presumably have higher levels of savings, being slightly more likely to draw upon this source. Just over one-third of all new firm founders used loans and overdrafts from the clearing banks, with those who were unemployed being rather less likely to start in this way than those who were employed. Again it is not possible to determine whether this is because of a reluctance of the unemployed to apply to the banks or whether they were rejected, having made an application. Perhaps the most notable differences occur in the use made of the 'other' sources. The unemployed are much more likely to use sources such as borrowing from friends and relations, from finance companies and using miscellaneous sources of trade credit. They were much less likely to use a second mortgage on a property — presumably because many did not own their own home. The informal finance market was also more likely to be used by those with previous business experience as an owner than by those starting in business for the first time.

Little difference was found between local and non-local entrepreneurs primarily because, although not brought up in the area, most had either been in business or in employment in the area for some years. During this period they had developed sufficient contacts to ensure that they were, statistically, indistinguishable from the native of Cleveland.

A second important set of personal characteristics of those establishing a business is whether or not they have educational qualifications and the level of these qualifications. Perhaps, as argued earlier, banks are more likely to lend to individuals with paper qualifications, since the latter should be able to present a cogent written case for their business proposition.

Survey results show that 19 per cent of the sources of finance mentioned by unqualified people starting their own businesses were bank overdrafts or loans. This was a significantly lower proportion than those with formal qualifications, and substantially lower than those with a degree or with professional qualifications (36 and 38 per cent respectively).

Personal savings received 54 per cent of mentions by those starting a business without qualifications, and does not differ significantly from those who were formally qualified. The main difference between the groups appears to be a relatively greater use of friends and relations, and of finance company lending amongst those without qualifications (or those who had qualifications at a lower level) and less use of the formal banking system.

The use of different sources of funds to start in business may also vary according to the age of the new firm founder. For example, personal savings and house mortgages are likely to be less important sources for the relatively young founder, whilst the banks are also likely to regard such individuals with suspicion because of their lack of time to develop a 'track record'. Conversely, personal savings might be of greater importance to the older entrepreneur who may also be reluctant to use the banks as a source of starting-up funds, for reasons of historical prejudice.

The survey confirms these hypotheses. It shows that in terms of the most important sources of finance, loans from friends and relations are of great importance to the entrepreneur who is under 30 years of age and of major importance for those under the age of 25. Loans and gifts, where they are made, are usually the only and hence the major source of finance. The table also shows that personal savings are of prime importance to the older (i.e., 45 year old) entrepreneur, for 79 per cent, for whom they constituted the most important source of finance. The banks are relatively more important in lending to the entrepreneur in the 30-45 age range — although even here, personal savings are absolutely of greatest importance. For entrepreneurs in the 30-45 age range the banks provided 30 per cent of them with their most important source of finance, compared with 20 per cent for other ages of founder. The very young entrepreneur therefore tends to start with loans and gifts from family and friends, whereas those in their 30s start with personal savings plus bank/finance company lending. The older entrepreneur tends to rely much more heavily upon personal savings although often supplemented from a variety of 'other' sources.

Initial sources of finance also vary with the social class of the founder prior to becoming an entrepreneur. For example, the majority of new firm founders come from the semi-skilled manual and non-manual groups plus the unskilled, which in very broad terms would normally be considered the working class.[3] Among this group, bank loans and overdrafts received 22 per cent of mentions as a source of start-up capital. The entrepreneur from this group is much more likely to obtain capital from his friends and relations or from finance companies than those in the professional classes. House mortgages, as would be expected, are mentioned relatively infrequently by these founders whereas the professional and skilled groups are more likely to use them. These latter groups are more likely to use the clearing banks — particularly those in skilled manual and non-manual occupations — and much less likely to use finance companies or loans/gifts from friends and relations. The use of personal savings is also substantially higher by the professional classes than amongst the partly skilled and the unskilled who make good this deficiency by obtaining assistance from friends and relatives and the finance companies. These conclusions do not seem to vary between 'mentions' of sources of finance and 'most important sources'.

8.6 Current Sources of Funding

All wholly new firms were asked to list the sources of funds upon which their business had drawn in the past twelve months. The results are cross-tabulated with the initial source of funds and are shown in Table 8.5. The major difference is the introduction into the existing business of retained profits. In fact, only five respondents did not claim to use retained profits as a source of financing their business at the time of the survey.

Table 8.5 shows there is a substantial decline in the role of personal savings in financing established, as opposed to start-up, businesses. Over 50 per cent of mentions in start-up firms were of personal savings, whereas this fell to ten per cent for established businesses. In terms of respondents, 23 per cent claimed to use personal savings, whereas 95 per cent claimed to use retained profits for financing established businesses. Bank lending was particularly important to established firms, being mentioned by 72 per cent of respondents. There also appears to be a tendency for established businessmen to make greater use of finance companies, than those initially establishing a business, with these being mentioned virtually as many times as was the use of the owner's personal savings.

A major distinction is made between 'mentions' and major sources of funding. Retained profits, although only receiving 44 per cent of all mentions were the most important source of finance for 71 per cent of all wholly new established businesses, whereas bank overdrafts and loans, although receiving 33 per cent of all mentions, were only the most important source in 13 per cent of cases. 'Other' sources of finance were of secondary importance, although where personal savings were mentioned they were likely to be the most important source of funding. This is probably because they were still being used to finance very recently established firms.

Perhaps the most interesting aspect of Table 8.5 is the switching of sources of finance which takes place as a new business develops. Unfortunately only 127 new firms provided sufficient information for this to be analysed, but the results are most illuminating. For example, 22 firms started without either personal savings or loans from the clearing

Table 8.5: Mentions of Current and Initial Sources of Funding

Initial	Current									
	Personal Savings		Bank Overdraft/ Loans		Others		Retained Profits		Total	
	No.	Prop.	No.	Prop.	No.	Prop.	No.	Prop.	No.	Prop.
1. Personal savings	20 (12)	0.13 (0.17)	48 (9)	0.32 (0.13)	14 (1)	0.09 (0.01)	70 (49)	0.46 (0.69)	152 (71)	1.00 (1.00)
2. Bank overdraft/loans	6 (3)	0.07 (0.09)	36 (6)	0.39 (0.18)	14 (0)	0.15 (0.00)	36 (25)	0.39 (0.73)	92 (34)	1.00 (1.00)
3. Others	7 (4)	0.10 (0.18)	20 (2)	0.28 (0.09)	13 (0)	0.18 (0.00)	31 (16)	0.44 (0.73)	71 (22)	1.00 (1.00)
4. Total mentions Total main source	33 (19)	0.10 (0.15)	104 (17)	0.33 (0.13)	41 (1)	0.13 (0.01)	137 (90)	0.44 (0.71)	315 (127)	1.00 (1.00)

banks as their major source of finance, yet by the time of the survey, i.e. once they were established, only one firm in the survey was relying on these 'other' sources for the majority of its finance. Few of these firms turned to the banks for their subsequent finance preferring to rely on retained profits, although some did negotiate relatively small loans with the banks.

Of those new firms financed primarily by either personal savings or bank loans only 17 and 18 per cent, respectively, continued to be financed primarily by these sources. Almost irrespective of the prime source of funds used to launch the business, approximately 70 per cent of new firms five years later relied upon retained profits.

In short, there are a number of firms in this sample who either do not use the clearing banks or whose use of them is limited. They are started either with personal savings or 'other' sources of finance and their development is financed by retained profits. An examination of the current most important sources of finance, of those starting primarily with 'other' sources of finance, shows that only nine per cent subsequently turned to the banks for the majority of their funding. This compares with 13 per cent for those starting primarily on personal savings and 18 per cent of those starting primarily with the banks themselves.

In Table 8.6 these current sources of finance are related to the current employment in the new firm. It suggests that in established companies personal savings of the founder are only an important source of financing in the smallest firms where they obtained 18 per cent of all mentions. Retained profits also become relatively less important as a source of finance in the largest new companies, although those new companies employing more than 25 people mentioned retained profits more frequently than all but the smallest firms. Loans from the clearing banks seem to be somewhat more important to the larger new firms although again they do not progressively increase their 'market share' with increases in employment size, since the new firms with employment in excess of 25 mentioned retained profits more often than assistance from the clearing banks. Perhaps the most surprising part of the table is the importance of lending from finance companies to those firms in the largest size category. Finance companies received 17 per cent of all mentions by firms employing more than 25 people compared with under seven per cent of the sample as a whole. This is particularly surprising bearing in mind that finance company lending was very rarely, as was shown in Table 8.5, the most important source of finance. To test whether this was due to industrial structure, current

Table 8.6: Current Sources of Finance and Current Employment Size (Mentions)

	_____ Employment Size in 1979 _____								
Source of Current Finance	1-4		5-10		11-24		25+		Total No.
	No.	Prop.	No.	Prop.	No.	Prop.	No.	Prop.	
1. Personal savings	14	0.18	6	0.08	5	0.09	1	0.04	26
2. Retained profits	40	0.53	35	0.47	21	0.39	10	0.44	106
3. Bank overdrafts/loans	17	0.22	26	0.35	21	0.39	7	0.31	71
4. Finance company lending	3	0.04	6	0.08	2	0.04	4	0.17	15
5. Other	2	0.03	1	0.02	5	0.09	1	0.04	9
Total	76	1.00	74	1.00	54	1.00	23	1.00	227

sources of finance were related to industry but there was no evidence that the propensity to use finance companies differed significantly between industries, except possibly being somewhat lower for new firms in professional services.

To test the extent to which current sources of finance were related to the profitability or otherwise of a new firm, Table 8.7 relates profitability in 1977-8 to sources of current finance. It shows that the banks, often criticised for their caution and selectivity in lending to new enterprises, were lending to a relatively high proportion of new firms that were not profitable and relatively few who were making high profits. Banks received half the total mentions made of sources of current finance by firms that made a loss in the years 1977-8, and by 38 per cent of those making a loss in 1976-7. In the sample as a whole for 1977-8 banks received only 32 per cent of all mentions. The finance companies, in this sample, however, were not mentioned as a source of funds by any of the firms making a loss. Such firms were predominantly financed in 1977/8 either by retained profits from better years or by the banks.

An examination of the most profitable new firms, i.e. those claiming to be earning rates in excess of ten per cent, shows that although bank lending facilities received 32 per cent of all mentions in the sample as a whole, they received only 30 per cent of all mentions by the most profitable group of firms. Retained profits were mentioned by 54 per cent of this most profitable group, compared with 48 per cent in the population as a whole, with lending from finance companies being 'over' represented in this group, receiving ten per cent of all mentions, compared with seven per cent in the sample as a whole. Personal savings receive a below average number of mentions in this group, with their major role seeming to be played in the only modestly profitable new firms.

8.7 Conclusions

The results derived on sources of finance are compatible with those of other studies which have concentrated upon manufacturing firms. Cross (1981), for example, found that personal savings constituted 44 per cent of all mentions of sources of initial capital, excluding sources such as the sale of property (4.5 per cent) which would in this chapter have been incorporated into the personal savings category. The Cross results, together with the IFT survey, suggest there is no reason to believe the

Table 8.7: Current Sources of Finance (Mentions) and Profitability in 1977/8

Source of Current Finance	Loss More than 10%		Loss 5-9.9%		Loss 0-4.9%		Break-even		Profit 0-4.9%		Profit 5-9.9%		Profit More than 10%		Total	
	No.	Prop.	No.	Prop.	No.	Prop.	No.	Prop.	No.	Prop.	No.	Prop.	No.	Prop.	No.	Prop.
1. Personal savings	0	0.00	1	0.13	0	0.00	2	0.29	5	0.14	5	0.12	4	0.05	17	0.09
2. Retained profits	2	0.50	2	0.25	4	0.50	2	0.29	16	0.44	20	0.49	41	0.54	87	0.48
3. Bank overdrafts/loans	1	0.25	5	0.62	4	0.50	1	0.14	11	0.30	12	0.29	23	0.30	57	0.32
4. Finance company	0	0.00	0	0.00	0	0.00	1	0.14	2	0.06	1	0.02	8	0.10	12	0.07
5. Other	1	0.25	0	0.00	0	0.00	1	0.14	2	0.06	3	0.08	1	0.01	8	0.04
Total mentions	4	1.00	8	1.00	8	1.00	7	1.00	36	1.00	41	1.00	77	1.00	181	1.00
Total respondents	3		5		6		3		25		25		47		114	

sample of new firms derived is in any way unusual or subject to major bias.

This chapter has attempted to go beyond a bald statement of sources of funds. It has tried to link firm performance to both the personal characteristics of the entrepreneurs and to the subsequent success or otherwise of the business. Here an attempt is made to investigate whether there are opportunities for the finance market in general to lend to potentially viable new firms.

Several points emerge from this examination. The first is that whilst banks and finance houses are an important source of funds – and they are as important in the non-manufacturing as in the manufacturing sectors – personal savings are consistently the most frequently used, and the most important single source of funding for the new business. The level of wealth in a local community must therefore be an important determinant of its capacity to add to its stock of businesses.

The clearing banks are the second most important source of funds for business starters, and they show little tendency to favour one type of industry rather than another. From a policy viewpoint the most interesting question is whether the banks are excessively risk-averse in their lending policies and whether they could improve their own profitability by directing a higher proportion of their lending towards the more profitable enterprises. The evidence presented in this chapter must be qualified by recognising that the sample of new firms is biased towards the 'average' firm. We have no information on the sources of finance of those firms which were established after 1973 but which had disappeared by 1979. On the other hand we have no information about new firms, formed after 1971 in Cleveland but who by 1979 had grown, such that they had either been taken over or had become parent establishments. Recognising these provisos it seems that the clearing banks are not particularly good at avoiding investments in loss-making companies. Perhaps more significantly they are not 'over' represented amongst those companies claiming to make the highest rates of profit in our sample despite the fact that the finance they offer is generally cheaper than that of the finance companies. One explanation may be that branch managers of local clearing banks are not particularly good at identifying whether an embryo business has the potential to develop profitably. An examination of the customers of the banks suggests that they tend to be more heavily concentrated amongst the middle class and the relatively educated, indicating that the local manager is more likely to accept a proposal from such an individual, even though the risk may be almost as high as from an individual without education.

Another explanation may be that the clearing banks, at least during the mid-1970s, did not actively market the services which they could provide for the small businessman. In contrast, the finance companies' representatives often arrived on the doorstep of the hard-pressed entrepreneur — making it much easier for him to do business.

We do not know whether new firm founders who borrowed from family and friends, or who used personal savings or who went to a finance company did, in fact, try to obtain funding from a clearing bank. Examination of the social class groupings of the banks' customers compared with those using the less formal financial network suggests, however, that these individuals were unlikely to have approached a bank. Several, no doubt, had no bank account until starting in business. The current results suggest there are a number of highly profitable business ventures where the clearing banks are not involved, either because they were never given the opportunity, or because they turned down such an opportunity. On the other hand finance companies seem very well represented amongst such firms, although they rarely provide the most important source of initial financing. To illustrate, finance companies seem well represented both amongst the most profitable new firms in 1977-8 and amongst those having the highest employment in 1979. This is a remarkable achievement since, in the survey as a whole, employment size and profitability are not significantly positively correlated.

There is also no suggestion that although new firms may begin with finance from sources other than the clearing banks, that once in business they gravitate towards the banks to finance further expansion. The current results suggest that those who begin without help from the clearing banks either tend to remain outside the formal banking sector or subsequently obtain only relatively small amounts of funding from the banks. To finance further expansion such firms use the retained profits of the business.

The banks almost certainly have had a substantial amount of defaulting on loans to new and small companies, and have not obtained as high a number of loans to profitable and trouble-free new companies as they might have liked. Nevertheless, it cannot be said that such lending opportunities do not exist. It is true that the vetting of small volume applications is expensive yet the opportunities of lending to small companies are currently being exploited by funds from the less formal financial sector. This supports the views expressed by Bannock (1981b) that lending to small firms is a potentially profitable opportunity which the banks should seize, rather than view it as an exercise in corporate responsibility. Unfortunately Bannock feels that even now the major clearing banks are insufficiently aware of the opportunities which the small firm sector presents, and are organisationally unsuited to exploit the markets. He feels that organisational centrality reduces their sensitivity to local business needs and reduces their identification with local communities. Finally, Bannock chastises the banks for not undertaking appropriately structured market research of the lending requirements of their customers and potential customers.

The opportunities for profitable lending may be interpreted as giving grounds for hope that the recent efforts of the clearing banks to market more actively their services will be successful and that the Loan Guarantee Scheme will bear fruit. For this to happen, it is clear that the banks have to market their services to all groups in society. It means that individuals, as a first step, have to be encouraged to start a bank account and that banks have to go out and visit firms rather than expecting such individuals to arrive on their doorstep. Secondly, the local branch manager has to be aware that individuals, possibly without formal education skills can, in certain businesses, be a highly satisfactory investment from the banks' viewpoint.

A more aggressive approach by the banks to the marketing of their services would benefit both the small firm sector and the banks themselves.

Notes

1. Note this does not mean that 52 per cent of all finance was provided by personal savings. It means that since each new firm founder was able to mention a number of sources of finance, 104 out of the 152 *respondents* mentioned personal savings. To normalise, however, by respondents would mean that the proportionate totals would sum to greater than unity.

2. Note again that the new firm founder can identify more than a single source of funds.

3. Note that relatively more new firm founders come from the 'middle classes' even though absolutely there are more working-class founders.

9 IMPACT ON THE LOCAL ECONOMY

9.1 Introduction

The establishment of a firm new to an area provides employment directly and may also stimulate existing businesses if it purchases locally produced goods. The extent to which such firms integrate into the locality may depend upon the size of the firm. Large plants, owned and controlled from outside the locality, may have little autonomy over purchases of inputs or over sales of final product. Such firms are more likely to have head offices, with central purchasing departments able to negotiate low cost bulk purchasing arrangements. Small volume local producers are unable to compete — even taking account of transportation costs, so that established firms new to the area may have a negligible impact on the local economy.

In contrast, the small local firm sector may have a greater impact. Small firms may purchase their goods locally, and be amenable to local incentives such as the provision of small premises and business advice. From the viewpoint of local and regional government they offer the prospect of a higher proportion of jobs being created for local people, whereas for every 100 jobs created by, primarily large firms, as a result of regional policy in the United Kingdom, only 30 people were removed from the local unemployment register (Moore, Rhodes and Tyler (1977)).

The small firm may also employ the type of labour available in the neighbourhood, since its recruitment is primarily local. The large firm may be less attractive to local government if its servicing costs are high. Many large firms, establishing new branches, often require housing to be made available to workers brought into the area. The provision of 'key worker housing' can cause resentment amongst local people on council house waiting lists. Large companies can also exert considerable pressure upon local authorities or other statutory agencies to provide road improvements, specific waste disposal facilities or worker training schemes. Skilful use of the local newspapers, media, etc. can often put pressure on the local authority to agree to these conditions, or risk losing the plant.

Such pressures are less likely to be exerted by small firms. They must accept the existing given conditions, although through its various associations the small firm lobby nowadays is increasingly vocal. Consequently most local authorities look favourably upon a programme of job creation, through stimulation of new small business ventures. The evidence currently available on the relative effectiveness of these strategies is, not for the first time, somewhat contradictory. McAleese and McDonagh (1978) in their studies of the Eire economy find that the entry of large, foreign-owned plants, have been associated with a rise in indigenous new firm formation rates. In contrast, Forsyth's (1972) evidence for Scotland shows large, foreign-owned enterprises have depressed the rate of new firm formation in Scotland partly because large firm patterns of purchasing have offered few markets for local small firms.

It is important to determine the impact which new firms have in a locality. Do large firms have less impact on the economy and do they reduce the likelihood of being able to initiate self-sustaining growth in a locality? In this chapter two important aspects of this matter will be examined, viz. the provision of job opportunities and the spatial distribution of the purchases and sales of the firm.

9.2 Employment by the New Firms

Table 9.1 shows the average and total numbers employed by firms new to Cleveland by sex and whether they are full-time or part-time employees. The figures include any employees who do not necessarily work at the employer's establishment but are based there.

Table 9.1: Employment by the Respondent Firms at the Time of Interview

	MALES		FEMALES		TOTAL		
	Full-time	Part-time	Full-time	Part-time	Full-time	Part-time	Total
Mean	18.8	0.5	4.5	1.1	23.2	1.6	24.8
Total	5,627	155	1,345	318	6,972	473	7,445

Note: Figures are based upon 300 responses. One firm did not know its employment level!

In total, 7,445 new jobs have been created by the sampled new firms, an average of almost 25 jobs per firm. The *general magnitude* of this figure can be compared with the net increase in employment in Cleveland of 17,000 jobs between 1972 and 1977. Thus, the new firms sampled accounted for almost half the *net* increase in jobs (but not the *gross* increase in jobs), the remainder being attributable to the net effect of *in situ* growth, *in situ* decline, closures of established firms and net growth in groups of firms not sampled. The author's work on Cleveland's *manufacturing* firms, showed that new openings created 15,322 jobs in the period 1965 to 1976, in 303 surviving establishments — an average of 50.6 jobs per firm (Storey (1981b)). The current survey showed that over a shorter time period, 3,572 jobs were found to have been created by 63 new manufacturing firms — an average of 56.7 jobs per firm. This suggests that new manufacturing firms are an important source of employment because their size is more than double the average of 24.8 jobs per firm for the sample as a whole and because 48 per cent of all employment created by the respondent firms is accounted for by manufacturing firms. This is high relative to the share of employment in manufacturing industry as a whole in Cleveland (39 per cent in 1977)[1] and against the background in the 1970s of decline in manufacturing employment, and increasing service employment. This shows that despite a decline in manufacturing employment new establishments continued to be created in significant numbers. In fact, because of their relatively large size, new manufacturing firms are the most important single source of jobs although this is mainly attributable to the large size of subsidiary plants — 21 such manufacturing establishments each employed an average of 126 people. Parent manufacturing firms also tended to be large but there were only three in the sample.

A high proportion of jobs in all firms new to Cleveland were created in relatively few enterprises. The five largest employers of male labour provided 34 per cent of all jobs for men and the five largest employers of female labour provided 44 per cent of all new jobs for women. Thus, relatively large employers are an important source of employment in firms new to the county although, in comparison with established employers in Cleveland, none of the sampled firms seems large: only two had more than 500 employees and none had more than 900 employees. In all cases the largest five employers were either new branches or subsidiaries of companies existing outside Cleveland prior to 1972.

The composition of the new employment opportunities in the

sample as a whole is of interest to those concerned with providing suitable jobs for both males and females in Cleveland. It is surprising because, as Marquand (1979) shows, much of new employment in the 1970s has been part-time jobs for females, to find that 76 per cent of the jobs in firms new to the county are for men working full-time and a further two per cent are for men employed part-time. Eighteen per cent of jobs were full-time for women while only four per cent were part-time female jobs. This latter result is remarkable when it is realised that 76 per cent of the *net* increase in jobs in Cleveland between 1971 and 1976 was in female part-time employment. Furthermore, part-time female employment grew by 50 per cent between 1971 and 1976. Although the distinction between *net* and *gross* new jobs has to be recalled, the discrepancy is puzzling.

Table 9.2: Male, Female, Full-time and Part-time Employment in Cleveland, 1971 and 1976

	Male		Female		Total
	Full-time	Part-time	Full-time	Part-time	
1971 no.	150,798	4,363	53,059	25,341	233,561
%	64.6	1.9	22.7	10.8	100.0
1976 no.	152,704	5,735	53,882	38,032	250,353
%	61.0	2.3	21.5	15.2	100.0
Growth 1971-6	1,906	1,372	823	12,691	16,792
%	1.3	31.4	1.6	50.1	7.2
Employment shares in sample %	76	2	18	4	100

Table 9.2 provides a partial explanation by showing that 12,691 additional female part-time jobs (net) were created in Cleveland between 1971 and 1976. Of these, over 11,000 were in the service sector, the main employers being either in distributive trades or in the public sector — public sector health and education services and public administration. Only in distributive trades could new firms have appeared in this survey — and even here the retail distribution sector was specifically excluded.

The increase in part-time female jobs in Cleveland in the 1970s which in its turn is the major source of *net* new jobs is therefore *not* attributable to new private sector firms, except perhaps in retailing. The major growth sector of such employment must have been the expansion of existing firms and the public sector. Conversely, new non-retail firms outside the public sector are an important source of employment for males seeking full-time work.

The male/female balance of jobs in the surveyed firms is similar to that of the registered unemployed in Cleveland; roughly three-quarters of each are male, which could be viewed as justifying policies to encourage new firm formation and the growth of new firms. In addition it has already been shown that firms new to Cleveland made a substantial contribution to net job generation in the 1970s, which could be taken to be a healthy foundation for local economic development.

However, small firm policies are directed primarily at independent firms and in the survey these firms contributed less employment than new branches and subsidiaries. Independent single plant firms provided 22 per cent of the jobs, parent plants ten per cent and branches and subsidiaries contributed 68 per cent of the jobs.[2]

The average size of the different plant types varied considerably. The smallest average-sized group is independent firms with 9.4 workers, followed by branch plants with 16.1 jobs per plant. Parent firms had an average size of 55.3 employees, while subsidiaries were the largest at 59.5 workers per plant. Wholly new firms employed an average of 9.5 workers. A policy designed to create jobs by raising the formation rate of wholly new firms could therefore take several decades before bearing fruit. The large, externally-owned manufacturing plants are the most important source of new jobs over the whole period.

The steady growth in employment of all firms new to Cleveland over the period 1974 to 1979 is due partly to additional firms coming into existence as the years progress, and partly to the growth of firms themselves. This is illustrated by dividing the sample into four cohorts according to establishment date, as shown in Table 9.3. All four cohorts have experienced, on average, continuous growth although it must be remembered that the sample only includes surviving establishments.

Table 9.3: Average Employment Levels of Four Cohorts of New Firms

Setting up Period	Mean Total Employment In:				
	1974	1976	1978	1979	N
Pre-1975	2,204	2,945	3,386	3,503	123
(Growth rate over previous years p.a.)	–	(17%)	(7%)	(3%)	
1975-6	–	1,451	2,226	2,638	116
(Growth rate over previous years p.a.)			(27%)	(19%)	
1977-8	–	–	790	944	50
Growth rate				(19%)	
1979	–	–	–	360	11

Table 9.3 might also be taken as preliminary evidence indicating that employment growth rates are highest in the early years of a firm's life. Thus, the *full* employment benefits of new firms do not accrue in the first years of a firm's life, although the vast majority accrue within five years. Hence a policy to create new jobs through the stimulation of new firm formation rates, even on the assumption that it can be achieved, requires a long period to bring results.

9.3 The Skill Level of Jobs Created by Firms New to Cleveland

The skill content of new jobs is important since only if the type of employment created matches the training and experience of the unemployed workers will newly created jobs reduce local rates of unemployment. All jobs created in firms new to Cleveland were classified according to their skill content and the results are shown in Table 9.4.

Table 9.4: Mean Numbers of Workers in Each Skill Category by Type of Firm: Firms New to Cleveland

	Skilled	Semi-skilled	Unskilled	Profes-sional/ Manag-erial	Clerical	Others	Total
Independent	2.9 (40)	0.8 (11)	1.1 (15)	1.4 (19)	0.9 (12)	0.2 (3)	7.3 (100)
Parent	16.1 (59)	0.4 (2)	0.9 (3)	5.6 (20)	4.1 (15)	0.4 (1)	27.5 (100)
Branch	3.9 (35)	2.1 (18)	1.3 (11)	1.7 (15)	1.9 (17)	0.5 (4)	11.4 (100)
Subsidiary	13.0 (30)	4.9 (11)	14.1 (33)	4.7 (11)	5.7 (13)	0.8 (2)	43.2 (100)
Number of jobs	1,859 (35)	592 (11)	1,327 (25)	744 (14)	708 (13)	118 (2)	5,348 (100)

Note: Percentages in parentheses.

The table shows that branch plants and subsidiaries are more likely to employ relatively large numbers of both unskilled and semi-skilled workers. Conversely, they are likely to employ rather fewer professional and managerial staff than independents or parents, although the number of parent plants is small.

Skilled manual workers account for a considerable share of employment in each type of firm: only in the case of subsidiaries does the share of skilled workers not exceed the combined share of unskilled and semi-skilled workers. Independent firms, whether they are single-plant or parents, make a considerable contribution to the enrichment of occupational choice in the local labour market judging by the numbers and proportions of workers in the professional and managerial, clerical and skilled manual categories.

Table 9.5 shows that the firms new to Cleveland had an average of 35 per cent of their workforce in the skilled manual category, almost as much as the proportion in the semi-skilled and unskilled categories taken together.

Table 9.5: Skill Levels of Cleveland Residents and in Firms New to Cleveland

	Skill Levels of Cleveland Residents* %	Skill Levels of Workers in Firms New to Cleveland %
Skilled Manual	33	35
Semi-skilled manual	20	11
Unskilled manual	11	25
Employers, managers and professionals	12	14
Other non-manual	24	15
Total	100	100

*Source: Cleveland Social Survey (1979), personal communication.

Further analysis reveals that the five largest employers of skilled labour provided 23 per cent (437 jobs) of all skilled jobs while the five largest employers of semi-skilled workers provided 35 per cent (209 jobs) of semi-skilled jobs. The five largest employers of unskilled labour, however, provided 69 per cent (915 jobs) of all unskilled jobs. This suggests that if new firms are to make a noticeable impact on the unemployment of unskilled workers in Cleveland, the area has to attract large employers, rather than rely upon a small firms strategy to cure unemployment.

The five largest employers of professional and managerial workers provided 24 per cent (181 jobs) of such jobs. Twenty per cent of firms however reported no jobs in this category and 38 per cent provided work for only one professional or managerial employee – normally the firm founder. Thus, jobs requiring higher level non-manual abilities were provided by relatively few firms in the sample. The pattern of clerical employment is similar with 34 per cent of firms not employing any clerical workers and 28 per cent employing only one. The largest five employers of clerical labour provided 37 per cent (261 jobs) of such jobs.

Table 9.5 crudely compares the distribution of new jobs with the skill levels of Cleveland residents as a whole. The major difference is in the manual workers categories, with new firms providing fewer semi-skilled and more unskilled jobs than existing employers as a whole.

This is due primarily to the presence of the five large employers of unskilled labour in the sample, although the exclusion of public sector and retailing employing from the sample is a contributory factor. Overall, there is a lower proportion of non-manual jobs in the firms new to Cleveland and the discrepancy may be explained by the relatively low proportion of service employment covered by the sample in comparison with jobs in existing industry. The corollary is the above average share of construction employment within the sample.

There is no reason why employment created by firms new to an area should necessarily resemble the existing distribution of employment. Like trees in the forest, some industries are expanding whilst others are contracting. In addition, the turnover of firms (births and deaths) differs between industrial classification. Nevertheless, the low proportion of non-manual jobs can be explained by the relatively low representation of service employment in the sample.

Table 9.6 confirms that amongst firms new to Cleveland, non-manual jobs are to be found primarily in services. The high proportion of unskilled workers in the firms is mainly attributable to a small number of manufacturing employers whilst semi-skilled and skilled manual workers are well represented in construction firms.

Data on wage levels were not collected and industrial and occupational data provide the only insight into the restructuring of employment. Throughout the 1970s well paid manufacturing jobs in chemicals, steel and mechanical engineering were lost to the local economy. In numerical terms new jobs in private sector firms and public sector jobs have more than compensated (see Table 9.7). But are these new jobs less well paid than the lost manufacturing jobs and can the area expect further job losses through reduced spending power? In particular, are the new private sector jobs (excluding retailing) well paid? We are unable to answer this directly but since manufacturing jobs are generally more highly paid than those in other sectors, the high proportion of new manufacturing jobs created suggests that average wage levels in the new employment may not be far below that of the jobs which have been lost.

Closer analysis reveals that 34 per cent of employment in the sampled manufacturing firms is unskilled manual work, however, and

Table 9.6: Mean Numbers of Workers in Each Skill Category by Industry of Firm

Industry	Skilled	Semi-skilled	Unskilled	Professional/ Managerial	Clerical	Other	Total
Manufacturing	14.8 (31)	5.1 (11)	16.5 (34)	5.0 (10)	5.7 (12)	0.8 (2)	47.9 (100)
Construction	5.8 (47)	1.9 (16)	0.6 (5)	2.1 (17)	1.6 (13)	0.3 (2)	12.3 (100)
Professional services	3.1 (39)	0.5 (6)	0.2 (3)	2.0 (25)	1.8 (22)	0.4 (5)	8.0 (100)
Distribution	2.7 (24)	1.4 (13)	2.6 (23)	2.3 (21)	1.7 (15)	0.4 (4)	11.1 (100)
Other	3.7 (45)	0.9 (11)	1.6 (19)	1.1 (13)	0.9 (11)	0.1 (1)	8.3 (100)
Number of jobs	1,859 (35)	592 (11)	1,327 (25)	744 (14)	708 (13)	118 (2)	5,348 (100)

this must tend to depress earnings relative to the average, since in 1979 only eight per cent of all employment in manufacturing firms in the area was for unskilled manual workers.

Table 9.7: Industrial Structure of Employment by Sampled Firms Compared with all Cleveland Employment

Industry	Sampled Firms %	Cleveland 1979[a] %	Change in Employment Cleveland 1972-7[b]
Manufacturing	48	43	− 6,635
Construction	24	9	+ 5,767
Professional services	10	13	+ 6,807
Distributive services	7	9	+ 1,979
Other services	11	26	+ 9,099
Total	100	100	+ 17,017

Source: a. Cleveland Social Survey (1979), personal communication; (b) Annual Census of Employment, personal communication.

Another indicator of wage levels might be shortages of skilled labour, resulting in its price (wage) being bid up. Skill shortages might also highlight specific requirements of new firms to which the local supply of trained manpower can only partially respond. Reliable survey evidence of skill shortages is very difficult to obtain because the *reason* for the shortage may or may not be apparent to the respondent firm. Lack of certain skills may be seen as a supply deficiency but be attributable to low wages, poor working conditions, poor public transport, etc.

To overcome these difficulties all firms new to Cleveland were asked to identify existing vacancies. In total 128 firms (45 per cent) reported difficulties in recruiting labour and 155 gave descriptions of types of worker that it was most difficult to recruit. New single plant independent firms which established in Cleveland (primarily wholly new firms) were less likely to have experienced recruiting difficulties but it is not clear whether this was due to local contacts or their small numbers of employees. Of the 155 descriptions of workers, 47 per cent could be clearly identified as skilled manual occupations, 16 per cent were junior non-manual workers, eleven per cent were semi-skilled manual occupations while the remainder were mainly in the managerial and professional categories. There was no obvious clustering of occupations revealing previously unknown skill shortages and the general tone of replies was that quality of potential workers was just as important as their training. Thus, 17 respondents qualified their description of occupation with the adjective 'good' or 'reliable' or similar, and a further 40 referred to the need for 'experienced' workers. Other qualifications to job descriptions were 'of the right type', 'prepared to travel', 'prepared to re-wire houses' (of electricians) and 'prepared to work late'.

Many responses could reflect genuine shortages to the individual firms because out of 155 occupations reported as presenting a recruitment difficulty, 81 occupations were also said to be required for an existing vacancy at the time of the interview.[3] Thus, firms new to Cleveland appear to be facing some skill shortages but they arise as much from the personal qualities of available workers as from their training, and they do not seem to be unique to new firms.

9.4 Spatial Distribution of Purchases and Sales of Firms New to Cleveland

The purchasing of supplies from 'outside' firms may also be considered a lost job opportunity. This could be true at several levels, the most obvious being the direct purchase of goods from a manufacturer. If there is sufficient demand from local firms, a new firm might establish a manufacturing plant in the area to meet that demand. Even if a manufacturing plant is not justified, demand may be sufficient to justify a distribution depot which would provide some employment benefits.

The extent to which a locality maintains employment and generates new employment in enterprises supplying other areas and gains employment to supply its own markets is one measure of progress towards the goal of self-sustaining growth.

It has been documented by Lever (1974) and others that firms moving into the area from elsewhere may continue to buy from suppliers who have met their demands in the past. Wholly new firms, on the other hand, are more likely to buy from firms known to them or select them at random or on the basis of price from trade directories. Once established, it might be expected that new firms, as a group, would become more familiar with local suppliers and perhaps switch their purchasing pattern towards local firms.

To examine these hypotheses all firms new to Cleveland were asked for purchasing patterns at these two points in time in the survey and the results are shown in Table 9.8.

Table 9.8: Location of Initial and Current Suppliers of, and Sales to Customers by Share of Value: Firms New to Cleveland and Wholly New Firms

Region	Mean of Supplies				Mean of Sales to Current Customers	
	Initially		Currently			
	New to Cleveland	Wholly New	New to Cleveland	Wholly New	New to Cleveland	Wholly New
Cleveland	50	61	51	60	70	78
Rest of northern region	16	16	14	14	12	9
Rest of UK	29	22	30	24	15	12
Abroad	5	1	5	2	3	1
Total	100	100	100	100	100	100

Note: All figures are given as percentages.

The mean proportion of supplies at each geographical boundary are remarkably similar between the initial year and the year of interview, although the reliability of retrospective questions is always open to doubt. The marginal increase in the share of supplies bought in Cleveland is less than any estimating error that may apply, and greater variation could have been expected from enforced changes of suppliers through firms going out of business. On this evidence the suggestion that firms new to Cleveland become more integrated in the local economy over time remains unproven.

New single plant independent firms establishing in Cleveland for the first time (i.e. those not moving into the county) might be expected to have more local suppliers and customers than firms moving into Cleveland; this is confirmed in Table 9.8.

The higher local proportions are achieved at the expense of trading with areas outside the rest of the north. There is little variation between the geographical sources of initial and current supplies for new, independent firms establishing in Cleveland for the first time, as was found for the sample as a whole. The high local proportions may be attributable partly to local contacts and partly to the type of industry represented by the wholly new, independent firms.

9.5 Conclusion

This chapter has questioned the role which wholly new firms are likely to play in reducing rates of unemployment in a locality, even when a total of 7,445 new jobs were created in all firms new to the area. Single plant independent firms created only 22 per cent of all these jobs suggesting that, as predicted from studies of wholly new manufacturing enterprises, the contribution of wholly new firms to job creation is low in the early years of the firm's life — even though this is a period of relatively rapid growth. These results suggest, in support of manufacturing studies, that policies designed to stimulate the birth rate of new enterprises will create relatively few jobs in the short run.

All current studies of the unemployed — for example Sinfield (1981) — show that in recent years there has been a sharp increase in the number of long term unemployed; i.e. those unemployed for more than six months. This is particularly true in localities of high unemployment, where this group is comprised primarily of unskilled manual workers. If there is to be a return to full employment these workers will either have to be employed or retrained. The results in this chapter provide little prospect of their being employed in wholly new firms. Amongst firms new to Cleveland the five largest employers (all of whom moved into the area from outside) provided 69 per cent of all unskilled manual jobs, illustrating that the wholly new firm, particularly if it is not in the manufacturing sector, offers virtually no opportunity for employment of unskilled labour. The wholly new firm appears to demand primarily skilled men with the right personal qualities, rather than those who have been off work for a long period.

The extent to which the establishment of firms new to Cleveland provides opportunities and markets for local firms is also examined. There is little to suggest that, over time, these firms become more integrated into the local economy. The group, as a whole, purchased an average of 50 per cent of its inputs, by value from local suppliers both at its date of establishment and in 1979. Single plant independent firms were significantly more dependent upon local suppliers and vastly more dependent upon local markets than the group of firms new to Cleveland as a whole. It again suggests that when these local markets are depressed this will be transmitted, *a fortiori*, to the small firm sector.

Notes

1. Since the survey excluded, by definition, the public sector and chose to exclude retail distribution in the private sector, manufacturing employment in 1977 provided approximately 46 per cent of employment in the remaining sectors.

2. Only five firms may have begun as independents and were branches or subsidiaries by the time of interview; they had only 244 jobs in total.

3. It should be noted that this result is significant because the vacancy question was asked before (but not immediately before) the recruitment difficulty question. If the questions had been asked in reverse order there might have been a suspicion that respondents felt obliged to report a vacancy to match a skill shortage. It seems less likely respondents would feel an obligation to match a skill shortage with a vacancy.

PART FOUR

IMPLICATIONS FOR POLICY

10 NEW FIRMS: THE REGIONAL PERSPECTIVE

10.1 Introduction

In Part Two, two separate explanations of new firm formation — or entrepreneurship as it has been called — were advanced. At the simplest level they describe the supply of, and the demand for, entrepreneurship, with the number of new firms actually founded as the outcome of this interaction. This theory together with the evidence presented in Part Three enables us to review the implications of a policy designed to raise the rate of new firm formation in an economy, with specific reference to the UK. In this chapter the regional implications are examined and in the final chapter a review and assessment of central government policies is presented.

Chapter 2 showed that wholly new firms in manufacturing make only a minor contribution to output and employment even after they have existed for a decade. It was also shown that the contribution made to employment by wholly new firms varied substantially from one region in Britain to another. In this chapter it is argued that this is due to differences, between regions, in latent entrepreneurship. The existing prosperous regions are shown to be more responsive to favourable conditions for new firm formation than the assisted areas. Hence national policies designed to assist new and small firms have a significant regional bias because those areas likely to benefit most are those which are currently most prosperous. Conversely areas currently experiencing high unemployment are likely to benefit relatively little from such policies.

10.2 Factors Affecting Entrepreneurship

In the eighteenth and early nineteenth centuries the north of England produced a rich crop of engineers and entrepreneurs including George Stephenson, whose designs of locomotives were, in their time, the most advanced in the world, whilst the Armstrongs and Parsons' on Tyneside and Pease on Teesside created giant enterprises in the engineering and metal industries.

For some reason this spirit of enterprise, so apparent in the north's population, or at least in a significant number of them, is less apparent today.[1] The Northern Region Strategy Team (1977) felt that 'a lack of entrepreneurship is one of the main weaknesses remaining in the Region's economy', and stated that 'a substantial effort is needed to encourage a faster rate of small firm formation and to encourage the survival and development of newly formed enterprises'. Whilst the Team were unable to document whether the relative absence of small businesses in the region, compared with the nation as a whole, was due to a low birth rate or to a high death rate they, like the Bolton Committee (1971), assumed the prime problem was low birth rate. The area, in the opinion of the Team, had come to rely too heavily upon large new manufacturing plants moving to the region to provide employment. The indigenous population, in general, did not regard it as 'the norm' to start their own businesses.

The injections of employment through the subsidised location of 'branch plants' became less frequent by the mid-1970s, and so the region has had to look towards alternative sources of new jobs. By the late 1970s it was being encouraged by central government, particularly after the election of a Conservative administration in May 1979, to direct financial assistance towards individuals currently in business in small firms or considering starting their own firm. Given that this shift of policy has taken place, it is important to ask whether assisted areas such as the north can pull themselves up by their own economic bootstraps and create a 'self reliant' form of economic development — Segal (1979). Are small firm policies likely to create a substantial number of new jobs in such areas to compensate for employment lost during the 1979-81 recession? Can new firms create employment within a 'reasonable' timespan, bearing in mind that movement to the assisted areas has mirrored the reduced growth rates of the national economy? What does our knowledge of entrepreneurs tell us about the prospects for the assisted areas in general, and the north of England in particular, of policies designed to induce a rapid rise in the number of new firms? In short, is the north likely to be responsive to incentives to create new enterprises and expand existing small firms?

Table 10.1 sets out several important factors associated with entrepreneurship which have been identified in previous chapters. It also shows that proxies may be found for these factors, so as to indicate geographical areas which either are, or have the potential to become, entrepreneurially fertile. In the remainder of this chapter an aggregate measure of regional entrepreneurship in the UK will be constructed.

The regional entrepreneurship score is constructed by taking an unweighted average of factors which have been shown in the earlier chapters to influence entrepreneurship, and for which there are recent regional data. Each of the eleven standard regions of Britain is scored on each of the criterion and is then ranked according to its position. Where the criterion in question is positively associated with entrepreneurship then a score of eleven points is awarded to the region obtaining the highest score. Where the criterion is negatively associated, the region with the lowest score is awarded eleven points.

Table 10.1: Factors Associated with High Levels of Entrepreneurship

Factors	High Entrepreneurship	Index
1. Size of 'incubator' firm	Small firms	% of small firms in the region
2. Occupational experience	Managerial experience	% of population in managerial groupings
3. Education	High levels	% of population with degrees
4. Access to capital	Easy access	a. Savings per head of population b. House-owning population
5. Entry into industry	Low entry barriers	% of population in low entry barrier industries
6. Markets	Wealthy local markets	Regional income distribution

Hence those regions with the highest number of points overall are regarded as the most, potentially or actually, favourable to entrepreneurship, or more specifically to a policy to encourage the development of small firms. In formulating the overall table, each index will be discussed in turn.

(a) Size of Incubator Plant

Johnson and Cathcart (1979b), Gudgin *et al.* (1979), Cooper (1973) and Cross (1981) all showed that small firms were, other things being equal, likely to produce more entrepreneurs than larger firms. Storey (1981b) also shows in comparing Cleveland and the East Midlands that new firm formulation rates, by industry, were generally higher in the region with the highest proportion of employment in very small firms.

Table 10.2 shows the regional breakdown of very small manufacturing units in Britain. It will be recalled that the smallest size band, i.e. less than ten employees, is the most 'productive' of all incubators, with productivity falling substantially as establishment size rises beyond 500 employees. For this reason the proportion of the manufacturing labour force in establishments employing less than ten people is chosen as the relevant index. Northern Ireland is shown to have the lowest proportion of its manufacturing population employed in very small establishments, followed by the northern region. The south-east has a substantially higher proportion of its workforce employed in these very small establishments than any other region.

Table 10.2: Size Distribution of Establishments, by Region

Region	Manufacturing in 1977				All Industries (1976)	
	% of Labour Force Employed in Plants Having Less Than Ten Employees	Rank	% of Labour Force Employed in Plants Having More Than 500 Employees	Rank	Employees in Employment in Size Band 1-10	Rank
Northern	2.2	2	57.1	1	11.8	3
Yorkshire and Humberside	3.6	7	39.8	8=	12.7	5
East Midlands	3.5	6	37.3	10	11.6	1=
East Anglia	3.8	8=	39.8	8=	14.7	9
South-east	6.2	11	40.6	7	13.4	6=
South-west	4.4	10	44.4	6	16.6	10
West Midlands	3.1	3=	48.2	3	11.6	1=
North-west	3.4	5	46.0	4	11.9	5
Wales	3.1	3=	50.1	2	13.8	8
Scotland	3.8	8=	45.8	5	13.4	6=
Northern Ireland	1.7	1	36.8	11	n.a.	—

Source: Manufacturing data are taken from Department of Industry (1977).
      'All Industry' data are taken from Regional Statistics (1980) Table 8.15.

We have postulated that large establishments are infertile incubators for entrepreneurs. Hence an area with a large proportion of its workforce employed in large establishments is likely to generate relatively few entrepreneurs. According to this criterion for entrepreneurship the north has the highest proportion of its population in these large infertile establishments but Northern Ireland, which has the lowest proportion of its workforce in very small manufacturing establishments, also has the lowest proportion in the largest establishments. The south-east which has the highest proportion of the labour force in very small establishments has only an about average proportion of the labour force in large establishments. The presence of Northern Ireland ensures there is no correlation between the rank positions of the regions according to the two indices, although the removal of Northern Ireland produces a weak positive correlation.

In considering the opportunities for new firm formation it could be argued that it is not simply the proportion of the manufacturing population employed in small manufacturing establishments that is relevant, but the proportion of employment in small establishments in all sectors of the economy. Data are not available for Northern Ireland but for all other regions the rank positions are similar for 'all the sectors' data for 'manufacturing', and so it makes little numerical difference which index is used. In constructing our final table, however, we have used the manufacturing rankings, primarily because all data on the fertility of difference sizes of incubator firms is derived from studies of manufacturing firms. Until work reported in Part Three was undertaken, new firms outside manufacturing have been virtually ignored by researchers.

(b) Managerial Expertise and Educational Qualifications

Cross shows that individuals are more likely to establish their own firm if they have had experience as a manager. This is particularly true of individuals who have worked in large firms. Nicholson and Brinkley support Smith's earlier results showing that those entrepreneurs with managerial experience are more likely to be successful than those coming from a craft background. Gudgin *et al.* show that closely related to managerial experience is educational attainment. Those individuals with higher educational qualifications, on average, create more successful firms than those with lower qualifications. Indeed for the most modern and technically sophisticated industries, Cooper argues that a degree in a science subject is necessary for at least one of the founders of the firm. Conversely the higher the proportion of the population without any managerial expertise or without any qualifications, the smaller is the pool of potential, and particularly potentially successful, entrepreneurs. Our own results in Chapter 6 are more equivocable than those of other researchers. From the Cleveland evidence for manufacturing entrepreneurs there was an association between educational qualifications and ultimate success. Yet it was not possible to identify such a relationship for non-manufacturing entrepreneurs. If anything the data suggested a negative relationship. Nevertheless, the consistency of this relationship in previous studies suggests that, at least for the manufacturing sector, this is an important influence on subsequent firm performance. Table 10.3 shows the regional distribution of educational qualifications of school leavers and of those persons classified as administrative and managerial grades, and those classified as manual.

Table 10.3: Regional Distribution of Educational Qualifications and Managerial and Manual Groupings

Region	Educational Qualifications				Occupational Groupings			
	% of School Leavers Going to Degree Courses	Rank	% of School Leavers Without Qualifications	Rank	Adminis- trative / Manage- rial %	Rank	Manual %	Rank
Northern	5.8	2	15.2	7	5.7	4=	47.0	2
Yorkshire and Humberside	7.0	6	16.8	4	5.7	4=	47.1	1
East Midlands	6.5	3=	15.6	6	6.5	8	46.1	3
East Anglia	4.8	1	15.0	8	6.3	7	35.4	9
South-east	7.6	8	12.9	10	10.4	11	34.1	11
South-west	6.8	5	11.3	9	6.2	6	35.1	10
West Midlands	6.5	3=	18.1	3	6.6	9	45.7	4
North-west	7.4	7	15.8	5	6.7	10	42.5	6
Wales	8.5	10	26.4	1	4.8	2	41.4	7
Scotland	8.4	9	n.a.	–	5.5	3	44.4	5
Northern Ireland	n.a.	–	25.9	2	4.8	1	36.6	8

Source: Regional Statistics (1980): educational data are from Table 7.3; occupational data are from Table 3.3.

The regional distribution of educational qualifications of school leavers is an imperfect proxy for the availability of educated entre- preneurs in the locality partly because it will be between 15 and 20 years before today's school leavers, on average, are in a position to establish their own firm. In addition, those leaving school and intend- ing to take a degree are the most likely to move out of the area to find work. The alternative proxy is to use census data, which gives the educational qualifications of the resident population by regions in 1971. This is also unsatisfactory because of its age, but more import- antly it reflects the net product of in- and out-migration from regions which has taken place in the past. In that sense it is an inadequate description of the region's potential to generate new firms in the future, although it is perhaps an adequate description of its current status.

In selecting occupational groups which were the most and least likely to produce new firm founders, the administrative and managerial group and the manual group were chosen. The administrative and managerial group includes a number of occupations which are essentially non-industrial, but it was thought that this grouping was slightly more relevant than the professional and scientific which seemed more orientated towards the public sector. In any event the ranking of the two groups was very similar.

These data are presented in Table 10.3. In three out of the four rankings the south-east has the highest position, but there are a number of interesting variations. East Anglia, for example, has the lowest percentage of school leavers going to university, whilst Wales has the highest. The north-west has the second highest proportion in the administrative and managerial grades, although it is well behind the south-east. In fact the orderings in this grouping illustrate the limitations of the technique since five regions have between six and seven per cent of their population in this grouping, so that 0.5 per cent makes a difference of four places in the groupings, yet the south-east in top place has over half again as high a proportion (3.7 per cent) in the group as second placed north-west.

In general these social characteristics of the population are rather more regionally diverse than other aspects of entrepreneurship, apart from the continually high scoring of south-east England. Even the north has a relatively low proportion of school leavers without educational qualifications and Northern Ireland has relatively few manual workers.

(c) Access to Capital

The willingness of a financial institution to lend to an individual wishing to start in business, possibly for the first time, will depend upon the inherent quality of the project on offer, upon any track record which the individual has either in that, or in any other previous business, and upon the security which the individual is prepared or able to provide.

The importance of personal savings cannot be underestimated. Cooper found that 40 per cent of technically orientated firms were financed primarily with the founder's own capital, whilst Litvak and Maule (1972), in a study of science-based companies in Canada found 35 per cent were financed primarily by the founder's own personal resources. The results presented in Chapter 8 for Cleveland entrepreneurs underline the importance of personal savings. Out of 152 respondents, 104 mentioned personal savings as a source of finance for starting their firm and 56 per cent thought it to be the single most important source.

One way in which low levels of personal savings may not act as a constraint upon raising capital is if the individual owns his home and is able to mortgage it to the bank. Chapter 8 showed that 12 out of 152 respondents raised capital through increasing their mortgage on property and in four per cent of cases it was the most important single source.

Table 10.4 provides data on the regional difference in savings per head of population, taken from Short and Nicholas (1980), and also on differences in the ability of individuals to use their home as collateral for raising capital from a bank or financial institution. Clearly the higher the proportion of the population living in council-owned or privately rented accommodation, the lower the number of entrepreneurs able to raise capital in this way. Equally the advances which a financial institution is prepared to make depend directly upon the saleable value of the house. Table 10.4 provides data on the regional differences in the house prices.

The data on savings should be treated with some caution partly because of the incomplete coverage of building societies and partly because there are other forms of savings which are not reflected in the table, and which a potential entrepreneur could draw upon — notably property, stocks and shares, etc. There are also differences from one region to another in saving habits. For example, the high position of the East Midlands in the rank order is due to its exceptionally high savings with the Trustee Savings Bank and National Savings, whilst the position of the north-west is due to its savings with building societies. Despite these deficiencies this measure is the best currently available.

It is unfortunate that data on owner-occupation are only available for England, but this shows it is the south-west that has the highest proportion of houses occupied by their owners, but the highest house prices are found in the south-east. Perhaps surprisingly the second highest prices are found in Northern Ireland followed by Scotland. Here again there is a substantial spread of values with average dwelling prices being over 50 per cent higher in the south-east than in Yorkshire and Humberside.

(d) Entry into Industry

The amounts of capital required by an individual depend upon the type of industry in which he is considering establishing a firm. In the timber industry or some forms of retailing industry capital requirements are low, whereas they are vastly higher in industries such as chemicals, shipbuilding (of the ocean-going variety) or metal manufacture.

Table 10.4: Regional Differences in Access to Capital

Region	Savings per Head of Population[a]	Rank	Housing Owner-occupied Dwellings as % of All Dwellings	Rank	Average Dwelling Price £	Rank
Northern	227.4	8	42.3	1	11,773	5
Yorkshire and Humberside	218.3	5	50.6	2	10,722	1
East Midlands	314.7	10	54.8	5	11,367	2
East Anglia	206.5	4	55.1	6	12,176	6
South-east	226.6	7	52.6	4	16,541	11
South-west	237.7	9	59.9	8	13,555	8
West Midlands	224.8	6	52.3	3	12,528	7
North-west	346.1	11	57.0	7	11,527	3
Wales	201.5	3	n.a.	—	11,673	4
Scotland	161.1	2	n.a.	—	14,236	9
Northern Ireland	132.2	1	n.a.	—	15,722	10

Note: a. Savings are defined to include net receipts by building societies 1975-7, Premium Bond net receipts 1975-6 to 1977-8, Trustee Savings Bank plus National Savings Deposits 1975-6 to 1977-8 plus banking sector current and deposit accounts 1975-6 to 1977-8. Doubts are expressed by Short and Nicholas on the magnitude of the building society figures, which are thought to be representative of the comparative savings by region, but the survey covered only 34 per cent of the total assets of societies.
Source: Savings data from Short and Nicholas (1980); housing data from Regional Statistics (1979), Tables 6.4 and 6.8.

It has been frequently noted throughout this book that most individuals establishing their own firm tend to start in the industry in which they were formerly employed. In the Cleveland case 60 per cent of new firm founders started a business in the same industrial order in which they were formerly employed. We have also seen that an individual working in a large establishment, irrespective of industry, is less likely to start his own firm than an individual working in a small establishment.

These two factors have an additive influence for the individual who is working in a large establishment in an industry where the optimum plant size is high, so that capital requirements upon entry are also large. Gudgin (1978) noted that slow growing industries were also likely to attract less entry. Table 10.5 represents an attempt to produce a single composite index to reflect these influences. It takes employment in the four industry orders where capital costs per operative are highest, and which have had generally slow rates of growth. It then examines the proportion of the labour force which is employed in establishments employing more than 500, and expresses this as a proportion of the total manufacturing labour force. This is designed to reflect the empirical observation that those regions with a high proportion of employment in such industries are likely to have a low number of entrepreneurs.

Table 10.5: Employment in Establishments of More Than 500 Employees as a Per Cent of Total Manufacturing Employment. 1977

Region	Chemicals	Metal Manufacture	Mech anical engineering	Ship-building	Total Employment	% of Total Manufacturing Employment in These Four Industries	Rank
Northern	35,757	34,038	33,852	43,102	146,754	33.5	1
Yorkshire and Humberside	18,119	62,312	31,272	1,500E	113,204	16.1	4
East Midlands	9,870	27,812	40,508	–	78,195	14.0	6
East Anglia	–	–	11,106	927	12,033	6.2	11
South-east	49,718	7,895	80,496	23,543	111,934	6.4	10
South-west	6,399	2,117	21,064	–	29,580	7.1	9
West Midlands	7,163	57,077	40,360	1,611E	106,211	11.0	7
North-west	54,157	6,218	42,397	5,000E	107,722	10.8	8
Wales	11,826	65,332	–	–	77,158	24.4	2
Scotland	17,462	21,859	47,199	25,000E	111,520	18.4	3
Northern Ireland	2,000E	–	10,000E	9,076	21,076	14.3	5

Note: E = estimates.
Source: Department of Industry (1977).

The table shows clearly that by far the largest concentration of individuals who are the least likely, for reasons of the industry in which they work, to start their own manufacturing businsses are in the north of England. Only Wales has an industrial structure which is comparable in terms of being such an unfertile breeding ground for entrepreneurs. The contrast with areas such as south-east England and East Anglia could not be drawn more starkly. The ranking system, here again, fails to do justice to the magnitudes involved.

(e) Wealth

Most firms when they start in business sell locally – Lloyd (1980) supports the data presented in Chapter 9 which showed that 78 per cent of the sales of wholly new independent firms in Cleveland were to customers within the county. The opportunities for growth in a depressed and poor local market, even for the most enterprising of firms, must be less than that for a similar firm established in a prosperous and growing region. New firms, whether of the technical and scientific type, or those operating in more traditional markets, begin in the locality in which the entrepreneur lives, because that is where he has his contacts for sales and for purchases. The individual located in a poor area has to decide whether to move out of his locality and risk losing his contacts, etc. or to stay in the area recognising that growth prospects are likely to be very limited. The third option, of course, is not to start the firm at all!

The above statements are major generalisations. Some firms are started solely to supply a major firm in the area with a specific product, so that 'wealth' locally is almost irrelevant, the prospects of the new firm being more closely dependent upon the fortunes of the larger firm. Other firms may be started by supplying a number of local companies, with again the wealth of local consumers being of only marginal significance.

Nevertheless, a majority of new firms will serve the local market and their growth prospects are closely related to incomes in the locality. For this reason in Table 10.6 data are derived from *Regional Statistics* on wealth. A number of indices could have been derived. Regional wage rates may be thought to be a relevant indication of wealth, as might holdings of personal assets. In the table, however, total income per head after tax is used. This includes profits and professional earnings, employment income, occupational pensions, National Insurance retirement pensions, family allowances less all deductions and tax. This index represents the spending power available in the individual family, and it is appropriate to include the redistributive function of government since this determines local levels of effective demand.

Table 10.6 shows that despite the role of government there is a considerable regional variation in total income per head after tax, varying from £794 in Northern Ireland to £1,289 in south-east England.

Table 10.6 Total Income After Tax per Head, by Region, 1976-7

Region	Income per Head £	Rank Position
Northern	1,082	5
Yorkshire and Humberside	1,128	9
East Midlands	1,105	6
East Anglia	1,117	8
South-east	1,289	11
South-west	1,077	4
West Midlands	1,137	10
North-west	1,108	7
Wales	1,015	3
Scotland	989	2
Northern Ireland	794	1

Source: Regional Statistics (1979).

10.3 An Index of Regional Entrepreneurship

In this section a composite index of entrepreneurship is constructed from the individual indices derived above, by using the rank position of each region in each index. The results are shown in Table 10.7.

Not unexpectedly it shows that the south-east of England is the region with the highest index of entrepreneurship, indicating that policies to assist small and new firms are likely to bear the greatest fruit in this area. Conversely the northern region of England has the lowest score, closely followed by Wales. In fact if the composite index had excluded consideration of school leavers going to degree courses the two regions could be considered as virtually identical.

The performance of the next batch of regions, Scotland, Northern Ireland, Yorkshire and Humberside and the West Midlands is variable. In particular Northern Ireland comes either at the top or at the bottom of the criteria — characterising it as an area of entrepreneurial extremes. Perhaps the most surprising inclusion in this group is the West Midlands, which is normally regarded as one of the more prosperous areas of Britain, and one where individual enterprise was 'endemic' in the population. Recently, however, it has been badly affected by the poor performance of the British economy, and Table 10.7 suggests it will not particularly benefit from a policy to place greater emphasis upon individual enterprise in small and new firms. Conversely, Scotland, which has been regarded by Cameron (1971) as lacking entrepreneurial dynamism, performs rather better than might have been expected, and its average score is virtually identical to that of the West Midlands, thus supporting the empirical work of Firn and Swales (1978).

The East Midlands occupies its traditional central place in the middle of the regional league table, with the north-west and East Anglia both being in high positions. The position of the north-west merits comment since Merseyside has for several years had a rate of unemployment substantially above the national average and part of the region has had assisted area status. In addition the South Lancashire area has shed a substantial number of jobs in the textile industry. Nevertheless, Table 10.7 suggests that the area as a whole has, at least in principle, the ability to develop new industries and new firms and the 'shake-out' of labour will have less effect in the long run than in Wales and northern England.

The south-west, and in particular the south-east, score heavily on most of the criteria and their average scores are substantially above those of the other regions, suggesting they have the greatest capacity for creating jobs in small and new firms. They have relatively little cause for concern over recent job losses since new firms are likely to be spawned to absorb labour shedding.

Although the ordering of some regions, notably the low position of the West Midlands and the high position of the north-west may be slightly curious, the general conclusions are not wholly surprising. The real value of Table 10.7 is that it shows that most regions, with the exception of Northern Ireland, take a fairly consistent position on most of the indices of entrepreneurship, with the northern region and Wales on only two indices obtaining more than a halfway position. Alternatively the south-east only once falls below halfway, indicating that the eventual groupings satisfactorily reflect the entrepreneurial potenial of the regions. It suggests that, as originally propounded by this author (Storey (1980b)), a policy of offering incentives to the small firm and to individuals to start their own firm is likely to result in take-up rates varying substantially between one region and another because of differences in entrepreneurial potential. Unfortunately, with the exception of north-west and the West Midlands of England, those areas currently suffering the highest rates of unemployment are also those with the lowest entrepreneurial potential. Hence a policy of assisting the small (at the expense of the large) firm risks being regionally divisive since the biggest take-up rates are in the areas which are currently the most prosperous. Only by giving greater encouragement and offering higher incentives to those in Wales and northern England will this side-effect of policy be reduced.

Table 10.7: An Index of Regional Entrepreneurship in Britain: Rankings

Region	Table 10.2		Table 10.3					Table 10.4		Table 10.5	Table 10.6	Average Score
	% in Small Manufacturing Plants	% in Large Manufacturing Plants	% Going to Degree Courses	% Without Qualifications	% in Admin. and Managerial Class	% in Manual Class	Savings	Owner-occupied Dwellings	Average Dwelling Price	Barriers to Entry	Disposable Income	
Northern	2	1	2	7	4=	2	8	1	5.	1	5	3.45
Yorkshire and Humberside	7	8=	6	4	4=	1	5	2	1	4	9	4.64
East Midlands	6	10	3=	6	8	3	10	5	2	6	6	6.09
East Anglia	8=	8=	1	8	7	9	4	6	6	11	8	6.91
South-east	11	7	8	10	11	11	7	4	11	10	11	9.18
South-west	10	6	5	9	6	10	9	8	8	8	4	7.64
West Midlands	3=	3	3=	3	9	4	6	3	7	9	10	5.27
North-west	5	4	7	5	10	6	11	7	3	7	7	6.64
Wales	3=	2	10	1	2	7	3	n.a.	4	8	3	3.70
Scotland	8=	5	9	n.a.	3	5	2	n.a.	9	3	2	5.11
Northern Ireland	1	11	n.a.	2	1	8	1	n.a.	10	5	1	4.44

10.4 Some Limitations of the Approach

Chapters 3 and 4 gave a more comprehensive description of the factors affecting new firm formation than it has been possible to incorporate into the scoring system described above. Some factors have been excluded because there are no readily available measurements on a regional basis, others are inherently non-measurable, whilst a third category might have been included, but would merely have duplicated existing measures. Nevertheless, it is important to be aware of factors not included in the above analysis.

Table 10.7 includes no direct measures of the psychological and motivational factors emphasised by McClelland. Unfortunately we have no data on the regional differences in the popularity of children's fairy stories! Certain regions have a long tradition of individual initiative whereas others have relied more heavily upon collective action. Thus the northern region of England, Scotland and Wales have a stronger tradition of collectivism than south-east England. The geographical settlement pattern in the former group of regions, associated with the working of natural resources such as coal and iron ore, meant that strong local bonds were forged within communities, with an unwilling- ness to move outside. Strong senses of regional and local identity were formed (Townsend and Taylor (1975)) leading to limited migration and occupational mobility. In such communities there was an inevit- able unification of individuals, faced with the threat from outside of the mine or from the pit owner and his management. These small independent local units offered little scope for enterprise since each community provided its own products and services, rather than purch- asing them from outside, even if this were cheaper. Hence the scope for consumer products was limited for reasons that were, at least in part, social.

The quality of management also affects a region's potential for development, but it is difficult to measure this quality, or even to obtain proxies which would enable the regions to be ranked. Never- theless it is our (wholly subjective) opinion, that if such data were available it would not significantly alter the rankings in Table 10.7. The social traditions of the areas again offer some explanation, since there is a history of paternalistic management by firms selling in local markets protected either by transport costs or by local tastes. Only with the movement into the areas by large firms, controlled from out- side the region, were new management styles developed, yet this move- ment proved a two-edged sword. Large enterprises, attracted by finance from central government, which located during the mid-1960s and early 1970s in the assisted areas, offered a greater diversity of employment to those in the locality. In one sense, however, they may have drained the area of the type of management potential which could have been used to establish a new firm. Take, for example, the case of a young man who lives in a relatively remote village in Co. Durham or in South Wales. After a modest education he may begin work with a company which has a production plant in the area but its headquarters outside the region, and possibly outside the country. If he shows real potential he may be promoted to one of the foreman positions, but it will become clear that if he is to advance any further, particularly within that company, he will have to move from the area, since the number of managerial positions in a production plant is relatively small and they are filled by experienced people. If he is ambitious he will move and the region will lose an individual who might otherwise have become an entrepreneur, if there had been a greater variety of managerial positions available to him. If he is lacking in ambition he will stay, but individuals lacking such 'drive' are unlikely to begin their own firms.

A third limitation of the table is that it takes no account of the interdependencies of the economy. For example, much of the strength of the West Midlands economy in previous years has been the subcontracting of work which encouraged individuals to start their own firms. Large firms, instead of undertaking the production of component parts 'in-house', purchased from small suppliers who were in vigorous competition with one another. This benefited the larger companies who were able to obtain the products at a low price, and also offered the incentive to an individual, with what he feels to be a marketable idea, to start his own firm. Traditions in the peripheral regions, however, oppose this process. Here giant firms in heavy engineering and shipbuilding undertake manufacture of most components 'in-house', often because these establishments specialise in producing 'one-off' products. The cyclical nature of demand for final products means that employees in such industries become accustomed to often fairly prolonged periods of unemployment and under-employment, returning to work once the economy became more buoyant, thus reducing the need to consider self-employment. Regional policies which brought new large production plants into the regions have done little to increase the amount of subcontracting in the area. Many plants purchased their inputs centrally so that small local firms encountered difficulty becoming approved tenderers, since this frequently required an agreement to supply, not simply the local plant, but all others in the group. In short, the impact which the new large firms made on the local economy in the peripheral regions of Britain was less than hoped for by the policy makers in the early 1960s.

In Eire, however, as noted in Chapter 9, McAleese and McDonagh (1978) argue that Irish entrepreneurs have reacted positively to the challenge of supplying the many foreign-owned firms which have been located in the Republic in recent years. Reasons for this difference between Eire and Britain are not difficult to find, but in the present context it is sufficient to note that if an index of opportunity for subcontracting were provided it is likely that Wales, Scotland and northern England would again be close to the bottom. Only the West Midlands might be expected to move up from its position in Table 10.7 with perhaps the north-west moving down.

10.5 Conclusions

The attributes of both the entrepreneur in general, and of the successful entrepreneur in particular, have been seen to be concentrated in certain regions in Britain — notably those which are currently prosperous. These disparities must be of concern, even to those policymakers only interested in national economic development, because it leads to different responses by each region both to government policy and to market opportunities. Since the capacity of the national economy to grow depends upon the contribution made by the constituent regions, a policy to increase the output of less 'responsive' regions will have 'national' benefits, when capacity is fully utilised in the more prosperous areas.

Since 1979 job losses have occurred through the closure of manufacturing establishments on a previously unprecedented scale. This has been due to a number of macro-economic factors such as high interest rates, high exchange rates, depression on the world economy, relatively high energy prices in Britain, the role of North Sea oil and reductions in, or alterations in the form of, public expenditure. In part, it has also been due to government being less willing to subsidise industry, so that firms which might have obtained assistance from government in the past were forced to cease trading. Government argued that these were likely to be either inefficient firms or ones where the demand for their product had disappeared, but that from the ashes of these fallen companies would arise new enterprises which were more dynamic, innovative and market orientated than their predecessors. Such firms would be able to compete, without public subsidy, for both home and foreign markets. It was necessary to die in order to be born again.

A knowledge of the characteristics of entrepreneurs suggests that such a strategy is likely to have significant regional implications. During the recessions of the post-war years labour was shed by firms, but then drawn upon, often by the same companies, in the upswing of the cycle. The effect of the post-war 1979 recession has been for closures to reach an unprecedented peak. No comprehensive data are available upon the size distribution of these closures, or even of their industrial or regional distribution, but it seems clear that medium and large establishments have been particularly severely affected. Let us, however, assume that the closures have no specific regional bias, other than that they are primarily amongst larger establishments, and that the net effect has been to reduce the manufacturing workforce by approximately ten per cent in one year.

Previous severe recessions have resulted in output recovering slowly partly because there are fewer firms in existence to take advantage of improved trading conditions during an upswing. Some output will be generated by wholly new firms but these take time to grow. The inability of domestic firms quickly to satisfy the increases in demand tends to lead to high import penetration, and effectively to a reduced market for home produced goods. The ability of individual regions in Britain to create self-sustaining economic growth by reacting quickly to improved conditions is likely to be determined partly by entrepreneurship in the area. In Scotland, Wales and the north of England relatively few new firms are likely to be created per head of population in a given time period. Establishment closures in the downswing of the trade cycle will result in proportionately fewer new jobs being created in those regions in the upswing, so that a policy which relies exclusively upon the closure of establishments, and upon stimulating indigenous entrepreneurship, risks being regionally divisive. This could only be off-set by increased demand inducing, once again, the movement of existing companies, wishing to expand, to the assisted areas.

The scenario assumes that a high average propensity is indicative of a high marginal propensity to start a firm, and to be successful in any region. There may be conditions when this may *not* be the case. For example, one region may have in its population a group who, by tradition, religious beliefs, etc., have high business acumen, and who form a large number of new firms. If they constitute a sizeable proportion of the population new firm formation rate in the region will be high, but once that group is fully employed the remainder of the population in the region may be only as likely to form new firms as the population in other regions. It is, however, these latter groups who determine the relevant marginal responsiveness to incentives. Whilst recognising that differences between marginal and average values could occur and that it is the unmeasured marginal, rather than the measured average, which is relevant to our conclusion, it seems unlikely, in practice, that this difference is significant. There is little evidence that entrepreneurship in the south-east is, for example, concentrated amongst certain groups, or that the number of potential entrepreneurs is almost exhausted, leaving a 'rump' whose propensity to form their own firm is no higher than populations elsewhere.

A policy which 'allows the inefficient to go out of business' may also result in a difference between the types of firm which disappear and those which replace them, even where the new firm is in the same industry. The post-1979 recession has seen the closure of an exceptional number of medium sized establishments of strategic importance, in the sense that they were suppliers to other parts of British industry. New firms which are being created, and will be created are normally only small (average of 15 employees after one decade) and are imperfect substitutes for those which have disappeared. It is a direct consequence that a proportion of the markets of these defunct firms will be satisfied by imported goods.

A second characteristic of new firms is that they often begin in sections of a general market which official statistics regard as miscellaneous – the so-called 'not-elsewhere specified'. In part this is due to the inability of government statisticians to classify a very small establishment on the basis of the limited information which it supplies. More probably it illustrates that new firms often begin, as would be expected, in low volume markets where economies of scale are irrelevant compared to the production of unique, one-off products.

The warnings in this chapter are clear. There is no evidence that, in manufacturing industry, large numbers of jobs can be created in less than a decade by raising the rate of formation of wholly new firms. Whilst for most of the 1970s, irrespective of the actions of government, the small firm sector has been growing at a time when manufacturing employment as a whole has been in decline, the capacity of new firms to create large numbers of new jobs is limited. Hence it is disturbing that government is allowing jobs to disappear in medium sized establishments, since in less than a decade these cannot be replaced by the creation of wholly new firms.

Taking a longer time perspective, all economies are constantly evolving in response to changes in relative prices, technology, tastes, etc., and it is frequently suggested that it is the failure of British industry to anticipàte, or even react to, these changes that is at the root of our relative industrial decline. In addition it is argued that pre-1979 government had removed monies from the most enterprising sections of society through high tax rates and used revenues for providing public services and for assisting the inefficient sections of industry.

Attempting to reverse this process is likely to be extremely painful in the short run, even if there are benefits over a longer period. The entrepreneur, upon whom so much faith is placed, is a complex animal and from the viewpoint of this book he/she is not evenly distributed spatially. A policy which relies upon the death of large industry as a precursor to reincarnation in smaller but more enterprising establishments risks low fertility and high infant mortality over large areas of Britain, even though the policy pursued does not have an explicitly spatial dimension.

Note

1. It should not be assumed that entrepreneurship is absent in the region. For example, Barratts of Newcastle are now the largest house builders in the UK, having increased their profit in the decade of the 1970s from £¾ million to over £30 million.

11 SMALL FIRMS POLICIES: A CRITIQUE

11.1 Introduction

The last 20 years have seen major changes in the economic structure of many developed countries. The period of the 1950s and 1960s saw rates of economic growth unparalleled in history, but this was brought to an abrupt end in 1973 when the price of oil was quadrupled. The 1970s also saw several LDCs notably in South-east Asia starting to compete with the developed countries in the production of many mass-produced industrial products.

Rising energy prices meant that it became less economic to construct major plants, since energy usage at the plant level increases at least in proportion with capitalisation. Less capital-intensive and hence smaller scale procedures are now favoured. Increased energy prices also increased the costs of transportation so that it has become more economic for units of production to be closer to either raw materials or final markets in order to reduce transportation costs.

Changes in energy prices, whilst they explain reductions in optimal *plant* size, do not explain why the decline of the small *firm* (enterprise) sector, which had been in progress for 30 years in some countries, was reversed in the early 1970s. Insights into this change must embrace three main strands. The first is a direct result of the oil price rise and the indirect effect which it had upon slowing the rate of growth of the world economy. Long periods of slow economic growth and of restructuring such as occurred in the 1930s and in the late 1970s meant that large enterprises substantially reduced output and labour creating a large pool of unemployed labour. A proportion of this labour, seeing few opportunities in wage employment will be more likely to consider, as an alternative to unemployment, the formation of their own business. The effect of recession is to increase proportionately the contribution made to total output by new firms. Recessions also de-unionise labour, through reduced employment in large firms where labour is likely to be unionised, and through individuals becoming entrepreneurs or working in small firms where they are less likely to be unionised.

Smallness became 'fashionable' in the 1970s as firms became aware of managerial diseconomies of scale such as impersonal management, difficulties of controlling disparate subsidiary plants, lack of motivation amongst workforces employed in repetitive tasks, etc. 'Fashion' changes, however, are more likely to be the result of underlying economic (and social) forces rather than the cause. In the same way that the oil crisis of 1974 cannot be regarded as an initiating cause of the reversal of the fortunes of the small firm, neither can 'fashion' since the 'small is beautiful' phrase was not even coined until 1972 with the publication of the book by Schumacher. It is true that Schumacher may have only been articulating the views held previously by many others, but it remains clear that, at least in Britain, the 30-year decline of the small firm sector had been arrested several years earlier.

A third, and more plausible explanation, is that small firms reversed their decline partly because increased incomes meant an increased demand for one-off products produced primarily on a small scale. The increased importance of electrical and electronic instrumentation meant that these industries, which could be entered relatively easily with little fixed capital equipment, represented a considerable opportunity for talented individuals to establish their own firms. At the same time there was a substantial shift in world production of heavy, capital-intensive products such as textiles, shipbuilding and heavy engineering, towards the LDCs.

Whatever the importance of these reasons it is clear that the small firm has become increasingly significant in the economies of most developed countries. Governments, almost irrespective of political complexion, are currently aware of the power which small firms wield in the national economy, and in response have offered increasingly valuable incentives to those wishing to establish their own firms. In the light of the empirical chapters of Part Three of this book it is important to review these initiatives to assess whether they are effective in terms of their own stated objectives, whether these objectives are appropriate, and whether major improvements in the delivery of policy may be effected.

11.2 Should We Have a New Firms Policy?

Whilst virtually all governments are actively concerned to assist the small firm there has been little assessment of the extent to which it is appropriate for governments to attempt to influence the rate of new firm formation. For those individuals intending to form their own firm it is in their own interest to argue that government should subsidise their initiatives. It is also in their interest, once in business, to argue that the small firm should be favourably treated and made exempt from various forms of taxation and legislation. Whether it is in the national interest is less clear.

Those favouring a market approach to economic problems argue that, subject to certain qualifications, the free market would provide an optimal number of new firms. New firms will be created in industries where there is an opportunity for profit and firms will disappear from industries where demand for the final product has declined. Government intervention is legitimate only where the social and private costs and benefits of new firm formation diverge, or where it is believed that the existing income distribution significantly reduces the extent to which willingness to pay reflects an individual or group's demand for a good or service.

It is not immediately clear to what extent subsidising the formation of new firms (and thus increasing, *ceteris paribus*, the existing stock of small firms) can be justified on any of these bases. Clearly, subsidies by government to those wishing to establish their own firms will result in an increased number of new firms and lead to an increased employment in the small firm sector. But subsidies to one group have to be raised by increased taxes or reduced reliefs to other groups, and it has never been shown that the *net* effect of subsidising small firms is to create more wealth in the community. In essence, the argument must always return to the basic issue that, if there are economic factors which currently favour the small firm, these would be exploited by that sector *without* the assistance of government.

Bannock states that the small firm sector is not claiming any advantage over other sized units, but rather that the disadvantages which have accumulated against small firms for generations be removed. He believes small firms have been discriminated against by finance houses, by the lack of availability of premises and by governments in various forms of legislation. The purpose of recent changes is to reverse these disadvantages and allow the small firm sector freedom to prosper. Yet it is extremely difficult to decide to what extent the disadvantages which the small firm encounters are 'natural' and the extent to which these are imposed 'unfairly' by larger firms or by government. It was argued, for example, in Chapter 7 that there was no reason to believe there could be a permanent shortage of premises in which the new firm could start in business. With an increased demand, prices of such property and hence rental incomes would be expected to rise, an increase in supply would be induced, with supply and demand subsequently being equalised — albeit at an increased price. The only 'shortage' would be amongst those willing to pay the old price but not the new. The chapter also showed that although the rents charged for small premises have probably risen faster than other forms of property, this could hardly be classified as discrimination against small firms. Indeed Chapter 7 suggests that, whilst there is currently an increased demand for small premises, this may be satisfied without any appreciable price rises due to the increased supply provided by public agencies.

The case for a public subsidy to small firms may also be based upon a possible divergence between social and private benefits. If, for example, it could be shown that assistance to small firms created more employment than comparable assistance to large firms this would be an argument for redirecting funds. Unfortunately this is not the case. The type of labour which new firms employ is primarily skilled, yet the unemployed labour available in most developed countries tends to be unskilled. Such labour is much more likely to be employed by large than small firms. We have also seen that although large manufacturing firms have been shedding labour and small firms have been increasing their labour forces it is not true, either in Britain or in the USA that 66 per cent of all new jobs are created in firms employing less than 20 people. Most new manufacturing jobs continue to be created in large establishments.

If it could be shown that workers in small firms were more contented this might be considered a worthy social objective justifying government financial support for small and new firms. Research evidence provides little support for such a hypothesis, suggesting that the probability of conflict between workers is invariant according to the size of the firm, and that whilst different attitudes towards work exist amongst workers in small and large establishments, these reflect differences in the importance of financial and non-financial rewards.

Governments in most countries finance scientific research and development because the benefits of modern technology and methods used in firms accrue, not only to the firm and its shareholders, but also to the nation. Benefits accrue to the employees in terms of higher wages and more secure employment when a firm is successful in national and international markets. The expenditure of these employees creates additional jobs. Much scientific research also has many of the characteristics of a public good — whereby those who have undertaken it cannot exclude others from benefiting from it — hence without government support such research would not be undertaken or be undertaken on a more limited scale. Similarly, financial support for small firms is also justified on the contributions which such firms make to research, innovation and invention. It is true that the small firm obtains more inventions per £ of R & D expenditure than the large firm, but this reflects the relatively few small firms which undertake any R & D. Lloyd (1980) in his pilot survey of new firms in Manchester and Merseyside found very few which had introduced any significant innovations in their early years and only one 'boffin businessman' amongst his sample of 60 small firms. The majority were '"family businessmen" or "hiver off" tradesmen with a handful of "wheeler-dealers"'. It would seem unduly optimistic to assume that an injection of substantial sums of public money will transform a collection of jobbers and wheeler-dealers into sophisticated technological entrepreneurs.

A third justification for government involvement in a market economy is where the existing distribution of income (in the view of the government) distorts the demand for certain goods. On this (and other) grounds governments have introduced national health schemes, since frequently those most in need of health care are the least able to pay. Precisely the opposite is the case with financial assistance to small firms. Those who benefit are the relatively wealthy, who are able to start new businesses. The results in Part Three support previous work by showing that although there are more 'working class' than 'middle class' entrepreneurs the chances that a middle-class person will form his own firm are substantially greater than for a working-class individual. Assisting the small firm will therefore be of greatest benefit to the wealthier sections of society.

11.3 The Dangers of Small Firms Policies

Policies to assist the small firm may not only bring relatively few benefits but they may also be damaging to countries as a whole, and to particular groupings. The effects upon the distribution of income have already been noted. The Bolton Committee recognised that it was possible to increase the importance of the small firm sector by redistributing income in favour of entrepreneurs. This the Committee rejected, despite the small firm sector having been in decline for 30 years, and there being a risk of it falling to a size where it could no longer perform its 'seedbed' function. In a brilliantly far-sighted paragraph, Bolton says:

> The simplest and probably most effective form of discrimination would be a tax concession to small firms themselves, their proprietors or potential investors in them; but to tilt the balance of forces in

favour of the small firm would require a concession of a size that we would judge to be politically unacceptable to the majority of the population, and which we could not defend on economic grounds . . . To justify [a cut in the effective rate of tax of more than 20 per cent] . . . to a group whose members are certainly not as a group among the less fortunate and underprivileged, and who include some of the more wealthy people in the country, would be impossible in the absence of much stronger evidence than is now available that the future of the small firm sector is in jeopardy to an extent that threatens national well-being. (para 8.15)

A second consequence of a policy to assist small firms is that it can, unchecked, have significant regional implications. It was noted in Chapter 10 that virtually all the indices of entrepreneurship were highest in the areas of Britain which are currently most prosperous. Conversely indices were lowest in the least prosperous areas, so that policies which rely exclusively upon small firms to generate jobs, risk having their greatest impact upon employment in prosperous areas and their least impact in areas of high unemployment. In this sense they risk being regionally divisive. In addition, the types of jobs which are created by small firms are less likely to be filled by those who are unemployed — and certainly not by the long-term unemployed.

The trade union and labour movements, at least in Britain, appear indifferent to the growth in importance of the small firm lobby. This is surprising since the increased importance of the latter has a generally unfavourable impact upon organised labour for several reasons. The first is that unionisation is much stronger in large establishments, and in most cases large firms, than in small. Reductions in the proportion of the labour force employed in large firms will reduce union membership and hence weaken union power. Secondly, a number of new firm founders will previously have been union officials who, having become their own bosses, are less likely ever to return to becoming union members. In this sense they are lost forever from the union ranks, and since they are likely to be amongst the more intelligent and articulate they represent a major loss to the movement. Thirdly, the small firm is not only less unionised, but tends to pay lower wages and perhaps be less scrupulous about issues of concern to unions such as employment protection, working conditions and safety. Growth in the small firm sector may therefore lead to a decline in pay and conditions of employment. Finally unions will, or should, be concerned about both the income distribution consequences of financial assistance to entrepreneurs partly for the reasons outlined above, but partly because the small firm in many respects is the antithesis of trade unionism. The former extols the virtues of independence and of personal achievement at the individual level. The latter sees the individual benefiting not from personal efforts but as part of the group through common effort. The absence of unfavourable reaction from organised labour to the increasing importance of the small firm may be due partly to the relatively small sums directed towards assisting the entrepreneur, at least in Britain, compared with government assistance to large firms.

However, the greatest danger of small firm policies in Britain is that they are currently designed to raise the expectations of the electorate that such policies will solve unemployment and recreate the conditions for prosperity. A recent opinion poll in Britain showed that the issue which most people identified as being central to government economic strategy was assisting the new firm.[1] The persistence with which Birch's work continues to be misquoted, and reluctance to quote any comparable British data, gives credence to the notion that small firms are being presented as the panacea for the problems of nearly a century of relative decline in the British economy. The real danger which such an approach brings is that of backlash when the effects of policies are not seen to bear fruit in a short period.

It has been stressed throughout this book that small manufacturing firms have, in the UK, been increasing their labour forces at a time when large manufacturing firms are contracting, and that there are several developments in the international economy suggesting these trends are likely to continue. Employment in most developed countries will, however, be determined in the short term by the performance of large enterprises, which will in turn be determined by the rates of growth of the world economy. The stock of small firms cannot be changed quickly. By definition, only if births exceed deaths will the stock be increased yet the typical new firm is likely to be highly unstable, and to die before it reaches its fifth year. To illustrate, again from the case of Cleveland, this economy created less than 2,000 new manufacturing jobs in wholly new surviving firms over an eleven-year period. In one day in 1980 the British Steel Corporation announced that, because of the world recession, output had to be cut and 3,000 jobs would be lost from the Cleveland area. This illustrates that the contribution to job creation over an eleven-year period made by new firms was more than negated by the contraction of the labour force of major plants.

Existing policies are likely to stimulate new firm formation, as is the recession itself, with the current rate of new firm formation being, as a result of these influences, at a record level. The jobs created in such firms will, however, only marginally reduce levels of unemployment prevailing in most developed countries. It would be unwise to pretend that small firms policies will have any noticeable impact in less than five years, with it taking perhaps 20 years before many of today's new firms become giants capable of influencing national economic prosperity. Nevertheless, it remains a fact that both central and local governments, of all political complexions, are wedded to policies designed to stimulate entrepreneurship. In the following section these policies are reviewed in a British context.

11.4 Central Government Policies to Assist the Small/New Firm in Britain

Table 11.1 provides a brief outline of the measures taken by a Conservative government in Britain to assist the small firm, and encourage more individuals to start their own business. In his first budget, the Chancellor of the Exchequer reduced the standard rate of income tax in the belief that this would encourage individuals to work harder since they would retain an increased proportion of their total income. He also believed that it would encourage more people to begin their own businesses.

Brown (1980) has demonstrated the difficulties of identifying a relationship between changes in the marginal rate of income tax and changes in the quantity of labour supplied, essentially because although income tax reductions increase take home pay, it may encourage those who have no wish for an increased income to work less hours and yet maintain the same income. Similarly, if income tax is reduced it may reduce the number of businesses formed, since it makes paid salaried employment (relatively) more attractive *vis-à-vis* unemployment or self-employment, because the majority of the benefits of reduced taxes fall to those in salaried employment.

The Chancellor has placed most of his efforts in stimulating new firms in a financial package for small firms which includes the business start-up scheme, loan guarantee scheme and other financial benefits. These schemes are estimated to cost the government approximately £90 million in a full year, and although the sums involved are relatively small it is difficult to argue that they do not constitute positive discrimination. As in Bolton's time the disadvantages which the small firm faces in raising finance are real, but they reflect the greater expense to financial institutions of lending to small firms from both the administrative and the risk of default viewpoint. Despite having introduced these changes government continues to be attacked by the small firms lobby for not going far enough. Restrictions over eligibility for the business start-up scheme have been criticised as have the high interest rates charged under the loan guarantee schemes.

Table 11.1: Government Initiatives to assist Small Firms in Britain, 1979-81

1. Business Start-up Scheme

   Outside investors buying shares in new small trading companies obtain tax relief at rates up to 75 per cent on investments of up to £10,000 per year.

2. Loan Guarantee Scheme

   Government will guarantee 80 per cent of new loans for between two and seven years, on values of up to £75,000. The remaining 20 per cent is carried by the financial institution making the loan.

3. Other Financial Benefits

   Corporation tax liability has been reduced. The VAT threshold has been raised. Trading losses can be offset against tax more generously. Redundancy payments of up to £25,000 are free from tax if the money is used to start a business.

4. Premises and Planning

   An extension programme of the building of small factory premises has been undertaken. Eleven enterprise zones have been created within which planning restrictions are much less onerous and where rates relief is given over a ten-year period.

5. Information and Statistics

   The number of forms which government issues has been substantially reduced. On the other hand, the businessman can obtain advice on a variety of topics from Small Firms Information Centres.

6. Employment Legislation

   This has been relaxed for small firms employing less than 20 people who are not liable for claims for unfair dismissal by workers employed by the firm for less than two years.

It is clear that the major beneficiaries of these schemes are the wealthy. The absence of incentives for individuals (an Aunt Agatha) with sufficient wealth to lend to an entrepreneur is often cited as a cause of low rates of new firm formation in Britain. Under the proposed scheme individuals lending to valid start-up companies can receive tax relief upon such investments. Clearly those paying the highest rates of tax have the greatest incentives under such a scheme, but early reports suggest that there could be considerable opportunities for tax avoidance in the scheme. Currently considerable efforts are being made to define tightly the types of company which would qualify for the scheme but this in turn is the subject of criticism by the small business community.[2] They feel that with any scheme designed to give incentives of this kind, there are risks of tax avoidance but that if there is an increase in the rate of new firm formation the 'price' will have been worthwhile.

At the time of writing the interest by small and new firms in the loan guarantee scheme seems to have surprised many analysts. The Department of Industry, responsible for monitoring the scheme, found that more than half the £50 million allocated for the scheme in the first financial year had been taken up within four months.[3] Under the scheme the banks may lend up to £75,000 to small firms with 80 per cent of this underwritten by the Department of Industry. Such loans are for clients who would, under normal commercial criteria, have been judged to be too risky. The surprising feature is that the take-up of funds has been so rapid since the effective interest rate paid by the borrower is high. The banks themselves charge at least two per cent above base rate upon such funds and the government charges three per cent on its 80 per cent. This makes the rate to the borrower at least 4.5 per cent above base rate, but if new firms in Cleveland are typical, many new firms began and expanded by using sources of funding which were almost certainly relatively more expensive than those available to small and new firms at the end of 1981. These developments by the banks, together with a more active policy of marketing their services to the small firm, are some of the most pleasing features of the changing attitudes to small firms. If the banks can be convinced to interest the entrepreneur, irrespective of social background, in the services which they provide, this will make a major contribution to raising the birth and survival of new firms.

Central and local government have attempted to satisfy the increased demand for starter premises through the construction of new units. In some cases the private sector has also become involved but this has tended to be only in the more prestigious projects in the prosperous areas of Britain. In the other areas central and local government have been the major initiators of development, although public and quasi-public bodies such as BSC (Industry) Ltd., Council for Small Industry in Rural Areas and Local Enterprise Trusts have also been involved. Local authorities have become increasingly aware that, in their redevelopment plans, account should be taken of the interest of small firms who might be displaced. The initiative of government on enterprise zones is also designed partly to encourage small firm development, although three early effects, none of them desirable, seem to be occurring. The first is that since the boundaries of the EZ are drawn precisely, the distinction between firms inside the zone who receive a substantial package of reliefs, and those outside, can be a matter of a few metres. This understandably generates great resentment amongst the latter firms. Secondly, most of the new locations in the EZ are very short distance movers so the net increase in number of jobs created over a wider area is minimal. Thirdly, the price of land within the EZ has risen substantially, so as to partly offset the package of reliefs available.

The information required of the small firm by government has been reduced and it is clearly in the national interest that firms should devote their time to producing goods and services rather than completing statistical returns. Nevertheless it is important that, since small firm initiatives are central to government strategy, the effectiveness of the strategy should be monitored, not solely by government. Unfortunately the reduction in the amount of information collected from the small firm sector has coincided with a reduced access to existing data for non-government researchers. Prior to 1981 it was also possible for detailed financial and other information on limited companies to be obtained for 5p, but this was raised by 2,000 per cent in 1981. The Companies Act 1981 also reduces the need to register companies and give names of directors. Finally in recent years the Business Statistics Office has begun to charge for many services which it previously provided at no cost. All these developments are dangerous since they suggest that government is intending to maintain a monopoly on information either by refusing outsiders access, or by charging a high price for information released.

The extent to which improved information and advice services will be utilised by those entrepreneurs most in need of their services remains open to question. Throughout these pages the loneliness of entrepreneurship has been stressed and the simplest forms of assistance can often ease considerably the problems of a business. Nevertheless the boom in organisations willing and able to advise the small businessman is reflected in Chapter 7. The number of such agencies must give rise to confusion and the poor 'after sales service' provided by the agencies, reported in the chapter, must also be a cause for concern. It is essential to rationalise the services of agencies, most of which are supported wholly or in part by public funds. This necessitates central and local government discussing with representatives of the small firm sector the criteria by which agency performance should be judged. All agencies should then be monitored according to agreed performance criteria.

Small firms have also become legally excluded from sections of the employment and safety at work legislation even though working in a small firm is not safer than working in a large firm. From the employee's viewpoint such legislative immunity cannot be beneficial. There is also no evidence that employees in a small firm are better paid and are so 'compensated' for the greater risks which they incur, either of industrial injury or of uncompensated redundancy. Whilst it is true that such legislation may bear particularly heavily upon the small firm owner, it is equally clear that the present immunities transfer the burden squarely on to the labour force in the small firm. Whether the current distribution of burdens is either fair or efficient has not yet been demonstrated.

11.5 Small and New Firm Policies: A Need for Redirection

Despite the recognition that small and new firms have an important role to play, governments continue to distinguish between certain types of firms which they regard as worthy of support, and other types of enterprise which they regard as less desirable. All small is not equally beautiful! In poll position in this hierarchy is the science-based small firm, established by a management-trained, graduate electronic engineer. Such an individual with only half a good idea would be in danger of being trampled in the rush of government and financial institutions wishing to invest in him and his idea. At the other end of the spectrum is the hairdresser whose husband has died and who wants to open a salon in order to work close to her children, or the man who cleans windows 'on the side' and would, since his redundancy, relish the opportunity of undertaking full-time work, or the man who would, in the absence of any other available local employment, like to make a business out of his hobby of woodcarving.

The science boffin is markedly less likely to be unemployed at the time of starting a business than the hairdresser, the window cleaner or the woodcarver. He is also, as is shown by the samples of new firm founders in Part Two, not the 'typical' entrepreneur and hence the employment created by such firms at least in the short run, is not high, yet he continues to be the prime target for policy. If there is to be a major increase in new firm formation, especially in areas of high unemployment, the link between the unemployment/social security system and self-employment has to be explored.[4]

Let us take as an example the man cleaning windows 'on the side', whilst receiving unemployment pay. By undertaking such work he is taking a considerable risk since government has recently announced a major increase in the number of benefit enforcement officers. If the window cleaner declares an income from his trade in excess of 75p per day he forfeits the whole of his unemployment pay for that day. In this context income and gross revenue from the business are identical, so that even if he incurs expenditure on petrol in driving to the place where the windows are to be cleaned, or if he incurs costs in providing materials, these are not allowable items which can be offset against his gross revenue. Thus whilst he is educating himself in the arts of entrepreneurship, building up a collection of clients, there is a powerful incentive for this to be done illegally without any payments being made to the state. The alternative, under current conditions, is not to undertake the work at all.

A change in these arrangements could induce a larger increase in the rate of new firm formation than is possible by any other single measure. If the unemployed were allowed their full unemployment pay for a period of up to twelve months when they were starting their business, provided that business paid all its taxes, this would have a number of benefits. First it would encourage those people, who currently find it too risky, to start a business by giving them twelve months to determine whether their idea is viable. The government will gain by receiving some tax revenue where it previously obtained none, and would be able to reduce its employment of enforcement officers. Consumers would gain by having a greater variety of goods and services provided at competitive prices.

The major beneficiary of such a scheme would be the working-class entrepreneur and the major impact would be in areas of high unemployment, and in both those senses it differs from existing small firm initiatives. There are also no regressive income-distribution consequences of the scheme, but it is true that the expected number of jobs which would be created in each firm would, on average, be less than those which would be created by the 'boffin-entrepreneur'. Almost certainly there would also be many failures, but in total it appears a more effective way of mobilising indigenous potential than any other single initiative.[5]

Finally it is worth reiterating the essential theme of Chapter 10 that current small firm policy in Britain risks being regionally divisive. It risks creating most jobs and wealth in areas that are relatively prosperous and fewest jobs in areas of low incomes. To reverse these trends requires government to reorientate the items of regional policy towards giving greater incentives for small firms in areas of high unemployment. For instance, at present, regional development grants are paid only to firms purchasing new capital equipment, but our investigations illustrate that many firms begin with second-hand or leased equipment and are not eligible for grant aid. Many firms also complained about grants only being available to manufacturing firms but excluding firms in services and construction. Why, they asked, should we be excluded since we clearly provide a service for which a market rate will be paid and in the supplying of which people are employed? There is a strong justification in their argument that if a regional balance is to be maintained grants should be available to the service as well as the manufacturing sector.

11.6 Conclusion

There has been a tendency to accept uncritically that all policies which help small firms are to be recommended since it is the small firm alone, which will in future create new jobs and new wealth. This book has tried soberly to review the existing evidence and provide new data.

It suggests that the observed trend of small manufacturing firms being net creators of jobs, and large firms being net shedders of labour, is primarily due to the depressed world economy, since these trends were also observed on the only other such occasion in the 1930s. If the world economy were to experience rates of growth similar to that of the 1950s and 1960s, then it seems possible that giant enterprises will again reassert themselves, probably by acquiring the successful firms spawned in the depressed 1970s. There are clear dangers of supporting a sector whose relative ascendancy is based upon depression in the world economy.

Other negative aspects of a small firms policy have been stressed in order to counteract the currently euphoric view of the potential contribution of this sector to economic development viz.: a higher proportion of small firms undertake no research and development than do large firms — although it is clear that economic prosperity in developed countries will depend increasingly upon technological advance. There is also no evidence to support the notion that working people in small firms are happier or more satisfied than those in large firms. Furthermore, they are in Britain at least, less well protected from accidents, lower paid and possibly have less secure employment than those in large firms.

Policies to stimulate the small firm also have mixed blessings. The jobs which have been created are relatively skilled and hence are less likely to be filled by those currently unemployed, yet it is the small firm sector alone which is the net creator of manufacturing jobs, and likely to remain so for a number of years. The type of entrepreneur most likely to create jobs is one with high levels of education, with managerial experience, access to capital and who has worked in a small firm and whose product will be sold in a buoyant (initially local) market. Hence he is most likely to live in the most prosperous areas and be relatively wealthy. Offering financial assistance to such an individual means that income is being redistributed in favour of the currently wealthy groups – such policies risk being regionally divisive.

The central question remains the extent to which governments should discriminate in favour of/reduce the discrimination against small firms. This book argues that there are forces which currently favour the small firm sector, irrespective of the actions of government, which will lead to an adjustment in both the nature and size distribution of firms in the economy. There is also recognition in banking circles, that the small firm sector offers opportunities for considerable new and profitable business. Whether, on top of this, governments, both local and national, should reinforce these trends by positive discrimination in terms of purchasing policies, constructing industrial property at subsidised rents, loan guarantee schemes, etc., seems less clear. Government is unsuited, by its bureaucratic nature, to assisting highly motivated individualistic entrepreneurs, with the entrepreneurs themselves often being sceptical and frequently unaware of the assistance available. Governments cannot commit public monies to projects without taking responsibility for these sums – a responsibility which takes time to implement and requires questions to be answered – both of which are an anathema to the entrepreneur. Even if assistance can be effectively delivered the income distribution implications are strongly negative. In a sentence, if small firms are in an economic ascendancy why has government to be involved?

This is not to argue that governments at local or national level should, as has happened on occasions in the past, ignore the interests of small firms. Local authorities in their redevelopment, green-belt and transportation policies should take into account the interests of all sizes of enterprises. Similarly central government should recognise that it is unwise to discriminate in favour of one size of firm because, when that group fails to deliver the promised jobs and wealth, it risks facing a powerful backlash. It is surely better to recognise that small and new firms will, irrespective of the actions of government, continue to make a modest contribution over a number of years to economic development, but that having an industrial base numerically dominated by small firms is not an insurance against economic decline. The example of the city of Birmingham, once referred to as the city of a thousand trades, and which was described by Wise (1949) as having a greater variety of firms 'more broadly based than that of any city of equivalent size in the world', is clear. Since the days of the 1950s the city has experienced almost unparalleled economic decline despite its diversified industrial base, the importance of small firms in its industrial structure and its historical traditions of entrepreneurship – Liggins (1977). Furthermore, Chapter 10 suggests that the West Midlands region is unlikely to reverse these trends, even if central government continues with present policies.

Our final word must be that new firms can perform a valuable function in the economy and that conditions are currently in their favour. Nevertheless, the small firm sector is a heterogenous combination of enterprises. It would be unwise to expect this collection of strange bed-fellows to reverse the relative decline of the British economy within the foreseeable future. In the 1960s the large firm was expected to transform the British economy, but it is now cast in the role of villain because of its failure to realise these expectations. The small firm sector should be wary that it does not follow this path. Small firm lobbyists should recognise that in the past the price to be paid for positive discrimination is unreasonable expectations of employment and wealth creation by government and electorate – a price which in the view of this author is not worth paying.

Notes

1. Commissioned by the McCann-Erickson Advertising Group, quoted in *Financial Times*, 9 September 1980.

2. A total of 16 amendments to the business start-up scheme were proposed by Michael Grylls, Tory MP and chairman of the Small Business Bureau, when the scheme was discussed in its committee stages. Virtually all were to increase the scope of companies eligible for assistance – *Sunday Times*, 16 July 1981.

3. *Financial Times*, 21 September 1981.

4. This follows Storey (1982).

5. In November 1981, after this was written, government accepted these proposals and launched a pilot scheme, as recommended in these paragraphs. This is a most welcome development.

REFERENCES

Aldcroft, D.H. (1975) 'Investment in and Utilization of Manpower: Great Britain and Her Rivals, 1870-1914' in Barrie M. Ratcliffe (ed.), *Great Britain and Her World 1750-1914: Essays in Honour of W.O. Henderson*, MUP, Manchester

Aldrich, H. (1980) 'Asian Shopkeepers as a Middleman Minority: A Study of Small Business in Wandsworth' in A. Evans and D. Eversley *The Inner City: Employment and Industry*, Heinemann, London, pp. 389-407

Aluko, S. (1973) 'Industry in the Rural Setting', *Proceedings of the 1972 Conference of the Nigerian Economic Society*, Ibadan University Press

Andrews, P.W.S. (1964) *On Competition in Economic Theory*, Macmillan, London

Ashton, T.S. (1948) *The Industrial Revolution*, Oxford University Press, London

Bain, J.S. (1956) *Barriers to New Competition*, Harvard University Press, Harvard

Bannock, G. (1972) *The Smaller Firm in Britain and Germany*, Anglo-German Foundation, Wilton House

—— (1980) Letter to *Guardian*, 22 August 1980

—— (1981a) *The Economics of Small Firms*, Basil Blackwell, Oxford

—— (1981b) 'The Clearing Banks and Small Firms', *Lloyds Bank Review, 142*, October, 15-25

Barbee, E.E. (1941) 'Reasons for Failure', *Credit and Financial Management*

Bator, F.M. (1968) 'The Simple Analytics of Welfare Maximisation', *American Economic Review*, March 1957. Reprinted in W. Breit and H.M. Hochman (eds.) (1968) *Readings in Microeconomics*, Holt, Rinehart and Winston Inc., New York (1968)

Baumol, W.J. (1968) 'Entrepreneurship in Economic Theory', *American Economic Review, 58*, 64-71

Bechhofer, F., Elliott, B. and Rushford, M. (1971) 'The Market Situation of Small Shopkeepers', *Scottish Journal of Political Economy, 18*, 161-80

Beesley, M. (1955) 'The Birth and Death of Industrial Establishments: The Experience of the West Midlands Conurbation', *Journal of*

Industrial Economics, 4, 45-61

Birch, D.L. (1979) *The Job Generation Process*, MIT Program on Neighborhood and Regional Change, Cambridge, Mass.

Bolton, J.E. (1971) *Small Firms: Report of the Commission of Inquiry on Small Firms*, Cmnd 4811, HMSO, London

Boswell, J. (1972) *The Rise and Decline of Small Firms*, George Allen & Unwin, London

Brough, R. (1970) 'Business Failures in England and Wales', *Business Ratios*, 8-11

Brown, C.V. (1980) *Taxation and the Incentive to Work*, Oxford University Press, Oxford

Brozon, Y. (1971) 'The Persistence of High Rates of Return in High Stable Concentration Industries', *Journal of Law and Economics, 14*(2), 501-12

Bruce, R. (1976) *The Entrepreneurs: Strategies, Motivations, Successes and Failures*, Libertarian Books Ltd., Bedford

Calvo, G.A. and Wellisz, S. (1980) 'Technology, Entrepreneurs and Firm Size', *Quarterly Journal of Economics, December* (4), 663-78

Cameron, G.C. (1971) 'Economic Analysis for a Declining Urban Economy', *Scottish Journal of Political Economy, 18* (November), 315-45

—— (1980) 'The Inner City: New Plant Incubator?' in A.W. Evans and D. Eversley, *The Inner City: Employment and Industry*, Heinemann, London

Chalkley, B. (1979) 'Redevelopment and the Small Firm', *The Planner*, September, 148-51

Chinoy, E. (1955) *Automobile Workers and the American Dream*, Doubleday, Garden City, New York

Churchill, B.C. (1955) 'Age and Life Expectancy of Business Firms', *Survey of Current Business*, 15-24

Clark, R. (1979) *The Japanese Company*, Yale University Press, London and New York

Collins, O.F. and Moore, D.G. (1964) *The Enterprising Man*, Michigan State University, Business Studies, East Lansing, Michigan

—— (1970) *The Organisation-Makers*, Appleton Century Crofts, New York

Commanor, W.S. and Liebenstein, H. (1969) 'Allocative Efficiency, X-Efficiency and the Measurement of Welfare Losses', *Economica, 36*, 304-9

Commission of the European Communities (1980) *Small and Medium Sized Enterprises and the Artisanant*, January, 1980. Reproduced in

Confederation of British Industry (1980) *Smaller Firms in the Economy*, October 1980, London

Cooper, A.C. (1973) 'Technical Entrepreneurship: What do we Know?', *R. and D. Management, 3* (2), 59-64

Coopers and Lybrand (1980a) *Review of Industrial Promotion Organisations*, Department of Industry, London

—— with Drivas Jonas (1980b) *Provision of Small Industrial Premises*, Department of Industry: Small Firms Division, London

Cox, J.G. (1971) *Scientific and Engineering Manpower and Research in Small Firms*, Committee of Inquiry on Small Firms, Research Report no. 2, HMSO, London

Cross, M. (1981) *New Firms and Regional Economic Development*, Gower Publishing Co., Farnborough

Curran, J. and Stanworth, M.J. (1981a) 'The Social Dynamics of the Small Manufacturing Enterprise', *Journal of Management Studies, 18* (2), 141-58

—— (1981b) 'A New Look at Job Satisfaction in the Small Firm', *Human Relations, 34* (5), 343-65

Dahmen, E. (1970) *Entrepreneurial Activity and the Development of Swedish Industry 1919-1939*, Richard D. Irwin, Homewood, Illinois

Davies, J.R. and Kelly, M. (1971) *Small Firms in the Manufacturing Sector*, Report of the Committee of Inquiry on Small Firms, Research Report no. 3, HMSO, Cmnd 4811, London

De Missie, S. (1975) 'Cross-cultural Entrepreneurship in African and Middle Eastern Countries, *Proceedings of Project INSEED*, Centre for Venture Management, Milwaukee

Department of the Environment (1977) *Policy for the Inner Cities*, Cmnd 6845, HMSO, London

Department of Industry (1976) *Report on Census of Production*, PA 1002, Summary Tables, HMSO, London

—— (1977) 'Analysis of United Kingdom Manufacturing (Local) Units by Employment Size', *Report on Census of Production*, Business Monitor PA 1003, HMSO, London

Department of Trade and Industry (1973-4) *Inquiry into Location Attitudes and Experience*, Memorandum submitted to the Expenditure Committee (Trade and Industry Sub-Committee on Regional Development Incentive) Session 1973-4, HC 85-1, HMSO, London, pp. 525-668

Derossi, E. (1972) *The Mexican Entrepreneur*, OECD, Paris

Dickerson, D.D. and Kawaja, M. (1967) 'The Failure Rates of Business' in I. Pfeffer (ed.), *The Financing of Small Business: A Current*

Assessment, Macmillan, Arkville Press, New York, pp. 82-94

Domar, E. (1968) 'Entrepreneurship in Economic Theory: Discussion', *American Economic Review, 58*, 72-3

Fagg, J.J. (1980) 'A Re-examination of the Incubator Hypothesis: The Case of Greater Leicester', *Urban Studies, 17*, 35-44

Falk, N. (1978) *Think Small*, Fabian Society Tract no. 453, London

—— (1980) *Local Authorities and Industrial Development – Results of a Survey*, URBED, London

Firn, J.R. and Swales, J.K. (1978) 'The Formation of New Manufacturing Establishments in the Central Clydeside and West Midlands Conurbations, 1963-72', *Regional Studies, 12*, 199-213

Forsyth, D.J.C. (1972) *U.S. Investment in Scotland*, Praeger, New York

Fothergill, S. and Gudgin, G. (1979) 'The Job Generation Process in Britain', *Centre for Environmental Studies*, Research Series no. 32, November

—— (1982) *Unequal Growth*, Heinemann Educational Books, London

Frazier, E. (1957) *Black Bourgeoisie*, Free Press, Glencoe

Freeman, C. (1971) *The Role of Small Firms in Innovations in the U.K. since 1945*, Committee of Inquiry on Small Firms, Research Report no. 6, HMSO, London

—— (1974) *The Economics of Industrial Innovation*, Penguin, Harmondsworth

Goldthorpe, J.H. (1980) *Social Mobility and Class Structure in Modern Britain*, Oxford University Press, Oxford

Goldthorpe, J.H., Lockwood, D., Bechhofer, F. and Platt, J. (1968) *The Affluent Worker: Industrial Attitudes and Behaviour*, CUP, Cambridge

Greenfield, S.M., Strickton, A. and Aubey, R.T. (1979) *Entrepreneurs in Cultural Context*, University of New Mexico Press, Albuquerque

Gudgin, G. (1978) *Industrial Location Processes and Regional Employment Growth*, Saxon House, Farnborough

Gudgin, G., Brunskill, I. and Fothergill, S. (1979) 'New Manufacturing Firms in Regional Employment Growth', *Centre for Environmental Studies*, Research Series no. 39

Hagen, E.E. (1962) *On the Theory of Social Change: How Economic Growth Begins*, Dorcey Press, Homewood, Illinois

Hannah, L. and Kay, J.A. (1981) 'The Contribution of Mergers to Concentration Growth: A Reply to Professor Hart', *Journal of Industrial Economics, 29* (3), 305-13

Harberger, A.C. (1954) 'Monopoly and Resource Allocation', *American Economic Review, 44*, 77-87

Harbison, F. (1956) 'Entrepreneurial Organisation as a Factor in Economic Development', *Journal of Political Economy*, August, 364-79

Harper, M. and Thiam Soon, T. (1979) *Small Enterprises in Developing Countries*, Intermediate Technology Publications Ltd

Hart, P.E. (1981) 'The Effect of Mergers on Industrial Concentration', *Journal of Industrial Economics, 29* (3), 315-20

Hart, P.E. and Prais, S.J. (1956) 'The Analysis of Business Concentration: A Statistical Approach', *Journal of the Royal Statistical Society*, Series A, *119*, 150-91

Hayek, F.A. (1949) *Individualism and Economic Order*, Routledge and Kegan Paul, London

Henderson, J.N. and Quandt, R.E. (1971) *Micro-Economic Theory*, McGraw-Hill, New York

Hitchens, D.M. (1977) *Business Efficiency in Iron Founding*, Technicopy, Stonehouse Gloucs.

HMSO, (1977) 'Policy for the Inner Cities, London, Cmnd 6845

Hoover, E.M. and Vernon, R. (1960) *The New York Regional Study Plan*, Harvard University Press, Cambridge, Mass.

Howdle, J.M. (1979) *An Evaluation of the Small Firms Counselling Service in the South West*, Bristol Polytechnic

Howick, C. and Key, A. (1980a) 'Small Firms and the Inner City: Tower Hamlets', *Centre for Environmental Studies, Policy Series no. 9*

—— (1980b) 'Small Firms, Entrepreneurship and the Industrial Regeneration of Inner Cities', paper presented at Manchester Business School, September 1980

IFT Marketing (1979) 'Survey of Financing of Small Firms in the Service Industries', in *Studies of Small Firms Financing*, Research Report no. 3 for Committee to Review the Functioning of the Financial Institutions (Wilson Committee)

ILO Mission (1972) *Employment, Incomes and Equality: A Strategy for Increasing Productive Employment in Kenya*, ILO, Geneva

Ingham, G.K. (1970) *Size of Industrial Organisation and Worker Behaviour*, Cambridge Studies in Sociology no. 1, CUP, Cambridge

Jewkes, J., Sawyers, D. and Stillerman, R. (1969) *The Sources of Innovation*, 2nd edn, Macmillan, London

Johns, B.L., Dunlop, W.C. and Sheehan, W.J. (1978) *Small Business in Australia: Problems and Prospects*, George Allen and Unwin, Sydney

Johnson, P.S. (1980) 'Unemployment and Self-Employment: A Survey', paper presented at Manchester Business School, September 1980

Johnson, P.S. and Cathcart, D.G. (1979a) 'New Manufacturing Firms and Regional Development: Some Evidence from the Northern Region', *Regional Studies, 13*, 269-80

—— (1979b) 'The Founders of New Manufacturing Firms: A Note on the Size of Their "Incubator" Plants', *Journal of Industrial Economics, 28* (2), 219-24

JURUE (1980) *Industrial Renewal in the Inner City*, University of Aston in Birmingham

Kamerschen, D.R. (1964) 'An Estimation of the Welfare Loss from Monopoly in the American Economy', *Western Economic Journal, 4*, 221-36

Kaplan, A.D.H. (1948) *Small Business – its Place and Problems*, McGraw-Hill, New York

Keeble, D. (1978) *Industrial Location and Planning in the United Kingdom*, Methuen, London

Kets de Vries, F.R. (1970) 'The Entrepreneur as a Catalyst of Economic and Cultural Change', unpublished Doctoral dissertation, Harvard University Graduate School of Business Administration

Kihlstrom, R.E. and Laffont, J.J. (1979) 'A General Equilibrium Entrepreneurial Theory of New Firm Formation Based on Risk Aversion', *Journal of Political Economy, 87* (4), 304-16

Kilby, P. (ed.) (1971) *Entrepreneurship and Economic Development*, Free Press, New York

Kirzner, I.M. (1973) *Competition and Entrepreneurship*, University of Chicago Press, Chicago

—— (1980) *Perception, Opportunity and Profit*, University of Chicago Press, Chicago

Knight, F.H. (1921) *Risk, Uncertainty and Profit*, Houghton Mifflin, New York

Kohn, M.L. (1977) *Class and Conformity: A Study in Values*, 2nd edn, University of Chicago Press, Chicago and London

Lees, J.P. (1952) 'The Social Mobility of a Group of Eldest-born and Intermediate Adult Males', *British Journal of Psychology*, General Section, *XLIII* (Part 3), 210-21

Leone, R.A. and Struyk, R. (1976) 'The Incubator Hypothesis: Evidence from Five SMSA's', *Urban Studies, 13* (3), 325-32

Lever, W.F. (1974) 'Manufacturing Linkages and the Search for Suppliers and Markets' in F.E.I. Hamilton (ed.), *Spatial Perspectives on Industrial Organisation and Decision-Making*, Wiley, London

Leys, C. (1973) 'Interpreting African Underdevelopment: Reflections on the I.L.O. Report on Employment, Incomes and Equality in

Kenya', *African Affairs*, October

Liggins, D. (1977) 'The Changing Role of the West Midlands Region in the National Economy' in F.E. Joyce (ed.), *Metropolitan Development and Change: The West Midlands: A Policy Review*, Teakfield, Farnborough

Lipman, A. (1965) 'The Social Background of the Bogota Entrepreneur', *Journal of Inter-American Studies*, April 1965

Little, A.D. (1977) *New Technology-Based Firms in the United Kingdom and the Federal Republic of Germany*, Wilton House, London

Litvak, I.A. and Maule, C.J. (1972) 'Managing the Entrepreneurial Enterprise', *The Business Quarterly, 37* (2), 42-50

Lloyd, P.E. (1980) *New Manufacturing Enterprises in Greater Manchester and Merseyside*, Working Paper no. 12, North West Industry Research Unit, Manchester University

Loebl, H. (1978) 'Government Financed Factories and the Establishment of Industries by Refugees in the Special Areas of England 1937-61', University of Durham, unpublished MPhil thesis

Lucas, R.E. (1978) 'On the Size Distribution of Business Firms', *Bell Journal of Economics*, 508-23

Lydall, H.F. (1958) 'Aspects of Competition in Manufacturing Industry', *Bulletin of the Oxford Institute of Economics and Statistics, 20* (4), November, 319-37

McAleese, D. and McDonagh, D. (1978) 'Employment Growth and Development Linkages in Foreign-owned and Domestic Manufacturing Enterprises', *Bulletin of the Oxford Institute of Economics and Statistics, 40*, 321-39

McClelland, D.C. (1961) *The Achieving Society*, Van Nostrand, Princetown, NJ

Macmillan Committee (1931) *Report of the Committee on Finance and Industry*, HMSO, London, Cmnd 3897

Mann, H.M. (1966) 'Seller Concentration, Barriers to Entry and Rates of Return in 30 Industries, 1950-60', *Review of Economics and Statistics, XLVIII* (2), August, 296-307

Mansfield, E. (1962) 'Entry, Gibrats Law, Innovation and the Growth of Firms', *American Economic Review, 52*, 1023-51

Marquand, J. (1979) 'The Service Sector and Regional Policy in the United Kingdom', *Centre for Environmental Studies, Research Series no. 29*, London

Marris, P. and Somerset, A. (1971) *African Businessmen – a Study of Entrepreneurship and Development in Kenya*, Routledge and Kegan Paul, London

Marshall, A. (1961) *Principles of Economics* (ed. G.W. Guilleband), 2 vols, 9th edn, Macmillan, London

Mitchell, J. (1979) 'I.C.F.C. and its Customers' in *Studies of Small Firms Financing*, Research Report no. 3 for Committee to Review the Functioning of the Financial Institutions

Moore, B., Rhodes, J. and Tyler, P. (1977) 'The Impact of Regional Policy in the 1970's', *CES Review, 1*, July, 67-77

Morley, R. (1979) 'Profit, Relative Prices and Unemployment', *Economic Journal, 89*, September, 582-600

Neck, P.A. (ed.) (1977) *Small Enterprise Development: Policies and Programmes*, Management Development Series No. 14, International Labour Organisation, Geneva

Nicholson, B. and Brinkley, I. (1979) 'Entrepreneurial Characteristics and the Development of New Manufacturing Enterprises', paper given at CES conference on 'New Firms in Local and Regional Economies', October

Nicholson, B., Brinkley, I. and Evans, A.W. (1981) 'The Role of the Inner City in the Development of Manufacturing Industry', *Urban Studies, 18*, 57-71

Northern Region Strategy Team (1977) *Strategic Plan for the Northern Region, Economic Development Policies*, HMSO, Newcastle upon Tyne

Oakey, R.P. (1979) 'An Analysis of the Spatial Distribution of Significant British Industrial Innovations', *CURDS*, University of Newcastle upon Tyne Discussion Paper no. 25

O'Brien, D.P. (1978) 'Mergers — Time to Turn the Tide', *Lloyds Bank Review*, 32-44

Oxenfeldt, A.R. (1943) *New Firms and Free Enterprise*, American Council on Public Affairs, Washington

Parish, R. and Ng, Y.K. (1972) 'Monopoly X-efficiency and the Measurement of Welfare Loss', *Economica, 39*, 301-8

Payne, P.L. (1978) 'Industrial Entrepreneurship and Management in Great Britain' in P. Mathias and M.M. Postan (eds.), *Cambridge Economic History of Europe*, Part I, CUP, Cambridge

Prais, S.J. (1976) *The Evolution of Giant Firms in Britain*, CUP, Cambridge

—— (1981) 'The Contribution of Mergers to Industrial Concentration: What do we Know?', *Journal of Industrial Economics, 29* (3), 321-9

Ray, G.F. (1979) 'Comment on Technical Innovation and British Trade Performance' in F. Blackaby (ed.), *De-industrialisation*, Heinemann/ NIESR Policy Papers no. 2, London, pp. 73-7

Regional Statistics (1980) no. 15, HMSO, London

Reilly, A.M. (1980) 'Small Business' Big Clout', *Duns Review, 15* (3), 69-71

Roberts, E.B. and Wainer, H.A. (1968) 'New Enterprises on Route 128', *Science Journal*, December, 78-83

—— (1971) 'Some Characteristics of Technical Entrepreneurs', *IEEE Transactions on Engineering Management, EM-18* (3), 100-9

Robinson, J.F.F. and Storey, D.J. (1981) 'Employment Change in Manufacturing Industry in Cleveland 1965-76', *Regional Studies, 15* (3), 161-72

Rothwell, R. (1975) 'Intracorporate Engineers', *Management Decision, 13* (3), 142-54

Rothwell, R. and Zegveld, W. (1978) 'Small and Medium Sized Manufacturing Firms: Their Role and Problems in Innovation Policy in Europe, the U.S.A., Canada, Japan and Israel', *SPRU*, University of Sussex

Rowley, C.K. and Peacock, A. (1975) *Welfare Economics: A Liberal Restatement*, Martin Robertson, London

Samuelson, P.A. (1975) *Economics*, 7th edn, McGraw-Hill, New York

Scase, R. and Goffee, R. (1980) *The Real World of the Small Business Owner*, Croom Helm, London

Schatz, S.P. (1965) 'N-achievement and Economic Growth: A Critical Appraisal', *Quarterly Journal of Economics, LXXIX* (2), May, 234-41

Schumacher, E.F. (1972) *Small is Beautiful: A Study of Economics as if People Mattered*, Abacus Books, London

Schumpeter, J.A. (1934) *The Theory of Economic Development*, Harvard University Press, Cambridge, Mass.

Scott, M.G. (1980) 'Mythology and Misplaced Pessimism: A Look at the Failure Records of New Small Businesses', paper presented at Manchester Business School

Segal, N.S. (1979) 'The Limits and Means of "Self-Reliant" Regional Economic Growth' in D. Maclennan and J.B. Parr (eds.), *Regional Policy: Past Experience and New Directions*, Martin Robertson, Oxford

—— (1981) 'Meeting all Property Needs of Small Firms', *Association of Independent Businesses, Annual Review 1979-80*, London, pp. 13-14

Short, J. and Nicholas, D.J. (1980) *A Study of Money Flows in the Regions of the U.K., 1974-75 to 1977-78*, Department of Economics, University of Durham

Sinfield, A. (1981) *What Unemployment Means*, Martin Robertson, Oxford

Smith, A. (1925) *The Wealth of Nations*, 4th edn (ed. by E. Cannan), University of Chicago Press, Chicago

Smith, N.R. (1967) *The Entrepreneur and his Firm: The Relationship Between Type of Man and Type of Company*, Michigan State University, Bureau of Business and Economic Research, Occasional Paper

Solomon, G.T. and Whiting, B.G. (1977/9) 'Casualties of Ignorance: The Dilemma of Small Business in the U.S.A.', *Siena Series* no. 16, Acton Society Trust Occasional Paper, London

Stanworth, M.J. and Curran, J. (1973) *Management Motivation in the Smaller Business*, Gower Press, London

Steindl, J. (1945) *Small and Big Business*, Basil Blackwell, Oxford

Stigler, G. (1976) 'The Xistence of X-inefficiency', *American Economic Review, 66*, March, 213-16

Storey, D.J. (1980a) 'Job Generation and Small Firms Policy in Britain', *Centre for Environmental Studies Policy Series no. 11*, London; reprinted as Minutes of Evidence presented to the House of Lords Select Committee on Unemployment, 7 May 1980

—— (1980b) 'Small Firms and the Regional Problem', *The Banker*, November; reprinted in P. Gorb, P. Dowell and P. Wilson (eds.) (1981) *Small Business Perspectives*, Armstrong Press, London

—— (1980c) 'Time to Re-think the Bolton Folklore', *Guardian*, 8 August

—— (1981a) 'Small Firms: Do They Get Too Much Advice?', *The Bankers Magazine*, March

—— (1981b) 'New Firm Formation, Employment Change and the Small Firm: The Case of Cleveland County', *Urban Studies, 18*, 335-45

—— (1982) 'New Entrepreneurs on the Dole', *Journal of Economic Affairs, 2* (2), January

Storey, D.J. and Robinson, J.F.F. (1981) 'Local Authorities and the Attraction of Industry: The Case of Cleveland County Council', *Local Government Studies, 7* (1), 21-38

Sylos-Labini, P. (1962) *Oligopoly and Technical Progress*, Harvard University Press, Cambridge, Mass.

Townroe, P. (1979) *Industrial Movement: Experience in the U.S. and the U.K.*, Saxon House, Farnborough

Townsend, A.R. and Taylor, C.C. (1975) 'Regional Culture and Identity in Industrialised Societies: The Case of North East England', *Regional Studies, 9*, 379-93

Von Mises, L. (1949) *Human Action: A Treatise on Economics*, Yale

University Press, New Haven, Conn.

Watkins, D.S. (1973) 'Technical Entrepreneurship: A Cis Atlantic View', *R. and D. Management, 3* (2), 65-70

Weber, M. (1930) *The Protestant Ethic and the Spirit of Capitalism* (1904) (translated by T. Parsons, Scribner, New York

Wedervang, F. (1965) *Development of a Population of Industrial Firms*, Scandinavian University Books, Oslo

Whitelegg, J. (1976) 'Births and Deaths of Firms in the Inner City', *Urban Studies, 13* (3), 333-8

Wilson Committee (1979) *The Financing of Small Firms*, Interim Report of the Committee to Review the Functioning of the Financial Institutions, Cmnd 7503, HMSO, London

Winterbottom, M.R. (1958) 'The Relationship of Need for Achievement to Learning Experiences in Independence and Mastery' in J.W. Atkinson (ed.), *Motives in Fantasy Action and Society*, Van Nostrand, Princetown, NJ

Wise, M.J. (1949) 'On the Evolution of the Jewellery and Gun Quarters in Birmingham', *Institute of British Geographers*, Transactions and Papers, *XV*, 57-72

Woodruff, A.M. and Alexander, T.G. (1958) *Success and Failure in Small Manufacturing Businesses*, University of Pittsburgh Press, Pittsburgh

Worcester, D.A. (1973) 'New Estimates of the Welfare Loss to Monopoly: U.S., 1956-69', *Southern Economic Journal, 40*, 234-46

World Bank (1978) *Employment and Development of Small Enterprises*, World Bank, Washington

Yamanaka, T. and Kobayashi, Y. (1957) *The History and Structure of Japan's Small and Medium Industries – With Two Specific Surveys*, The Science Council of Japan, Division of Economics and Commerce, Economic Series no. 15, Tokyo, Japan, March 1957

Yamey, B.S. (1972) 'The Bolton Committee Report on Small Firms', *Three Banks Review*, September, 20-38

For Product Safety Concerns and Information please contact our
EU representative GPSR@taylorandfrancis.com Taylor & Francis
Verlag GmbH, Kaufingerstraße 24, 80331 München, Germany